FRENCH ENTR
BRITTA

FRENCH ENTRÉE 14
BRITTANY *Encore*

A Gatwick Eat and Sleep Guide
Patricia Fenn

Quiller Press

First published 1995 by Quiller Press Ltd
46 Lillie Road, London SW6 1TN
Previous Editions 1986, 1987, 1989, 1991

Line drawings: Ken Howard
Area maps: Paul Emra
Cover illustration: Tim Jaques
Cover design: Jim Reader
Design and production in association with
Book Production Consultants plc, Cambridge

ISBN 1 899163 03 4

Photoset by Rowland Phototypesetting Ltd
Bury St Edmunds, Suffolk
Printed in Great Britain by
Cox & Wyman Ltd, Reading, Berks.

Contents

Notes on using this book   vi
Foreword   vii
Author's Preface   viii
Introduction   1
Introduction to Brittany   9
Special recommendations   21
Maps   23

BRITTANY   28–187

Wines and spirits by John Doxat   188
Condensed glossary of French wine and ancillary
terminology   192
Glossary of cooking terms and dishes   194
Other titles   200

Notes on using the book – and an appeal

1 The area maps are to help the reader to find the place he wishes to visit on his own map. Each place is given a reference on the relevant area map, but they are not designed to replace a good touring map.

2 A number in brackets at the beginning of a telephone number is the area dialling code, used when making calls from outside the area.

3 o.o.s. stands for 'out of season'. Other abbreviations such as f for francs, are standard.

4 L, M or S in the margin stand for 'L' = Luxury, 'S' = Simple and 'M' for those in between.

5 H stands for Hotel and R for Restaurant in combination with 4 above, ie (H)S, (R)L etc.

6 stc means service and taxes are included (*service et taxes compris*).

7 The ➤ symbol means the establishment fulfils exceptionally well at least one of the author's criteria of comfort, welcome and cuisine – see also pages 27–8.

8 Prices, correct at time of going to press, represent a room for two people, except for demi-pension, which is per head.

9 ![thumbs up] and ![thumbs down] stands for readers' reactions, for and against.

10 (New) = new since last edition of FE5.

Author's appeal
In order to keep *French Entrée* up to date I need all the latest information I can get on establishments listed in the guide. If you have any comments on these or any other details that might supplement my own researching I should be most grateful if you would pass them on.

Please include the name and address of establishment, date and duration of visit. Also please state if you will allow your name to be used.

Patricia Fenn,
c/o Quiller Press
46 Lillie Road
London SW6 1TN

FOREWORD

The unique and gentle charm of Brittany on the northern coast of France made it a magnet for turn of the century artists, who revelled in its stunning scenery and traditional lifestyles. Today, it is even more popular as a mecca for travellers, a paradise within easy reach of Britain.

The Breton town of Brest, served daily from London Gatwick by Brit Air, is just one of dozens of destinations in France offered by the airport. This new Entrée to Brittany guide is designed to help you make the most of your trip to this beautiful region.

For many people the holiday begins at the airport and at London Gatwick we have invested in a major £100 million redevelopment programme to make sure it's an enjoyable experience, whether you are flying on business or pleasure.

A smooth and efficient service from checking in to boarding the aircraft is complemented by a whole host of tax and duty free shops, including familiar high street and internationally renowned brand names, as well as a selection of bars and restaurants which cater for everyone's tastes. At London Gatwick we have created a truly world class, world beating airport.

We hope that you find this Entrée guide a valuable source of information when planning your trip and that your holiday, from start to finish, is an all round success.

Eric Lomas
Managing Director
Gatwick Airport Limited

AUTHOR'S PREFACE TO
FE14

The first edition of *French Entrée* 5 was the result of a year's single-handed research. Every entry was personally vetted.

However, the day of the visit might have been depressingly grey or encouragingly bright, I might have just got up or be longing to go to bed, the chef might have been on top form or just walked out, and I readily admit that these are unavoidable limitations on my judgment.

But now the immeasurable benefit of further assessment by an army of volunteers, in all kinds of weather, in all manner of moods, can be added to the original text and second, third and fourth editions. Brittany has inspired an even larger number than usual of kind readers to share their experiences.

In this new book, I have been able to indicate reaction to my suggestions by the thumbs-up or down symbols. Up means that the majority is decidedly in favour, down means a boo-boo. Where opinion is split down the middle, both signs indicate the indecision; where there is no sign, there has been no feedback.

There have been an amazing number of changes in the region, and not only with the prices. Times are obviously hard and sadly several establishments have given up or been taken over. That said, it is encouraging that I have a bumper number of readers' recommendations.

I hope that from these new ideas more and more successful holidays will result and I am most grateful to all my intrepid and eloquent aides.

Feb 1995   Patricia Fenn

INTRODUCTION

F.E.14 aims to cover one area of a vast and diverse country in the kind of depth that should leave the reader in no doubt what he's in for. Michelin, the eatin' sleepin' man's bible, uses symbols between which the tourist must search for a hint that the hotel is next to an early morning market or the church clock, or that the chef has just run away with the patronne; I hope to paint the picture more vividly so that the reader can decide for himself if it's right for him.

The arrows (see p. 21 for a list) are the ideals, worth arranging a holiday around, tested and verified. But it's no use suggesting only these paragons; they may be too far, too full, too expensive for the occasion and this is when second-best is far far better than none at all. So other ideas, with suitable reservations, have been included to offer a range of choice. Where there is an outstanding restaurant or hotel, hard to miss, but not to be recommended, I have described it too, in order to warn away as well as towards.

However I make no claims that this is a dispassionate book. As it is the work of a committee of one, it is unashamedly subjective and often prejudiced. As long as you know what those prejudices are, I believe you can choose wisely and go prepared.

For instance you will find few large chain hotels included, not necessarily because they are not worthwhile, but because it is not difficult for any fool to locate one without my help and they are so predictable that they need no description. My preference is for smaller hotels, preferably family-run to ensure continuity of interest, with lots of 'character'. This gets me into no end of trouble of course. The play-safe plastic cube would be an option I sometimes sigh for when a reader complains 'my wife found some fluff under the bed in a hotel you recommended'. (What was she *doing* under the bed?)

But generally readers have agreed, and have shared their own discoveries of the kind of hotel and restaurant that rarely gets into the smarter guides or package tours. Their help continues to be invaluable for updating purposes, whether written in approval or more in sorrow than in anger. By answering every letter personally I hope to show my gratitude.

Hotels are still much cheaper in France than they are at

home because the French sell rooms not beds. Two can sleep as cheaply as one, but for a third occupant you will probably have to pay a small supplement. Family rooms represent excellent value for a cheap one night stand. Children are usually welcomed and treated like adults so long as they behave like adults. Sunday lunch sees them clamped to their dining chairs for several hours with scarcely a wriggle or a whine.

Children's menus are sometimes on offer but never hesitate to ask for an extra plate so that they can share yours. Ask for an extra plate for adults too if you wish. A *menu gastronomique* between two is not at all a bad idea, as is a *menu dégustation* – small portions of many courses – giving the opportunity to sample new dishes.

Insistence on eating one meal in the hotel is a problem. Make quite sure when you book what the form is, to avoid inevitable ensuing unpleasantness (and only the French can be quite so tight-lipped). I was told that compulsion was illegal but came across it so often that I checked again with a senior tourist official. 'Madame,' he said, 'in France we have good laws and bad laws. We obey the first and ignore the second.'

Eating must come top of many reasons for going to France. Sadly I would claim that more guidance is necessary nowadays, since not every restaurant serves the kind of French meal we dream of. The deep freeze has arrived and been welcomed, short cuts are not uncommon. The course I mourn most is the vegetable. Time was when it was invariably served as a treat in its own right – a little entrée, perhaps a gratin or soufflé, would precede the meat, accompanying veg were as much evidence of a chef's judgment and skill as the main course. But now all too often its flaccid tinned beans and indiscriminate *frîtes.*

That said, the value is indoubtedly there *if you know where to look.* At all levels it is possible to eat better for less than at home. At the top, this is the time, if ever there were, to splurge on a gastronomic adventure. Save up for at least one meal at a starred restaurant if you care at all about good cooking.

Markets   We Brits go to France to sleep cheaply, eat well and to shop. The markets are more than just a utility – they are part and parcel of the French scene and everyone loves them. Take your time strolling round the colour and hubbub, and experience the pleasure of buying from someone who knows and cares about his wares. The man selling you a kitchen knife will be an expert on knives and will want to know what you need it for; the cheesemonger will choose for you a cheese ready for eating today or in a couple of days' time, back home. Trust them. Choose for yourself the ripest peach, the perfect tomato, and buy as little as you need and no more, so that you can buy fresh again tomorrow. Stock up on herbs and spices, pulses and dried fruits, soap scented with natural oils, honey from local bees, slices of farmers' wives' terrines – every village a veritable Fortnums on market day.

Closing Times The markets, like the rest of the town, snap shut abruptly for lunch. I regularly get caught out by not shopping early enough; if it's going to be a picnic lunch, the decision has to be made in good time. From 12 p.m. to 2.30, and sometimes 3, not a cat stirs. At the other end of the day it's a joy to find shops open until 7 p.m. Mondays tend to be almost as dead as Sundays and its likely to prove a grave disappointment to allocate that as a shopping day.

It does not pay to be casual about the weekly closure (*fermeture hebdomodaire*) of the restaurants. It is an excellent idea to ensure that not every restaurant in the same town is closed at the same time, but do check before you venture. Thwarted tastebuds are guaranteed if you make a special journey only to find the smug little notice on the door. 'Sun. p.m. and Mon.' are the most common and often it will take a good deal of perseverance to find a possibility open then.

Booking Sunday lunch is the Meal of the Week, when several generations settle down together to enjoy an orgy of eating, drinking, conversation and baby-worship that can well last till teatime. You should certainly book then and on fête days (list on pp. 13–14). Make tactical plans and lie low, or it could be a crêpe and a bed in the car.

As Brittany, especially in the coastal areas, has so short a season, it is particularly important to book ahead if you have a special choice in mind. If you do not speak French, try and find someone who does to make a preliminary telephone call. If necessary, write in English and let them sort it out but make sure when you get the confirmatory letter that you understand what you've booked. Many hotels nowadays will ask for a deposit.

Make good use of the local tourist bureaux, where you will find English spoken. Let them do the booking for you if you have problems. This is the place to pick up maps and brochures.

Maps and Guides	Good maps are essential and I must stress that those in the front of this book are intended only as an indication of where to find the entries. Michelin 230 covers the whole of Brittany, but if this is a bit cumbersome, best buy 58, 59 and 63. I recommend the purchase of the Green Michelin guide to Brittany too. It is published in English and will fill in all the cultural gaps.

The red Michelin, apart from all its other virtues, has useful town maps. It's a bit slow to spot a newcomer though, unlike its rival Gault-Millau, also now in English, though I prefer the French version. This gives more specific detail but has less comprehensive coverage; it is useless for the really basic hotels and restaurants.

Logis de France do a good guide to their hotels, obtainable at the French Government Tourist Bureau at 178 Piccadilly. This is the place to go for general advice, free maps and brochures and details of the admirable gîtes system, which provides simple self-catering accommodation in farmhouses and cottages. We have stayed in gîtes all over France and found them invariably reliable and cheap, and often more comfortable and interesting than hotels, but you have to be quick off the mark to book the best in peak season.

Hotel chains issue their own guides; that of the Châteaux Hotels Indépendants is well worth following up. These are hotels converted from châteaux, mills, manor-houses, often with owners newly converted themselves to hotel keeping, and trying hard. I looked at all those in Brittany and several are recommended highly.

The Relais et Châteaux chain is decidedly upmarket and getting more so by the minute. At best, they are sublime – superbly luxurious, with wonderful food, ideal for a special occasion, and by English standards not expensive for the standard they offer. At worst, they are over-priced, pretentious and full of Americans. The Breton bunch are generally a disappointment and I have said so and why.

The Relais de Silence badge is worth looking out for, since it guarantees a quiet night – very high on my priorities.

Categories	I think I must be the only guide-writer who claims to visit every entry personally. Another difference is that French Entrées are not designed for one income group. My theory is that we all have need of different kinds of bed and board on different occasions (even the poor have birthdays, even the rich lose their credit cards). So the categories: 'L' for

luxury, 'M' for Medium and 'S' for Simple, are designed to suit some of the people some of the time.

'L' will meet only exacting standards. Not only must the hotel be comfortable, it must be special in some way – its building, its service, its furnishing, its site, its food. For my favourite 'L' hotel, the Ti al Lannec at Trébeurden, everyone of these desirables is fulfilled.

Anything above 600f a night for a double room would come into the 'L' category, and quite a few below. When you consider this is equivalent to £34 a head, you can realise that luxury hotels will be available in France to readers who could never consider their equal at home.

I would expect recommended 'L' restaurants to cook exceptional food and serve it in elegant surroundings. The chef should be able to add a touch of genius to mere professional competence. If the limited choice on the lowest menu happens to appeal, you'll get a bargain, often cheaper than at humbler establishments, and cooked with the same flair as the à la carte extravagances. These menus are often only for lunch and rarely at weekends. Otherwise expect to pay upwards of 200f in this category.

The best 'M' hotels are comfortable and pleasant, well equipped and, by virtue of being mainly family-run, assuring a warm welcome. Essentially bourgeois and proud of it.

The food in this category should be good enough for *demi-pension* to be acceptable. This is where the modest stars can be found – the *chef-patrons* who lack only the long professional training to equal the big names. Their ingredients, though more modest, should be just as fresh and preferably local; their dishes, though less elaborate, should show some individuality and no short cuts. The price range is roughly from 250–500f for a double room with bath, or around 200f without, and from 90–200f for a meal.

When judging the 'S' group, bear in mind that there is nothing quite like them at home. At under £9 a head for a bed, and £10 for three courses, certain allowances should be made. It is still perfectly possible to get a double room for 160f and a meal for 70f. For this you should expect undoubted cleanliness, hot water in bedroom washbasin and shared bathroom, but not powerful lightbulbs, thick piled carpet, fleecy towels and free packets of bath oil, nor even soap. Above all, the welcome is important in these modest, invariably family-run establishments. Here is where you are most likely to get to know the patron and/or the locals. You'll get atmosphere even if you have to forget your back-home standards.

I get more excited letters about 'S' establishments than for any other. And I can understand the thrill of the chase for a bargain. However a bad meal is never a bargain and it is all too easy to end up with a waste. Don't even think of asking the *patron-chef* to come up with something too *recherché* for his limited talents. Stick to the simplest dishes on the menu and if he buys honestly and freezes nothing, you're on to a winner.

Wine

Restaurant wine is a common hiccup in more ways than one. Somehow they creep up to ridiculous mark-ups. It is not uncommon to find the bottle of plonk that costs 10f in the supermarket on the menu for six times that amount. The patron's local reputation stands or falls by his house wine, so at least try the 'Réserve de la Maison', 'Choix du Patron', though these are more likely to be red than white. Travelling alone, I often want just a glass of wine, and this is maddeningly difficult to achieve. Wine bars may have arrived in Paris but certainly not in Brittany.

Breakfasts

A sore point. The best will serve buttery croissants, hot fresh bread, home-made preserves, a slab of the slightly salted butter favoured in Brittany, lots of strong coffee and fresh hot milk, with fresh orange juice if you're lucky. The worst – and at a price of between 15 and 60f this is an outrage – will be stale bread, a foil-wrapped butter pat, plastic jam, a cup of weak coffee and cold sterilized milk. Synthetic orange juice can add another 20f to the bill. If you land in a hotel like this, get out of bed and go to the café next door.

Bread

Everyone loves French bread but debutantes to France may not realise how much it varies. Look for the boulangerie with the longest queue and buy your *baguette* or *pain* there. Ignore the plastic-wrapped hypermarket specimens – you'd buy better French loaves back home. It all goes stale very quickly, so unless you can get it in a freezer promptly its not worth stocking up however delicious the freshly-baked specimens might be.

Similarly croissants can be very nasty from an inferior *patisserie.* 'Au beurre' are the richest and best, but cost a bit more.

Speciality bread shops selling dozens of different varieties of bread are a new breed in France, and still only to be found in big towns. I like the brown variety with hazelnuts embedded, but generally the traditional crusty white is too good to forego.

Take with You
Soap and a decent towel if you're heading for the S group and can't stand the handkerchief-sized baldies. If self-catering, take tea, orange juice, breakfast cereals, biscuits, Marmite, marmalade – all either expensive, or difficult to locate, or horrible.

Bring Home
Beer is a Best Buy and the allowance is so liberal that you can let it reach the parts of the car that other purchases fail to reach, i.e.: load up. Coffee is much cheaper; cheeses are an obvious choice if the pong is socially acceptable. I buy fresh fish if I see a boat coming in while I'm homeward bound, and early expensive vegetables like asparagus, artichokes, mange-touts and the wonderful fat flavoursome tomatoes. Electric goods are often cheaper, le Creuzet pans, glassware. John Doxat's notes on p. 191 will help choose the best bargain of all – the wine.

Tipping
Lots of readers, used to the outstretched British hand, worry about this. Needlessly – 's.t.c.' should mean what it says – all service and taxes included. The only exception perhaps is to leave the small change in the saucer at a bar.

Changing Money
Everyone has their pet method, from going round all the banks to get a few centimes advantage, to playing it the easy and very expensive way of getting the hotel to do it. It depends on how much is involved and how keen a dealer you are as to how much trouble is worth it. I change mine on the boat, where I have always found the rate to be very fair. If you get caught outside booking hours, the *bureaux de change* stay open late.

Telephoning
Most of the public telephones in France actually work. You put your 1f piece in the slot and watch it roll down for starters, then as many more pieces as you estimate you will need. If it's too much, out it all comes at the conclusion of conversation.
    To dial U.K. from France: 19, wait for tone, 44, then STD code minus 0, then number.
    Inter-departmental: 16, then 2-figure code, then number.
    To dial France from U.K.: 010, pause, 33, 8-figure code.
    Emergencies: Fire 18; Police 17; Operator 13; Directory Enquiries 12.

How to get there:

My research in Brittany, both for this book and for the new 'Bed and Breakfast in France' guide, has involved many weeks spent driving around the countryside, investigating every corner. Because I took my car, crossings have usually been by Brittany Ferries, whose ships seem to get bigger and better all the time. No guide on Brittany eating would be complete without a reference to the excellent value and comfort to be found in their restaurants, run with French flair, so that the holiday begins and ends in Plymouth, or Poole. Their Breton ports are St. Mâlo and Roscoff. Information from Plymouth – 01752 221321 – or Portsmouth – 01705 827701.

There are also daily flights out of Gatwick to Brest – much recommended.

* * *

I am often asked how I go about the inspections: 'Do they know who you are?'. Well, generally, no. Never in the case of a restaurant and only where necessary in a hotel in order to see as much as possible. No question ever of special treatment. 'Do you go alone?' Sometimes and increasingly often. In the early days of 'F.E.1.' (which I realise now were a doddle) I needed friendly support and found no shortage of willing volunteers. As I got tougher and more sceptical, though, I found them too nice, enjoying every minute of this lovely break, and it became hard to spoil everything by criticism. Nowadays it is only family that I subject to the rigours of a much speeded-up routine. Only they, I feel, can be asked to put up with a heavy lunch when a beautiful day indicates a picnic, or a 'S' dinner when they feel like putting on the Ritz. Only they can be expected to work all day and stay awake all night because the mattress is so hard or the disco so noisy.

I can't say I like going it alone, especially in the evening, when there's no-one to grumble with over an awful meal or a one-watt bulb, but there's no doubt that this is when the eye is beadiest and the observation gains accordingly.

INTRODUCTION TO BRITTANY

Brittany – a rich and rewarding province, but a devil to research for a guidebook. The first thing I had to learn was that it was not a bit like next-door Normandy. Normandy, with its autoroutes, proximity to Paris, and industry, keeps going year-round, whereas most of Brittany dies for six months of the year. It's on and around the coastline that the essential flavour is to be found and there's a helluva lot of coastline to see in six months.

Of this time, July and August are out for casual booking – the regulars reserve a year ahead, and as their season is so short, hoteliers like you to eat in. So for the freewheeler, one-nighter, eater-outer, like me, the prospect is, to say the least, difficult.

Doggedly resolved to make some use of the fallow months, I tried some off-season sorties, but the power to write convincingly about best beaches, best views, best balconies, deserted me in the face of windswept rocks, sea fogs, peeling paint and stacked plastic recliners. A meal eaten alone in a frumpy dining-room takes on an altogether different aspect from one on a sunlit terrace overlooking sparkling water.

Inland kept me going for a while. The autumn was a perfect time to explore the canals. I can't recommend too highly the pleasures of picking up a little boat at Redon or Josselin, or whatever other station appeals (details from the French Government Tourist Bureau) and proceeding at jogging pace through a green and lush Brittany – quite a contrast to the drama of the coast, and in many ways more real, more substantial. The lockkeepers' wives sold us vegetables as we waited for the water to change levels, the simple restaurants along the route were pleased enough to see us but generally relied on local trade more than tourists and cooked and charged accordingly. Cycling along the towpath, foliage draped with glittering cobwebs, for the breakfast baguette, buying and cooking the best of the local market's produce and eating it pulled up under a willow, is a very agreeable way to get to know Brittany. But as the leisurely pace tends to slow down to the point of inertia, it would take more time than I had available to cover the extensive canal and river network, and winter was setting in.

November was a good time for Rennes, though I grew to

hate the drive down from Cherbourg in the early darkness and unkind weather. Still I found, shaking somewhat after manoeuvring round the *périphérique*, that I could be in my hotel room by six o'clock, and at any other time of the year I would recommend this timetable – the morning boat from Portsmouth and an early afternoon drive-off makes a very civilised start to the holiday.

Nantes is another good off-season choice – I did my Christmas shopping there. The most sophisticated of Breton cities, lively year-round, the best shops, good restaurants. Dinan's mediaeval charm and diversions don't rely on summer weather; in fact without the traffic jams and tourists its probably nicer o.o.s.; but then of course you'd have to go again to have the pleasure of sitting out in a café terrace down by that picturebook port and to take that obligatory trip up the Rance.

Quimper and Vannes fitted in nicely to a spring visit but when I tried to tack on a few of the coastal resorts between them, I knew it wouldn't do. Without their visitors, some looked more attractive, some less, but none typical. I should have to come back later, stay longer.

And so the summer was spent covering practically every resort, every point, every bay around the truly staggering coastline. I found such contrast of stark rock, soft dunes, pink granite, azure sea, fierce rollers, gentle estuaries, dizzy heights, boggy marsh, bleak moor, fertile farms, fishing village, jazzy resort, that it was hard to believe all this could be encompassed in one country let alone one province. Add a mystery of fairy legend, a history of relentless warfare, a glimpse of starched coiffes, a severity of bleak granite, an economy of fish and farm, and you just begin to get the flavour. I doubt if any foreigner gets more.

Because of this variety, Brittany is perfect touring territory. You can drive from rocky north to sandy south in a couple of hours, taking in a mediaeval village, a river, and a canal or two along the way.

Or you can stick to the coast and just keep on driving, left hand down, from Mont St. Michel to Nantes, which is the route I propose to detail now.

Two shortcomings I have to admit: Where does Brittany end? I had pictured the Loire as its south-eastern limit; when I asked people in the north some said yes, some said they didn't rightly know; when I asked those in the south they were sure it stretched across for a slice of the other bank too.

The Loire-Atlantique is a hybrid *département*, coming under the 'Pays du Loire'; by the time I had established that historically some of the south bank should indeed count as part of Brittany, it was too late to go back. So the SE limits for this book stop a bit short.

The big industrial ports – Brest, Lorient, St. Nazaire – are deliberately omitted. This is a holiday book.

So, a brief summary from NE to SE to help plan the holiday:–

From **Pontorson** both road alternatives are bad. The N. 176 is both bad and dull, so take the coast road to **St. Malo** for preference. At least there is some interest in the oyster and mussel beds that line the flat coast from **Le Vivier** northwards.

Cancale is a charming little port and resort. From then on the drama begins, with rocks, cliffs, islands, to **St. Malo**, a No. 1. choice in and out of season. Across the beautiful river Rance **Dinard** has fine beaches and a Riviera setting.

Then along the **Emerald Coast** comes a chain of little family holiday spots, unsophisticated, good sands, spectacular views – **St. Briac**, **St. Jacut**, **St. Cast**. The coast dips into sand dunes at **Sables d'Or**; **Erquy** and **Le Val André** are small fishing harbours.

I have to say I do not care for the stretch between **St. Brieuc** and **Paimpol**. Diligently I followed most of the lanes leading off the D. 786 to the coast and found often enough good sands and sheltered bays, at **Binic** and **Étables** for example, but they lacked charm; **St. Quays'** tawdriness I positively loathed. Worth making a détour from the fishing port of **Paimpol** to **Arcouest** and the **Île de Bréhat**, and from then on it all starts getting really interesting – undoubtedly one of my favourite regions. Hundreds of islands dot the seascape, rivers provide safe anchorages. **Tréguier** and **Trébeurden** are the pearls on this unique **Pink Granite Coast**; between them are dozens of beguiling bays and beaches. **Perros** is the biggest and noisiest resort, in a superb natural setting, **Lannion** is a pleasant inland market town.

Immense sandy bays follow one another from **St. Michel-en-Grève** westwards, with the nice little port of **Locquirec** facing all directions at the tip of the point. **Morlaix** is an old and interesting river port and the minor coast road from there to **Carantec** is a delight. More islands and lovely beaches here, up to **Roscoff**, a colourful port and resort, with the time-warped **Île de Batz** just offshore.

At this stage I would head inland and visit some of the unique parish closes (see p. 15) but if you stick to the coast it is back to sand dunes and a rather uninteresting stretch until **Brignogan Plage**, where the rocks take over again.

Then the remote area of the *abers* – creeks that cut deep inland – with few tourist amenities, round the wild west coast to the industrialisation of **Brest**. The **Crozon** peninsula is green and soft to the north, grey and harsher after **Camaret**, round to **Morgat**, a little fishing harbour.

Inside the **Bay of Douarnenez** are low sandy beaches, like **Ste. Anne-la-Palud**, round to the busy fishing port of **Douarnenez** itself, from whence it all gets mighty impressive, with high cliffs and crashing seas, around the daunting **Raz**. Softer again to the port of **Audierne**.

Then a dullish stretch, low and windswept, to the bleak fishing port of **St. Guénolé** and round the grim little harbours of the south of the **Bigouden** peninsula.

Sheer delight from then on, with the deep estuaries of green-banked rivers, **Odet**, **Aven**, **Belon**, **Laïta**, slicing into the Mediterranean-style foliage, and charmers like **Benodet**, **Concarneau** and **Pont Aven**. **Raguénés-Plage** has an unbelievably beautiful beach. The stretch between the pretty little port of **Le Pouldu** and **Larmor Plage** is a bit of a let-down, but beyond **Lorient**, **Port Louis** has charm and a good beach.

Everyone finds the **Quiberon** peninsula fascinating, with **Carnac's** contrasting attractions of megaliths and beach, and **Belle-Île** would be well worth a visit. **La Trinité** is a modern yachting centre.

Then another favourite area, full of interest, around the **Gulf of Morbihan**, with its dozens of islands and picturesque **Auray** and **Vannes** to explore. The little fishing ports of **Locmariaquer** and **Port Navalo** are the tips of the arms that enfold the gulf; the **Rhuys** peninsula to the south is only moderately interesting and I wouldn't bother to divert through the flat countryside to the little resorts in the sand dunes to the south, except perhaps for the rocky point of **Pen-Lan**.

The mighty river **Vilaine** is good to explore by canal boat, with **La Roche Bernard** an attractive town on its banks. Don't miss the walled **Guérande** on the way to sophisticated La Baule, with fabulous beach, light years away from the simple family holiday villages of the north. Take a drive to **Le Croisic**, a photogenic fishing port, to eat the freshest seafood, and then its foot down along the motorway to elegant **Nantes**, 'little Paris'.

Although I believe most travellers will be seeking coastal holidays along the coast, or 'Armor' region, the 'Argoat' or inland regions, have their high spots too. I would pick for outstanding interest: **Dinan**, **Josselin**, the **Paimpont/Brocéliande** forest, the **Regional Park of Armorica** and the parish closes of **Finistère**, and I have also tried to indicate stops along the main routes.

THE BRETONS

Ignored by industry, poor communications with the rest of France, a history of warfaring – it's not hard to see why the Bretons are known for their spirit of independence. By clinging doggedly to regional dress, customs, legends, language, they have succeeded in maintaining a unique charm and interest that, combined with their extraordinarily beautiful coastline, has made Brittany the second most popular tourist destination in France.

The costumes are passed down through the generations and are most likely to be seen in the south, at Quimper, Pont Aven, Pont l'Abbé, Plougastel, Douarnenez, Auray. It is worth planning a holiday around the 'Pardons', the colourful local religious processions, to see them being worn. Here is a list of the chief *pardons* and local events of special interest:

2nd Sunday in May	Quintin
May 19	Treguier
Whitsun	Moncontour
Whit Monday	Carantec
Friday before Trinity	St. Herbot
Trinity	Rumengol
June 23	St. Jean du Doigt
Sunday before June 24	St. Tugen
Last Sunday in June	Le Faouët
Last Sunday in June	Plouguerneau
Eve of 1st Sun. in July	Guincamp
3rd Sunday in July	Douarnenez, Blessing of the Sea
3rd Monday in July	Roscoff
4th Sunday in July	Quimper, festival of Cornouaille
4th Sunday in July	Bubry
July 25 and 26	Ste-Anne d'Auray
July 26th	Fouesnant
1st Sunday in August	Pont Aven, Festival of the Golden Gorse
August 15	Perros-Guirec
August 15	Plougastel-Daoulas

August 15	Guelven
Sunday after August 15	Carantec
Sunday after August 15	Ploerdut
Penultimate Sunday in August	Concarneau, Festival of the Blue nets
Last Sunday in August	Audierne
Last Sunday in August	St. Anne-la-Palud, Grand Pardon
1st Sunday in September	Camaret
1st Sunday in September	St. Nicholas-de-Pelem, Blessing of the Horses
September 8 or Sunday before	Le Folgoet, Grand Pardon
September 8 or Sunday before	Penhors
2nd Sunday in September	Carnac
2nd Sunday in September	Josselin
3rd Sunday in September	N.-D de Tronoen
Last Sunday in September	Hennebont
December 4	Le Faouët

Every Breton would claim that the Quest for the Holy Grail and the rest of the Arthurian legend centred on Brittany not Britain, as most of us supposed, and certainly in the Forest of Brocéliande around Paimpont (see p. 110) the magic is potent, carefully fostered by the tourist board. Otherwise it is in the north-west that the Breton affinity for myths and fairy tales is most strong. The local saints, many of them monks coming from Britain in the 5th and 6th century, have villages named after them – St. Ivy (Pontivy), St. Suliac, Île Tudy. The miracles they performed still work for the believers, the spells are still potent, the tabus formidable.

The Breton language in a written form is surprisingly evident but nowadays only a few of the older peasants in the remotest northwest villages do not understand French. There is a strong movement to re-introduce Breton to the young and it is taught in schools all over 'Lower Brittany' – the line from St. Brieuc to Vannes – where the feeling for independence is strongest. You can buy Breton dictionaries, but some of the most common prefixes are: *plou* (look at the list of place names in this book) = parish, *tre* = congregation, *loc* = holy place, *ker* = house, *gui* = town, *tro* = valley, *goat* or *coat* = wood, *lan* = sacred ground.

CHURCHES

It is not surprising that in an area as poor as Brittany was in the Romanesque period (11th and 12th centuries), when some of the outstandingly beautiful cathedrals were being built in Normandy and elsewhere, few churches of any stature were achieved here. It therefore comes as an additional shock of pleasure to find the startling richness of the Gothic and, particularly, Renaissance periods, when the wealthy Dukes were in power, in the interiors of churches often built in humble villages.

The parish closes – *enclos paroissiaux* – (see Lampaul Guimiliau, St. Thégonnec) are the most outstanding example of what I mean and no-one visiting Finistère should fail to witness this unique Breton phenomenon of parish vying with parish over several centuries to produce the most glorious combined effect of triumphal arch, calvary, ossuary and brilliant church interior.

However the local material they had to work with on the exteriors was still the unmalleable granite and any delicacy and lightness was achieved with difficulty. The carvings often appear crude to the point of caricature, but are nonetheless fascinating in the stories they tell.

Calvaries

In the most famous, at Guimiliau, are 200 figures depicting episodes of the Passion; at the other extreme is the simple cross to be found at the roadsides all over Brittany. The oldest remaining calvary is at Tronoën, dating from the end of the 15th century, but they were still built two hundred years later. Those in the late 16th century were intended to ward off the plague or as a thanksgiving to have escaped from it.

A LITTLE HISTORY

A common Breton phenomenon are the megalithic monuments of prehistoric times. Anyone interested in depth should make for the display and explanation in the Musée de Bretagne in Rennes, or the Museé Préhistorique Finisterien in St. Guénolé, but, very briefly; – dolmens mark huge collective graves dug at a time of a cult for worshipping the dead. Menhirs (lit. tall stones) probably mark a sacred spot but, in spite of many theories over the years, nobody has ever satisfactorily explained their existence. The puzzle remains too as to how they and the dolmens, some weighing over 100 tons, were erected at that time.

After the mysterious builders of the megaliths came, in

the 6th century BC, the Celts, of whom the most powerful tribe were the Veneti, around Vannes. After much resistance, they were conquered by the Romans in 5 BC. Having drained the land by fierce taxation, the Romans left Armorica to degenerate again into savagery until about 460 AD when the first settlers arrived from Britain. These intrepid seafarers settled mainly in the Nort-west, often in communities ruled by the monks who later became locally sanctified and gave their name to their villages. They also gave a new name to Armorica – Brittany, or Little Britain.

Charlemagne's forces conquered Brittany in 799 AD but the Breton rebellious spirit hardly faltered and only 44 years later Duke Nominoë from Vannes defeated Charles the Bald at Redon and founded an independent ducal dynasty.

Here the sense of territorialism worked against the new country, for the Dukes persistently quarrelled amongst themselves and, divided, were an easy target for Norman invasion. William the Conqueror used Brittany as a buffer state between his England and his Normandy.

From the 12th to the 15th centuries, Brittany, a hub of maritime trade routes, was a prize coveted by both French and English monarchs, while powerful dukes, kings in all but name, whose names are commemorated in fortresses, villages and streets throughout the province – Montfort, Rohan, Clissons – were contending for control of the duchy. The weak duke Conan IV had to call in Henry II of England to help deal with his opponents and feebly ceded the throne to Henry in 1166, ensuring a period of chaos with no clear ruler. The War of Succession in 1341 had the French supporting one contender, Charles de Blois, and Edward III the other, Jean de Montfort. It was in this war that that indefatigable warrior, much revered by the Bretons, Bertrand du Guesclin, made his name (even though he was fighting on the losing side – the de Montforts won).

The Dukes of Montfort, virtually sovereigns, paid only scant homage to the King of France. Under their rule in the 14th and 15th centuries, Brittany enters its most successful period, economically and artistically.

In 1491 Anne, Duchess of Brittany, the best remembered of all Breton rulers, married Charles VIII of France, but on his death, seven years later, she returned to her duchy for a year (see St. Mâlo) before marrying another king of France, Louis XII (she seems to have had quite a way with her since both these monarchs had to repudiate previous wives to marry her, and she herself did some two-timing by rejecting her first proxy marriage to the future Emperor of Austria). When Anne died in 1514 her daughter, Claude, inherited the duchy and ceded it to France on her marriage to the future Francois I, finally linking the two states, but with a partially independent parliament for Brittany.

But the Bretons hardly ever stopped rebelling against irksome control, either from the French or from anyone else. When their Governor in 1588 tried to make a Catholic take-over, they rebelled against him too and called in the French for help! The Edict of Nantes in 1598 brought a temporary halt to the religious conflict.

The 17th and 18th centuries saw many other uprisings, against taxation, the Jesuits, the Republicans (from welcoming the Revolution as a defeat for autocracy, the Bretons came to resent the new disciplines as much as the old.)

The last rising organised by the colourful Duchesse de Berry (said to have invented sea-bathing) petered out in 1832 but the resolution to achieve a free Brittany for the Bretons has never faltered.

FOOD AND DRINK

This is no place for complicated gastronomy. With prime materials – other mens' luxuries like lobster and oysters, turbot and sole, artichokes and strawberries – what need, argued the wise forefathers, to taint the pure Breton lily with the superficial gilt of Paris elaboration. I believe they were right, and in my travels I came across very few successful examples of cuisine haute or nouvelle. But throughout the province is to be found some of the best seafood in Europe and I have yet to taste a dish more sublime than a lobster freshly plucked from Breton waters, plainly cooked to show off his freshness. The 'Armoricain' version (so often wrongly tagged 'Americain') has to be treated circumspectly. Rich and delicious in skilful hands, it is no dish for pretentious amateurs.

The *beurre blanc* sauce that hails from Nantes is a natural and delicious accomplishment to fish. (It incorporates two Breton products, dry white wine and butter; the wine is reduced to intensify the flavour and the butter judiciously whisked in.) Not as simple as it seems – it can end up swamping the plate and the flavour.

Perhaps this is the moment to clarify the great crustacean mystery. *Langouste, homard*, labour, crayfish, crawfish, *écrevisse, langoustine*, Dublin Bay prawn, scampi, shrimp, *crevette rose*, not to mention crab, spider crab, *étrilles*, *tourteaux* and *crabe* become hopelessly confused in minds and on menus, and as most of them will be encountered some time in Brittany, a little light should be thrown.

Homard (lobster) rules O.K. The king of the sea, ink-coloured in the *vivier*, turns an angry red (who can blame him!) when cooked. *Langouste* is the spiny lobster or crawfish, covered in shell pimples, reddish brown alive, scarlet when boiled, not so fine a flavour as *homard.* Delicate *langoustine*, pale pink, with long spindly claws = Dublin Bay prawn = scampi, except that most 'scampi' are not scampi at all but glorified prawns – *crevettes* in French, shrimp in American. Are you still with me?

Crevettes roses look and taste delicious when pink and briefly oiled; on the fishmongers' slab they appear outer-spaceish, weirdly transparent. Baby shrimps caught in the rock pools are *crevettes grises* – fiddly to shell but with a unique salty flavour that brings just reward for the labour.

Écrevisses are freshwater crayfish, sometimes wrongly termed crawfish. Red-clawed, like miniature lobsters, they are a great delicacy, fashionable in the *nouvelle cuisine.*

Tourteaux or *crabes* are the kind we know back home, full of meat; *araignée*, the spiny spidercrab, has more flavour, less meat, and *étrilles*, the tiny grey swimming crabs have no meat at all but are good for soups. Do I make myself clear?

Fresh scallops, lightly poached in Muscadet or cider from the rocks around Erquy I particularly relish, and one taste of their pearly moistness is enough to make you foreswear their frozen aunties forever. Baby scallops are *pétoncles.* Local mussels and clams (*palourdes*) are cooked simply *à la marinière* or stuffed (*farcis*) on a half-shell (try the clams for a change).

Oysters are The Best Buy, especially if you can pick them up from the market stall or the stands along the coast at Le Vivier, Cancale, Le Pô, Bélon, and serve them yourself (having first purchased an oyster knife in the market). They are cheap enough to make you (a) understand why they used to be considered poor man's food in England, and (b) wonder how they can possibly be so expensive there now. Bélon's (see p. 37) are the best. Even in restaurants they will feature on inexpensive menus with a lavishness that makes the fancier's eyes glisten.

The fishing boats also bring in a good supply of flavoursome sole, turbot and bass, which I prefer any day to the modish monk-fish. If you can find a good restaurant grill, who will stripe these fish over a hot flame and serve them simply with perhaps a sprinkling of herbs, lemon, butter, stick with it.

What *bouillabaisse* is to the Med., *cotriade* is to Brittany, except its potentially better because cold water fish have more flavour. Well-prepared, the drabness of its components (cheaper variety of fish, like mackerel, whiting, *eel*, plus potatoes) is relieved with the corals of mussels and scallops, the flavour sharpened with sorrel, enriched with cream; carelessly prepared, its a sorry grey mess, unmitigated with the saving saffron of *bouillabaisse.*

Lamb from the salt marshes – *pré-salé* – near Mont St. Michel or the Crozon peninsula is the meat to look for, ready slat-flavoured, killed pathetically young, served pink. The juices round a *gigot à la bretonne* comes thick with white beans. *Kig-ha-Fraz* is a hotch potch that combines several courses in one – a sweetened buckwheat pudding with meat – beef, ham, oxtail – and vegetables. You have to be both hungry and brave to try that one. Duck from the Grande Brière region, usually described as *canard nantais,* is justly famous, often served with *petits pois.* From Morlaix comes the products of the pig – *andouilles, saucisson, jambon.*

Breton puddings – *'far'* – cater for hearty northern appetites. Heavy is the word I hesitate to use. *'Far breton'* is like a Yorkshire pudding with raisins (prunes from the Loire region are a better idea) *Gâteau breton* is a pound cake made with the slightly salted breton butter.

Brittany is one area in France where you need never have problems finding a snack. *Crêperies* abound, turning out the lacy pancakes and *galettes,* made from flour or buckwheat (*sarrasin*) and stuffed with every imaginable combination of filling, sweet and savoury. They used to provide the basis for a three course meal for the breton worker – the first crumbled into his soup, the second wrapped around a sausage and the third spread with sugar or jam. The aroma from the *galettières* – the open air griddles – in the markets, along with gaulois and garlic, is part of the instantly recognisable flavour of France.

CHEESES

Trust the Bretons to be different. Here is one of the few provinces in France where cheese is not revered. Only two indigenous species are likely to be tracked down:–
'Campenéac', made by the nuns in the Campenéac convent, is similar to *St. Paulin*, round with a very smooth

ochre rind and a light yellow inside, very fine holes and strongish flavour. 'A good buy' says Androuet. The other, also made from cows milk and similar in appearance and flavour, is the '*Nantais*' or '*Fromage du Curé*', because it was invented last century by a priest from the Vendée. This one is now factory-made, square with a straw coloured smooth rind, 'A fairly good buy'.

'*Maingaux*' (or *Mingaux* or *Mingots*) *de Rennes* is a combination of fresh and soured cream beaten together and eaten with sugar and perhaps fruit. It used to be a speciality of the crêpe-makers, each one of whom would jealously guard the proportions of the delicious filling for his pancakes, but I should very much like to know of any *marchand de galettes* nowadays who would take the trouble.

The local drink is cider, the best coming from Fouesnant, but generally inferior to the Norman variety. Muscadet is claimed as the local wine, but the vineyards in which the grapes from which it takes its name are grown spill over from the area around Nantes into the neighbouring Anjou. The best are to be found on the gentle slopes bordering the Loire.

The best sub-district within the *appellation controlé* is Muscadet-de-Sevre-Maine, another – Muscadet-des-Coteaux-de-la-Loire comes from outside the Brittany border. Gros Plant, made from the Folle Blanche grape (Gros Plant) is a VDQS from the area around Nantes.

Muscadet ages quickly and is best drunk young. '*Sur lies*' indicates that the wine has been left to mature in the cask on their lees, giving a distinctive fruity taste.

SPECIAL RECOMMENDATIONS

ARROWS These are special recommendations, tried and tested, many of them inherited from four editions of FE5 and approved over nine years. Criteria for inclusion are one or several of the following virtues:- good food, comfort, welcome, situation.

Arradon: *Les Vénètes* (H)M. *Les Logoden* (R)M.
Belle-Îsle-en-Terre: *Le Relais d'Argoat* (HR)M.
Cancale: *Restaurant de Bricourt* (R)L.
Combourg: *Hotel du Château* (HR)M. *l'Ecrivan* (R)S.
Dinan: *Le Relais des Corsaires* (R)M-L. *La Mère Pourcel* (R)M.
Dinard: *Le Vieux Manoir* (H)M.
Dol-de-Bretagne: *Le Grabotais* (R)S.
Fouësnant: *Hotel d'Armorique* (HR)S.
Guenrouet: *Le Relais St. Clair* (R)M.
La Jouvente: *Manoir de la Rance* (H)M-L.
Lannion: *La Ville Blanche* (R)M.
Pacé: *La Griotte* (R)M.
Perros Guirec: *Les Vieux Gréements* (R)S.
Plancoët: *Chez Crouzil* (HR)M.
Pleugueuneuc: *Château de la Motte Beaumanoir* (HR)L.
Plonéour-Lanvern: *La Mairie* (HR)S.
Plouer-sur-Rance: *Le Manoir de Bigourdaine* (H)M. *The French Connection* (R)S-M.
Pointe du Raz: *Hotel de la Baie des Trépassés* (HR)M.
Pont l'Abbe: *Hotel Bretagne* (HR)M.
Port Blanc: *Hotel des Îles* (HR)S.
Quimperlé: *Bistro de la Tour* (R)M.
Raguerès Plage *Men Du* (H)M.
Riec-sur-Bélon: *Chez Jacky* (R)M.
Roscoff: *Temps de Vivre* (R)M.
Ste Anne d'Auray: *l'Auberge* (HR)M.
St. Brieuc: *La Vieille Tour* (R)M-L.
St. Malo: *La Duchesse Ann* (R)M-L. *La Villefromoy* (H)M-L.
St. Servan: *St. Placide* (R)M.
St. Suliac: *La Grève* (R)M.
Trébeurden: *Ti al Lannec* (HR)M-L.

Treguier: *Kastell Dinech* (HR)M.
La Trinité-sur-Mer: *l'Azimut* (R)M.
Val André: *Au Biniou* (R)M.

MAPS

Saint-Malo

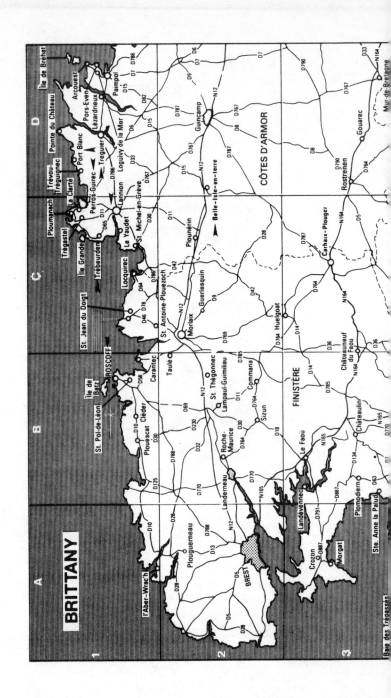

24

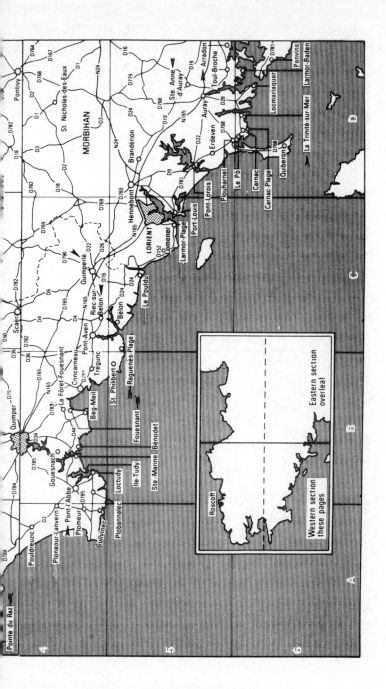

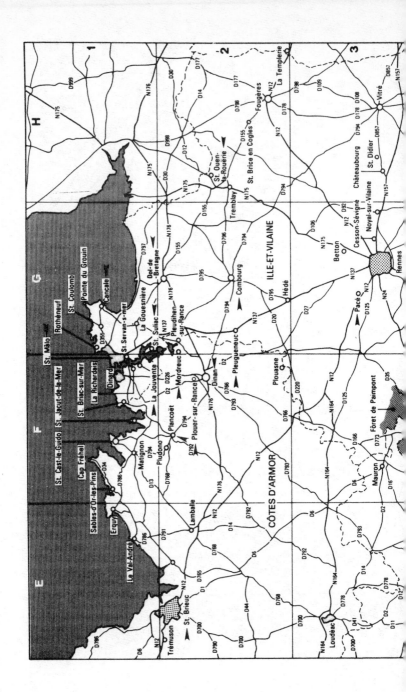

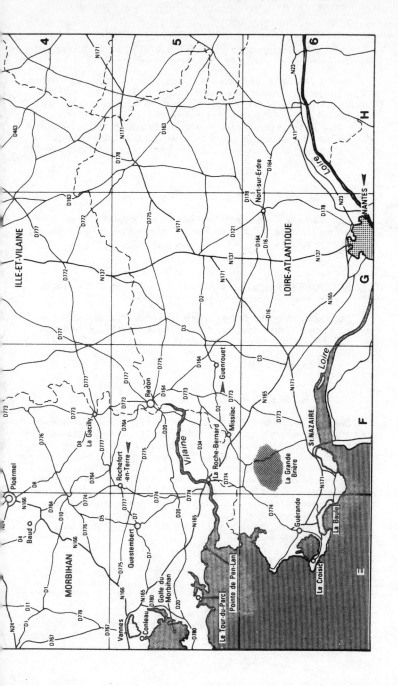

Map 1A   **ABER WRACH** Landéda 29214 (Finistère) 28 km N of Brest

The extreme north-west-coast of Brittany, low and rocky, is sliced by wide estuaries known as 'abers'. No ports or big towns around here, just a few unsophisticated holiday spots and tiny harbours, with little in the way of accommodation or restaurants.

Aber Wrach is attractively sited on a wide estuary, useful for sailing. The hotel I went to look at, the Bellevue, was desolate and shuttered, and apart from the activities of a sailing school, not a lot was going on, even in August.

Baie des Anges
(H)S   *98.04.90.04 Cl. mid Nov.–Easter*

Just 17 rooms in this simple little hotel, blissfully peaceful, in a lovely setting. No restaurant but good advice offered from the management on local options. 190–395f.

Map 1D   **ARCOUEST** Ploubazlanec 22620 (C. d'A.) 6 km N of Paimpol

The point of Arcouest is the depot for the boats that leave every half hour to the Ile de Bréhat (see p. 47). Even better is to take one right round this enchanting island, or along the coast and up the river Trieux.

Right on the point is:

Le Barbu
(HR)M   *96.55.73.87 Fax 96.55.73.87 Cl. 3/1–15/2*

The exterior is dignified, creeper-covered, with a large hydrangea-brimming terrace from which to observe all the activity; I did feel however, on a recent visit, that the interior is a bit naff in view of the prices, which seem to have escalated alarmingly. The cheapest room is now 450f and the ones with the best views command 900f in high season. While it has to be admitted that La Barbu has one of the best natural positions in Brittany and that the food has won plaudits from many readers (menus from 150f), the downside is that hordes of tourists mill around in high summer, waiting for boats to the island, and the bill is beginning to seem unjustified. More reports on whether this is so would be welcome.

Map 5D   **ARRADON** 56610 (Morbihan) 7 km SW of Vannes

The gulf of Morbihan loops and curves and juts, with as many promontories and bays as there are islands. Any of the side turnings of the D 101 will lead to water and boats, and often to a little hotel or bar.

One of the most pleasant is down to the Pointe d'Arradon, which is just a cluster of houses and a little dinghy harbour. Via sea walls and beaches you can walk for miles around this stunning bay. One golden autumn evening I did just this, from Arradon towards Vannes, and met only half-a-dozen people – children dawdling on the beaches, a fisherman sitting in his pulled-up boat, an elderly couple walking their dog – in an hour's perambulation at the water's edge, with island succeeding island over the sparkle, and only the chatter of halyards and an occasional phut-phut to disturb the calm.

We liked it so much that we returned for a second look, arriving on a hot Saturday in June and hardly believed our eyes at the sight of our quiet little bay overrun with sunbathers, promenaders, windsurfers and all. Dying for a swim after a long sticky ride, I had to pick my way over the bodies to reach the decidedly murky water. Another favourite bites the dust?

But no, next morning was cooler and the beach stayed reasonably free all day. During the marvellous weather of the week that followed, spent exploring this exceptionally beautiful area, we had it all to ourselves and the conclusion must be that anywhere as attractive as Arradon, so near to a big town like Vannes, must be busy at peak periods. Still a lot of calm to go round, and with the bonus of:

➤ **Les Vénètes**
(HR)M   *97.44.03.11   Cl. 1/10–1/4; rest. cl. Tues.*

 H

 R

The Vénètes were the earliest Armoricain seafarers, rough and crude – not a bit like this smart little hotel. Right on the water's edge, with terrace and dining-room enjoying the view.

The rooms vary a lot in size and price but all are extremely well-fitted, bright and cheerful. Those on the front, with balcony, are well worth the 460f, but all have some view of the sea, and a tiny one at the side was perfectly agreeable at 300f with bath.

The brothers Tixier, Jacques and Henri, who run the little hotel, are exceptionally friendly and helpful and although they do have a restaurant (menus from 110f), there were no sour looks when we ate out.

The combination of superb site, comfortable hotel and congenial management make this my no. 1 choice for Morbihan and an arrow, but there have been some doubts about the food. Demi-pension unfortunately is insisted on in high season, at 368–450f per person.

➤ **Les Logoden**
(R)M   *97.44.03.35   Cl. Wed.; Thur. o.o.s.   EC, MC, V*

The Logoden are the humpbacked islands opposite Arradon, and M. and Mme Gabriel Pellan are true Morbihanais. Their delightful little restaurant opposite the Poste in the bourg of Arradon, 2 km away from the Pointe, was the find of the week. We went initially because it was open on the difficult Sundays and Mondays, but would go back any night of the week for such exceptional value.

There are perfectly good menus at 75f and 95f, including oysters and seafood, but the 120f menu was irresistible. For me, a huge platter of

Les Vénètes

langoustines, home-made mayonnaise; for husband, six fat oysters, grilled and scattered with almonds. Then *saumon cru mariné* – a kind of gravadlax – and *coquelon de pêcheur* – scallops and white fish gratinéed in an excellent sauce. The third-course sole covered the plate and would have justified the menu price alone, and husband's herbed beef, cooked on skewers over the charcoal fire, was served exactly as he requested. The cheese-board far exceeded normal expectations for a modest country inn, and the strawberries were lavish and served with *crème fraîche*.

Gabriel Pellan is more than just an adequate patron-chef, and is not content to dish up the standard fishy menus, admirable but undemanding, of the area. If you want a plain *sole meunière*, you can have one here for 90f – one of the lowest prices for this fish I found – but he will also offer it with a lobster stuffing. And sorrel soufflés like his don't come ten a penny in many un-sung Breton villages. Go soon.

The restaurant has recently been smartened up pushing this erstwhile S restaurant into the M category, but the quality, value and atmosphere are unchanged. Highly appreciated.

Map 4A   **AUDIERNE** 29770 (Finistère) 15 km E of the Pointe du Raz, 35
km W of Quimper

A big fishing port, especially for tuna and crayfish. Sheltered from the
west, it nestles in the estuary of the Goyen, approached from a bridge
from the Plouhinec side, with the beach. Overlooking the port is:

Le Goyen, le port
(HR)L   *98.70.18.77   Fax 98.70.18.77   Cl. mid Nov.–mid Dec.; Mon.–Tues. lunch
o.o.s.*

At the time of my inspection, M. Bosser was waiting for authority to
convert an old fish processing plant on the other side of the estuary
into an ambitious new venture, so judgment on the accommodation
will have to be suspended.
   In any case it is the food for which La Goyen is chiefly famous, after
36 years of M. Bosser's tenure, and I don't suppose that will change
much whatever the situation. That said, he is not averse to including
dishes like a carpaccio of salmon, unheard of when he first donned his
toque, in his impressive repertoire of skilful, mostly fish, dishes. Mid
week lunch costs 160f, otherwise the cheapest menu is currently 260f.
Goodness knows what effect the move will have on prices, but I fear
they can hardly move downwards, so we are talking special occasions
here, but the loyalty of local clients is good testimony to reliability and
good value in this category.

Roi Gradlon
(HR)M   *98.70.04.51   Fax 98.70.14.73   rest. cl. Mon. Sun. p.m. o.o.s.; 10/1–22/2*

For lighter budgets the Roi Gradlon, on the beach, fills the bill. The first
menu at 100f offers plenty of seafood, and if you must have lobster
you can do so just as well here as at the Le Goyen, if with fewer frills.
Hotel rooms cost 310–350f and half pension is a good buy here at
340–370f.

Map 5D   **AURAY** 56400 (Morbihan) 18 km E of Vannes

An enchanting town, split into two distinct parts by the river Auray, on
which in high season you can take a *Vedette Verte* out to the Gulf of
Morbihan.
   The little port of St.-Goustan, once one of the busiest in Brittany,
is pure picturebook, with its cobbled square and old grey stone
houses brightened with masses of flowers. Benjamin Franklin landed
here in 1776 to seek French support for his country's War of
Independence.
   We sat there, under one of the multicoloured parasols, one hot
summer day and watched the local children dive from the old bridge
into the fast-flowing river, to be carried along, squealing happily, to the

far river bank, or hang on to the bridge supports to get a free jacuzzi from the powerful stream.

On the other side of the bridge a path zigzags upwards through the trees to the Promenade du Loc, for a good view of the colourful harbour from the other, more down-to-earth Auray, with shops, a market square and the Office du Tourisme. The 18th century St.-Gilda's church is up here, with a fine reredos behind the high altar.

Nearby is:

Hotel de la Mairie
(HR)S *32 pl. de la Mairie   97.24.04.65   Cl. Oct.; 2/2–15/1 Sat. p.m.; Sun. o.o.s.*

An unpretentious little Logis, much used by locals, whose patron, M. Stephant-Guidelo, cooks good-value meals from 65f and has rooms from 150–275f with bath.

I didn't think there were any hotels down by the river, since none proclaim their existence, not even:

La Closerie de Kerdrain
(R)L *20 r. L-Billet   97.56.61.27   Cl. Tues. Mon. p.m. o.o.s.; 3/1–18/1; 6/11–16/11.*

An affordable special-occasion luxury. La Closerie is a lovely manorhouse set in a colourful garden, in which it is a great pleasure to eat in high summer. Fernand Corfmat is dedicated to Breton ingredients, but serves them in a highly sophisticated style, which makes a pleasant change occasionally in this largely unsophisticated part of the world.

Try his roast turbot flavoured with bay leaves and cider to see what I mean – the clever harmonising of flavours makes the prices seem good value. The lunch menu (not Sundays of course) at 100f makes downmarket choices look bad news. And the 145f dinner menu could hardly be bettered.

More favourable reports on this new addition for an arrow.

Map 1B   ÎLE DE BATZ 29253 (Finistère) 1.5 km off Roscoff

A truly enchanting place, permeated with a serenity that is catching. No one hurries or flusters on Batz, not even the weather which is as calm and mild as its inhabitants. Mediterranean plants – mimosa, figs, oleanders – thrive alongside the early vegetables which are transported to the mainland once a day on the bulky carrier ship that returns with the islanders' supplies.

The ferry from Roscoff crosses every half hour, or thereabouts – they tend to wait for their regulars who may not have quite finished lunch or depart a bit early if someone's got a train to catch. It takes fifteen minutes to reach the 3 km-long island, with a choice of twenty little *plagettes* to decide upon, according to the wind direction and inclination for solitude or company.

Walks are marked around the island, through narrow streets lined with grey cottages, flowers a-tumble everywhere, down to the little fishing harbour where the boats land the shellfish that proliferate on the surrounding rocks, to the beaches where the other 'industry' of the island – seaweed gathering – is carried on by the fishermen's wives.

Just by the landing stage is the inaptly named **Grand Hotel** with a terrace overlooking the water, and I highly recommend an excursion to this lovely island combined with a platter of *langoustines* eaten here or in the large bustling dining-room. For 110f (other menus at 75f) we ate a huge perfectly fresh quantity of these crustaceans, followed by a delicious seafood *feuilleté*, followed by sole, followed by cheese and dessert. Not at all smart, very French *familial*.

M. Morvan has simple rooms available too, but in August they were all full and unvieuable. A weekend here would certainly be away from it all.

Mme Ressot's *crêperie* **du Port** makes a good cheap snack alternative, open every day from April to October.

Map 4E   **BAUD** 56150 Morbihan. 15 kms N of Pluvigner 35 kms SW of Josselin.

---

l'Apollinaire
(R)S–M *Le Pont de Baud.* 97.51.03.66 *Cl. Wed. o.o.s.*

A discovery while researching chambres d'hotes on a wild and wet June day when the surrounding forests in which we had hoped to picnic were dripping despondently and so were we. It was late for French lunch and a brasserie on the main road was not what we had hoped for, but how lucky we proved to be.

All the advantages of a good brasserie were here – a fairly substantial lunch of excellent steak and frites for Him and something lighter for Her – an interesting and well balanced salade composée, two dishes which reveal nothing on the carte, but can be superb or dire. There were many more adventurous options on the good value menu and we left considerably cheered, to find that the sun was shining.

Three courses 60f, omelettes 22–42f, fresh fish 33f. Cheerful service.

Map 6E   **LA BAULE** 44500 (Loire-Atl.) 136 km SW of Rennes, 58 km W of Nantes – *Mkt: Tues., Fri., Sun.*

Of the many youthful memories of La Baule – stylish/mostly pine trees/ expensive – only the last, sadly, is valid today. The pines have retreated one by one further from the beach, invaded by the inexorable march of the apartment blocks. A street or two away from the prom they are still to be found, shading the little hotels and causing the quiet roads to twist around them.

The chic has departed with them, it seems; the main street goes in more for jeans than Balenciaga, cafés and fast foods are easy to find, good restaurants are not. The 'best beach in Europe' is still very fine indeed, but now that the backdrop green has gone, so has a lot of its character.

Jam-packed on sunny weekends, entirely deserted on grey days after mid-September, it's hard to hit it right. Most hotels shut up firmly for six months and charge enough for the other six to compensate. Those that do stay open are full if the weather is good, and in fairness it often is – La Baule enjoys a microclimate that gives it more sunshine than its latitude would seem to expect.

Castel Marie-Louise
(HR)L   *espl. Casino*   *40.60.20.60*   *Cl. 30 Jan.–6 March*   P.   *AE, DC, V*

I call 195f a bargain, in this expensive town or anywhere else, for the chance to sample the sublime cooking of Henri Reverdy in this odd Gothicky 'villa' set in the pine trees on the Esplanade. The dining-room is not large and you must certainly book, since I am not the only one to appreciate the excellence of his *gâteau de pintade et de jarret de veau* or his *marinière de lotte aux artichauts*, his irresistible pastries and even the home-made breads, all served in surroundings as elegant as one would expect from a member of the *Relais et Châteaux* chain.

The bedrooms are expensive – from 790f–1,870f! – but so comfortable and with such perfect service that the cost might seem justified, especially if full use were made of the swimming pool and tennis courts.

La Palmeraie
(HR)M   *7 allée Cormorans*   *40.60.24.41*   *Fax 40.42.73.71*   *Cl. 1/10–1/4*

You name it – Gault-Millau, Michelin, Logis de France, Bottin Gourmand – and many more guidebooks laud **La Palmeraie**, so it's not easy to get in. Certainly an attractive little hotel, in a good position a few quiet roads back from the promenade, set in pine trees. It recently won a special prize for being more 'fleuri' than any other hotel in France; the front garden is ablaze with colour, around a dazzlingly white courtyard, with steps leading up on to a well-equipped terrace. And the palm trees are no idle boast – very lush and healthy they look and as polished as the rest of the horticulture. Little white balconies are clapped on to most of the rooms, from which to survey the pleasant scene below.

Inside, the riot of colour and pattern continues – all a bit too busy for my taste, but still patently clean and shining. Outside it's great but in such a midget-sized room, where one occupant has to stay in bed while the other gets dressed, it all gets a bit oppressive. The plumbing here is unavoidably near your ear and too raucous to be used nocturnally without the certainty of waking up your neighbours. In the morning rush-hour the building nearly got lift-off.

It's a very noisy hotel altogether in fact – that gleaming white terrace got harshly scrubbed at a very early hour with unacceptable cheerful chatter, and gallic cops and robbers shot it out irrepressibly in the TV room beneath our bedroom to an audience of (deaf?) elderly residents.

We were the only eaters-out and crept guiltily down those steps, to escape the no-choice menu of the day – cauliflower soup, poached fish, ice cream: 130f. Perhaps it was more exciting than it sounded, but it didn't seem worth the risk.

So – clean, central, not expensive (360–420f) but best for the hard-of-hearing dwarf.

Délice-Hôtel
(H)M   *19 av. Marie-Louise   40.60.23.17   Fax 40.24.48.88   Cl. 23/9–15/5*   P.

All modern, bright and cheerful, set in a quiet road not far from the front. Good sized bedrooms, all with bathrooms, are from 300f with shower to 350f for four beds, with variations of bath; twin beds, in between. No restaurant.

Hôtel Ty-Gwenn
(H)S   *25 av. de la Grande Dune   40.60.37.07   Cl. 15/11–15/12; 7/1–15/2*

In La Baule-les-Pins, at the southern end of the bay. The little old-fashioned-style hotel is in a quiet road, in a garden, and chosen because it stays open longer than most. The rooms are simple, but warm and comfortable. From 210–330f.

La Ferme du Grand Clos
(R)M   *av. de Lattre-de-Tassigny.   40.60.03.30   Cl. Wed. o.o.s.; 15/3–31/3*

A useful place to know, this light and cheerful little 'fermette' if the kids are starving and the purse is light. You can fill them up with the very best crepes, of sarrasin and froment, while you tackle simple wholesome dishes like osso buco and fresh pasta. No menu but expect a bill of around 130f.

La Marcanderie
(R)M   *5 av. Agen   40.24.03.12   Cl. Mon. except July and Aug. and Sun. p.m. o.o.s.*

The best choice in town when feeling in need of a treat. Even when its raining outside, the sun shines in La Marcanderie, a villa, decorated in pastel tones with a pleasant hostess to welcome you. Jean Luc Giraud's cooking is enough to banish the blues – take his 150f menu to put a smile on your face. Lots of fish, like a superb turbot cooked with a cream flavoured with oursins, salad langoustines and smoked salmon and worth-waiting-for desserts.

Map 4B   **BEG MEIL** 29170 (Finistère) 19 km W of Concarneau by D 44 and D 45

One of the saddest results of the hurricanes that have blasted the Brittany coasts of recent years has been the devastation of the pines on the front at Beg Meil. They were so much a part of the little town, for picnicking and courting and sheltering and strolling under, that it is hard to recognise the reincarnation. However, there are still many blessings like magnificent beaches and rocks and the lovely walk round the cliff edge by the lighthouse, with more sandy beaches, inaccessible at high water, facing across the glittering bay to Concarneau. Whichever way the wind blows, there will always be a sheltered bay in Beg Meil.

The big disadvantage is the lack of recommendable hotels. The same old name keeps cropping up:

Thalamot
(HR)M   *Le Chemin-Creux   98.94.97.38   Fax 98.94.49.92   Cl. Oct.–19/4; All credit cards*

One row back from the beach, set in a shady garden, an eccentric old-fashioned-looking hotel, recently smartened up. The rooms are simple but well equipped and cost a modest 260–300f. Menus from 195f; demi-pension obligatory in season.

I have been duly chastised for recommending the Thalamot, even with reservations. I suppose it is because I am so fond of the little town that I had to include *something*. One irate reader offered the following alternative, on which I should very much like to have comments:-

'Why you continue to mention the Thalamot is beyond me (except that you warn away, with which I agree). We first went to the Hotel de la Plage ten years ago and were thoroughly charmed. There are doubtless acres of fluff under the bed, the towels are bald, the plumbing is noisy, the beds sag, the welcome is not exactly effusive, but what a position, what lovely gardens and, best of all, Mr. Hulot himself seems about to appear round every corner. Not a place for all the comforts of home but quite marvellous. Rooms from 95–250f (in high season in Beg Meil!), menus from 75f.'.

He could well be right.

Map 2D   **BELLE-ISLE-EN-TERRE** 22810 (C. d'A.) 10 km W of Guincamp

Turn off the busy N 12 motorway just one km to find this pretty peaceful little village, whose name derives from its site – an island between the rivers Léguer and Guic.

➤ Le Relais de l'Argoat
(HR)M *96.43.00.34 Cl. Sun. p.m. Mon. Feb.*

Should I be pleased or sorry that this find of mine should have been generally discovered and that the description of simple little inn with country cooking is no longer altogether appropriate? Pleased on the whole, because Pierre Marais deserves his success. His terrines are still superb, though nowadays they tend to be of foie gras rather than rabbit, his tasty entrecôte Marchand is replaced by tournedos with sauce Béarnaise and, his apple tart gives way to nougatine glacé. Never mind, the cheeseboard has improved and his portions are as generous as ever. Prices have inevitably jumped (the cheapest is now 110f) but offers a good seafood salad and a choice of monkfish or quail before the dessert.

The rooms are comfortable, especially the quieter ones at the back, now costing a reasonable 265–320f, and the welcome is still warm.

With so many readers in favour I think the arrow is justified even though some of the character has changed.

'A huge bedroom with splendid elephantine Second-Empire furniture and a brand new carpeted (there's novelty for France) bathroom for 195f and a menu at 160f which was more than good provincial, all very high quality and the work at a guess of an untrained chef but a genuine food lover and experimenter. Ebullient welcome and departure routine, beginning and ending at your car, as M. Marais takes charge of unloading and loading. Worth making a journey for. An undoubted arrow.' (Deepest apologies – I can't read the signature.)

Map 4C   **BÉLON** (Finistère)

The Bélon is an enchanting river. Trees grow right down to its edge, reflecting their green in its deep waters. It twists and turns disorientatingly so that each vista is a new one, luring you on to discover the next. Little settlements, some just a few houses and as many boats, punctuate the water line. One of these is the **Port du Bélon**, where, near the bottom of a steep hill, with sublime views round a wide sweep of water dotted with yachts, and across the river to **Chez Jacky** (see Riec), you'll find a bar, La Cabane, for a plateful of shellfish.

Map 4B   **BÉNODET** 29950 (Finistère) 16 km S of Quimper

I must declare a weakness here – if I had to pick one holiday spot in the whole of Brittany, it would be Bénodet. Not particularly clever this – the Brits (me among them) discovered the little town on the mouth of the Odet (Bén-Odet) years ago and have colonised the place ever since. It's like saying you've found a little French resort called Cannes to recommend Bénodet to an Englishman. It's obvious and not even particularly French. They say in summer (when I refuse to see for myself) the population swells from 2500 to 35,000 and it must be another story then from my experiences at Easter, in June, in September, which have been pure gold.

Particularly pure gold in that the resort faces due west and when Ste.-Marine across the estuary is dark in shade, gets the benefit of the evening sun, so that late strollers along the river path, around the point, past the old lighthouse, towards the little port and maybe even as far as the marina, continue to bask in the unusually warm air and spectacular sunsets.

There are splendid sandy beaches to the south but the intrusion of concrete beach huts into the pine trees does not please and I prefer the river aspect, where the coves are still sandy, more sheltered, and more interesting, with the never-ending fascination of water traffic. It all reminds me very much of beloved Salcombe.

A boat trip up the beautiful river Odet makes a most agreeable excursion, from Bénodet to Quimper, or vice-versa. I've never tried the lunchtime or dinner gastronomic trip but I'm told they're good value for money and certainly the restaurant looks classy. Personally I'd rather sit outside on the upper deck for a better view of the variety of scenery passing by.

From wide estuary, dotted with yachts, under the Pont de Cornouaille, the river shrinks to fjord-like proportions, still and very deep, then widens into a lake just short of Quimper. Always tree-lined, herons posing along its banks, châteaux to admire, the river offers a peaceful way to spend a couple of hours. An alternative trip on a calm day is to the offshore islands of **Glénan**.

Le Minaret
(HR)M   *98.57.03.13   Cl. 30/9–25/3   rest. cl. Tues. from Apr.–June*

A strange white building, prominent with the odd tower that gives the hotel its name. They say it was built by some eastern potentate for the local doctor who had saved his life. The interior carries out the theme with oriental carpets, a tapestry or two and the odd gong. No, it's not for the incongruous decor, nor the bedrooms, some of which anywhere else I would reject as on the small side and poorly furnished, that I would return to the Minaret whenever able. It's the position that wins hands down. To sit on the balcony with all that truly fabulous panorama of sea, river, rocks, boats, gardens, lighthouse, spread around is worth a lot. A lot in this case is from 260–420f depending on aspect, and here it's worth going for the best.

The elegant dining-room also makes the most of the view but, as I had heard poor reports of the food, we didn't eat in. Now, at least so I hear, it is vastly improved, but herein is the snag – between June and September demi-pension is insisted upon, and if the food is only indifferent, what starts off as a very good deal indeed becomes insupportable. I enjoy eating in occasionally but neither want (nor am able) to do so every night, so for me the Minaret can only be an o.o.s. experience (other reports welcome), but that's when Bénodet is at its considerable best anyway.

There is a lovely formal garden to walk through en route for beach

Le Minaret

just below, shady pines to park in and a new pagoda-like tea-room, which I would have liked even more had it not been for the dreaded pop deafener.

Menez Frost
(H)M   *98.57.03.09   Fax 98.57.14.73   Cl. 30/9–12/5; 30/9–12/5*

A substantial villa, modern extension at rear set in a lovely garden, with sizeable heated swimming pool, all seeming well worth keeping open a little longer than five short months. Centrally placed just behind the post office (but nowhere in Benodet is very far from the sea).
  'We had only allocated ourselves two days but heartily endorse your description of this attractive little town. We stayed at the 3-star Menez-Frost, right in the centre of town. Beautifully situated in a prize-winning garden. The little 80 year old in the flat hat clipping the hedge turned out to be the owner. The manager, M. Cornec, is very friendly and helpful.' L. I. Loch.
  50 rooms cost between 420 and 750f, some of them with 'cuisinettes'.

Ferme du Letty
R(L) *Letty* *98.57.01.27* *Cl. 1/10–20/10; Wed. Thurs. lunch.*

2 km SE on the D 44 and VO. Letty is on an almost enclosed inland sea between the Pointe de Bénodet and the odd strip of land that spits out from Moustelin. Known as the Mer Blanche, the peaceful lagoon, perfect for fishermen, is now a popular sailing centre, with the shallow water providing ideal conditions for falling into.

The best meal we had in Finistère was eaten at this old stone farmhouse now cleverly converted into a smart restaurant without going over the top tapestry-chair, heavy-drape-wise. Here one can still be cosy and romantic, rustic definitely, while appreciating the classy *couverts.* French windows open on to a summer terrace, log fires burn cheerfully in winter, flowers everywhere and Quimper pottery on the walls. Very nice indeed.

And the food! (Menus 98f lunchtime except Suns., at 195f.) A bill – of around 250f – emerges at the end of a three course meal, helped no doubt by the bargain wine list, with excellent house wine.

I ate an inspired *crêpe*, stuffed with *mousserons* (wild mushrooms) and crab, then an escalope of *lotte* with an interesting creamy red pepper sauce, while husband tucked in to a dozen oysters, thoughtfully produced as two half dozens in sequence, so that the debris shouldn't get out of hand, followed by the cheapest item on the menu – a farm chicken roasted on the spit over the fire, for 65f.

But the justly famous course at the **Ferme** is the dessert. Mme Guilbert wheels round a vast lazy-Susan apparatus on whose tiers are strewn the kind of puds that weaken even the most dedicated dieter. Noting that all the locals chose at least three, we felt able to do as the Romans do and allow Madame to serve generous portions each of a wonderfully tangy *tarte au citron*, a dark and rich chocolate mousse cake and a *bavarois* of orange. With dollops of *crème fraîche* . . .

I liked particularly the atmosphere, with parties of locals, all obviously regulars, being greeted by name by M. and Mme Guilbert, locals themselves, who have clearly made a huge success of this project – once a modest *crêperie*. Now a Michelin star.

Domaine de Kereven
(HR)M *rte. de Quimper Clokars-Fouesnant* *98.57.02.46* *Fax 98.66.22.61* *Cl. Oct.–Easter*

Peacefully situated a km or two north of Bénodet. All very pristine and straightforward. The comfortable well-equipped rooms, each with its own good bathroom, are 345–395f and the menus are 125f. They prefer demi-pension but do not insist out of season. There is a terrace, a salon and a nice dining-room; all so nice and respectable and blameless that if all French hotels were so exemplary I should have nothing to write about.

Map 3G   **BETTON** 35830 (I. et V.) 9 km N of Rennes – *Mkt: Sun.*

Take the N 776 road north out of the city and turn left at the traffic lights in the village of Betton to find the river Rance and canal, running side by side. Just before them is:

Hôtel de la Levée
(HR)S   *r. Amérique   99.55.81.18   Cl. 15 days at end of June; rest. cl. Sun. p.m.; Mon.*

A simple country Logis, whose modest décor is more than compensated for by the friendliness of the owners M. and Mme Louazel. She speaks some English and they welcome regulars each year, who make this a convenient and cheap stop-over on the road from Normandy to the South.

The value is excellent; a double room is 110–230f; a three course simple meal is 49f, but for 85f Jean-Claude shows what he can do – *pâté de saumon maison aux deux sauces* or eight *huîtres portugaises chaudes, beurre à l'ail*, followed by *lièvre marinadé* or *canard à l'orange.*

Map 5D   **BRANDÉRION** 56700 (Morbihan) 7 km W of Hennebont

Leave the *Voie expresse* at Landévant, heading west, on to the N 165.

Hotel l'Hermine
(H)M   *97.32.92.93   Cl. 5/1–15/3*

A practical choice for those who might wish to eat at Locguénolé (see p. 85) but are not prepared to pay the exorbitant price for a room. The nine rooms here are immaculate, not very large, comfortable, and quiet if you ask for one at the back away from the main road. At 345–370f they are not a bargain, particularly as the grooming of the terrace and garden has cost the owners little or nothing, but a reliable contingency choice.

Map 1D   **ÎLE-DE-BRÉHAT** (C. d'A.) (see Arcouest)

For me, a magical island, partly due perhaps to an arrival by sea one evening, after a fretful storm-bound week in St.-Malo, to find the glowering sky and sea suddenly yield to a spectacular sunset, deep blue water, pink rocks and pine trees. Anchor dropped in horseshoe bay, we swam ashore, feeling like Robinson Crusoes.

That must have been September because I remember a powerfully golden light and the stillness and shadows of late summer. This July it was a more prosaic approach by packet from Arcouest, accompanied by scores of twittering schoolchildren. There was barely room enough on the sand of the little beach for Man Friday to leave his footprints, but still the charm was there. The climate is so oddly mild that oleanders and palm trees flourish, the rocks really are pink, the water just as blue.

You arrive at little **Port Clos**, where there are bars and a hotel and walk through narrow car-free lanes smelling of broom and hydrangeas to get to the beach. Or, as I did, hire a bicycle and explore all 3 km of what is really two islands, joined by a causeway. In the centre is a lively little *bourg* centring on a square for boules, stalls, craftwork.

I wouldn't at all mind the chance of staying the odd night here:

La Vieille Auberge
(HR)S   *96.20.00.24   Cl. Nov.–Easter*

You eat at a central courtyard under the trees, and the hotel itself is set back well away from the main thoroughfare. The rooms are more modern than you might suppose; with dinner and breakfast they cost 285–320f per person. Menus from 90f.

Map 1D   **BRÉLIDY** 22140 Begard. (C. d'A.) 13 km N of Guingamp

---

From Guingamp take D 8 towards La Roche Darrien, then after 11 km onto D 15 to Brélidy. Then follow signs for the Château.

Château du Brélidy
(HR)M–L   *96.95.69.38   Fax 96.95.18.03   Cl. from Nov.–Easter*

Many changes here since I last wrote about Mme Yoncourt's four bed and breakfast rooms. There are now two distinct characters to the heavily-restored 16C chateau – one is the chambres d'hôtes, which I describe in the new bed and breakfast guide, and the other a luxury hotel. Visitors to both have the benefit of the huge baronial rooms mellowed with lots of flowers, huge fires, tapestry chairs and objets d'art. Those in the hotel get really luxurious rooms, some with four-posters, and cossetting bathrooms for 440–695f. Dinner is available for residents at 175f (not Mondays o.o.s.), but I would eat out.

Map 1B   **BRIGNOGAN-PLAGES** 29890 (Finistère) 26 km N of Landerneau; 53 km NW of Morlaix.

A quiet village, with a sheltered sandy beach, bordered by bizarre boulders. Make sure the weather's right for a visit here, because it can get a bit grim when the grey of the sea meets the grey of the granite. Offshore are dozens of little islands, battered by the waves. A good spot for a family holiday, with lots of natural wonders, and the base for wonderful coast walks along the dunes.

Castel-Régis
(HR)M *Plage du Garo.   98.83.40.22   Fax 98.83.44.71   Cl. 1/4; rest. cl. Wed.*

Right on the sea, so that the dining-room and the bedrooms have amazing views. Most of the accommodation is in rustic bungalows among the trees. Two have private jacuzzis and two are specially adapted for the disabled. There is an outdoor terrace for drinks and good public rooms. M. Plos cooks traditional Breton recipes, making much use of local ingredients. Menus are 120 and 195f with an 80f lunch menu. Rooms cost 260–420f. Good value, considering there is also a large swimming pool and tennis court for residents.

Map 4D   **BUBRY** 56310 (Morbihan) 24 km NE of Lorient

Auberge de Coët-Diquel
(HR)M   *97.51.70.70   Fax 97.51.73.08   Cl. 1/12–15/3*

Twenty rustic rooms in this new discovery, set in pleasant woodland, through which runs a trout stream. A heated swimming pool and tennis court add to the attraction. Rooms are a reasonable 275–320f and good cooking features on the 85f menu. Demi-pension at 295f obligatory in season.

'A delightful hotel, set in lovely woodland with a mill stream. All very peaceful. Lots of outdoor games for children like table tennis, swing, roundabout etc. plus indoor swimming pool. The bedrooms are fine with good bathrooms and the cooking is very good and unpretentious. We did notice that a lot of French people used it, which is always a good sign.' – Mrs. C. L. Hodgkin.

Map 1G   **CANCALE** 35260 (I. et V.) 14 km E of St. Malo, 59 km from
Avranches – *Mkt: Every day*

A picturesque little fishing port looking east across the Bay of St.-Michel. Wonderful walks along the cliff edge, via the old Customs Officers' path, as far as the **Pointe du Grouhin** (see p. 82). For centuries Cancale has been famous for its oysters, which used to be the finest in France. A mysterious disease decimated the population some twenty years ago and now the young spat comes from Bélon (see p. 42). Stocks are building up again and there is no shortage in evidence in the numerous cafés and stalls round the harbour advertising stand-up *dégustation.* Like Southend but classier. There's a very jovial atmosphere to be induced by strolling about the harbour, out along the jetty to watch the fishing boats unload, and then partaking of a little refreshment, both liquid and marine-based. Plenty of choice down here.

Along the quay in Cancale stretches a line of unashamedly fishy eateries, some upmarket restaurants, some mere degustations depots, where a dozen oysters can be washed down with a glass of Muscadet ridiculously cheaply compared with the equivalent in Britain. For the latter you don't need my recommendation – just stroll along and see which one has the best atmosphere, which one has the cheapest molluscs – they're all going to be fresh. If you're looking for something more substantial I would choose the restaurant with most French people therein, check the menu to see that its what you want and make sure there's a table free on the terrace if its that kind of day. My last sampling, and very good too, was at:

Le Cancalais
(R)M   *11 quai Gambetta   99.89.61.93   Cl. Sun. p.m.; Mon*

A good covered terrace provides the vantage point from which to observe all the activity of the port. My 109f menu yielded a dozen local creuzes, grilled salmon and dessert, and the short wine list was not exorbitant.

Continental
(HR)M   *au port   99.89.60.16   Fax 99.89.69.58   Cl. 20/3–11/11; rest. cl. Mon. Tue. lunch*

The best position in the town, overlooking the harbour, with smart yellow awning to sit under and watch all the activity. The bay must twist round here to face west because it gets all the evening sun and it is so pleasant to settle down for a meal on the terrace that the slowness of the service shouldn't annoy; when the food does arrive, it's excellent. 132f buys nine oysters, sole, cheese and *pâtisserie*, but for 250f you get lobster for the second course and there is now a limited 98f menu.

The rooms are very pleasant too, especially if you get there early enough to pick one with a good view; with bath, it will cost 680f. The cheapest is 440f.

The place is obviously thriving, which unfortunately involved escalating prices; I feel that they should stop here.

'We have visited this hotel many times. Prices are on the up presumably because the rooms are being done up – but we don't really want a TV, especially in pretty Cancale. The food was excellent of course. We had the 152f menu, but wine was expensive.' Richard and Charlotte Bass

L'Emeraude
(HR)M   *Quai Thomas   99.89.61.76   Fax 99.89.88.21*

Another seafront alternative with agreeable terrace to make the most of the situation and a rustic/marine decor inside. The food is not as good as that at the Continental but is somewhat cheaper at 90f for the first menu and perfectly acceptable as long as you stick to the staple fish, especially the plâteau de fruits de mer. The 11 rooms here have recently been redecorated and are good value at 285f–470f and there is

a turretted annexe on the cliff overlooking the bay with another five
spacious rooms, complete with magnificent view and complete quiet.

La Bisquine
(R)M   *4 quai Gambetta*

Newer, and as yet untried, but said to be particularly promising.
Certainly looks most attractive, with Art Deco décor. Fishy menus start
at 95f.

These are good of their kind, but for something quite exceptional it is
necessary to leave the port, drive up the hill to the town:

➤ Restaurant de Bricourt
(HR)L   *r. Duguesclin   99.89.64.76   Fax 99.89.88.47   Cl. 30/11–1/3; Tues.; Wed.;
except dinner in July and Aug.   All cards*

Still my No. 1 restaurant in Brittany. An elegant old manorhouse, with
antique furniture, gilded mirrors, chandeliers, and two small dining-
rooms, whose tables are set with beautiful china.

One is led through the house to an unexpected garden behind, to sit
under the parasols by the pond and contemplate the delights of the
menu.

I feel a strong proprietary interest here, in that de Bricourt and its
young patron-chef Olivier Roellinger were my first 'scoop', spotted at
the very beginning of his career as a genius and subsequently backed
for one Michelin star and then another. It is very satisfying to see his
talent now generally recognised, and the innovations that seemed so
daring ten years back – the use of spices in unconventional
combinations, inherited from his Malouin forbears who brought back
culinary treasures from their forays to the West Indies, for example –
now accepted in any good cook's repertoire.

Because Olivier genuinely loves cooking as a science (he was
originally a chemist), he still experiments tirelessly; it would seem
impossible that he should ever be bored with his metier. You may
confidently expect a memorable meal here, and bearing in mind the
absolute perfection of the ingredients and the skill with which they are
presented, the prices are fair. Especially if you go for lunch when three
courses during the week are still the best bargain in the book at 130f.
For dinner its serious money – around 350f, and the wine is not
cheap.

Thank goodness, for all its success, the restaurant de Bricourt is not
an awesome temple of gastronomy, overly gilded. This is a bourgeois
manorhouse, typically Breton, with antique furniture, modest
chandeliers and two small dining-rooms, whose tables are set with
beautiful china and glass. One is led through the house to an
unexpected garden behind, to sit under the parasols by the pond and
contemplate the delights of the menu.

Olivier and his wife Jane obviously like a challenge. Having reached
the summit restaurant-wise they looked around for ancillary activities
and settled for two hotels and another restaurant in the
neighbourhood. It makes sense to list them all here:

Les Rimains

(H)L   *address and telephone as above*   *Cl. 5/1–5/3*

Perched on the clifftop, on the Sentier des Amoureux, with fab views of the oyster beds below, St. Michel swimming in the distance, this was previously just a 1930s granite villa; it has now been converted into a luxurious six-bedroomed hotel, where pampered pensionnaires can complement their superb de Bricourt dinners with breakfasts the next morning of equal quality. 650–750f.

Maison Richeux

(H)L   *Le Point du Jour at St. Meloir des Ondes, 7 kms SE of Cancale by the D   76.99.89.25.25   Fax 99.89.88.47   Cl. 14/11–15/12*

An extraordinary Gothic 1930s mansion, pinacled, turretted, balconied, which on the wild wet day we visited, with wind howling and whipping up the grey seas below, looked like something from a horror movie. Inside the courage which must have gone into the purchase is totally justified. The rooms are vast, the dining-room is panelled, the floors are expensively patterned in different woods and the bay windows make the most of the (normally) wonderful views.

The bedrooms are named after the different spices so dear to Olivier's heart – 'Fenugreek', 'Saffron', 'Gingembre'. They are all different and furnished with the flowery fabrics that the French call 'le style Anglaise'. The 750–1,250f includes a London taxi to ferry you from Cancale.

Le Coquillage

(R)M–L   *Address and telephone as above.   Cl. Tues. lunch, Mon.; 14/11–15/12*

This is billed as a 'bistro de la mer'. Some bistro! True the decor in the tall-ceilinged dining-rooms has been kept simple – no curtains at the tall windows to obscure the view and no carpet on the floor to hide the wonderful parquet, but the simple and cheap alternative I had been looking forward to, with Roëllinger cooking and modest prices hardly materialised. Even on a horrible mid-week April day, on which we had felt no need to book, we were lucky to grab the last table, so obviously it is a huge local success.

Our 100f no-choice lunch started badly with a 35 minute wait for a first course of fish soup. It came in a pudding basin and if you'd consumed the lot there would be little space for anything else, but there was no temptation to do so, since it was thin and unexciting – a far cry indeed from anything sampled at de Bricourt. Things bucked up a bit with course two, which introduced me to **cretons** – baby skate – which I had not encountered before but would certainly search out again, so tender and sweet they proved to be. They came in a lovely light butter sauce with appropriate strips of carrot, asparagus and new potatoes accompanying. Lemon tart with crême anglaise liberally flecked with vanilla was equally satisfying. The formula works well if you like fish for lunch as much as I do and I shall assume that the soup was a one-off hiccup. Big spenders next door were tucking into the most amazing plâteau de fruit de mer I've ever seen in a long career of p.d.f. de m. observation. Two ladies, two men and a boy demolished lobster, crayfish, langoustines, oysters, crabs, you name it, diligently picking and scooping until only a mound of shells remained.

Map 1B **CARANTEC** 29660 (Finistère) 15 km N of Morlaix

Follow the highly scenic D 73 from Morlaix along the river Frout, through Locquénolé to the estuary, up to Carantec, a charming little holiday resort on a peninsula, with beaches and bays in all directions. Smashing views from Pen Lan point, but you have to leave the car under the pine trees and scramble down a long sandy track to see the panorama of Île Louët, the 16th-century Château du Taureau built on a reef, and numerous small islands, part of a bird sanctuary.

Excellent walks abound, like those to La Chaise du *Curé*, a promontory overlooking the Baie de Morlaix, the estuary of the Penzé, St.-Pol-de-Léon and Roscoff, but it is more fun to discover some for yourself – no matter which road you take, past gardens full of hydrangeas, it is bound to end up with a rewarding seascape.

The little town itself is lively and very busy; I was driven away by mind-blowing pop music relayed from every corner, but I hope that was just an unlucky one-off. Its chief industry, apart from oyster-farming, is tourism, and very popular it is too. The several hotels are all full in the season and demi-pension is generally obligatory.

Pors Pol
(HR)S *98.67.00.52   Cl. 20/9–16/5*

A family hotel with a nice garden overlooking the little beach of Pors Pol. Good value cooking on menus from 90f. 30 rooms from 235–270f, but all occupied so I could not check. Children particularly well cared for. Demi-pension is 260f per person.

Readers' recommendations here are *Le Cabestan*(R)M a little fishy restaurant in the port, which unusually, stays open year-round; *Les Ondes*, a bar-restaurant in the avenue des Francais, is also open throughout the winter, and *Aux Delices de la Mer*, an exclusively fish restaurant run by a co-operative of professional fishermen. This one is to be found near the church and sounds particularly well worth investigation. Carantec obviously inspires readers – here is yet another suggestion – *Les Iles* on the Plage du Kelenn, which has a lovely view over the water and is a fish restaurant cum creperie.

Map 3C   **CARHAIX PLOUGUER** 29270 (Finistère) 44 km SW of Guincamp

It wasn't until I started to research Carhaix that I realised that La Tour d'Auvergne was a man not a building! He was this dairy market town's most famous son, campaigning for the Breton language in the 18th century. On June 27 and 28 Carhaix still celebrates his name.

Once a Roman settlement, still the hub of five main roads, Carhaix makes a good base from which to explore the pleasant country of the Argoat, the Montagnes Noires to the south and the Regional Park of Armorica to the north, but accommodation in this area is unfortunately sadly limited. The best I could find is:

Gradlon
(HR)M   *12 blvd République   98.93.15.22   Fax 98.99.16.97   Cl. 15/12–15/1; rest. cl. Fri. p.m.; Sat. o.o.s.*

An aggressively modern hotel in the centre of the town, offering a strictly functional possibility for an overnight stop. Rooms are 245–290f, menus from 78f.

'In my opinion this hotel warrants three stars in view of its standard of comfort and efficiency. The 5-course dinner at a mere 85f was in quality, quantity and service the most outstanding gastronomic feast of our journey. Carhaix and its amenities deserve your further research.' – Eric Sheldon.

Auberge du Poher
(R)M   *98.99.51.18   Fax 98.99.55.98   Cl. Feb.; Mon. 1st fortnight in Feb. & 1st fortnight in Sept.*

6 km to the south on the D 769, a pleasant ride through wooded countryside to a pretty little restaurant specialising in Breton dishes, like *tripes Bretonne* and local *andouilles*.

Large helpings of traditional cooking on the 85f menu. Stick to this, or other menus at 115f or 150f, since the à la carte prices are prohibitive, and the wine is not cheap.

Map 6D   **CARNAC** 56340 (Morbihan) 13 km SW of Auray on the D 768, on the bay of Quiberon

Divided into two distinct and very different areas – the Carnac of the historic monuments and the Carnac-Plage that cares more about Ambre Solaire than *alignements*.

Flaubert said that Carnac has had more rubbish written about it than it has standing stones and, as there are 5,000 stones, I shall not add to the rubbish. A specialist guidebook is clearly necessary for the serious *dolmen* fancier. I admit I find the serried rows of crude megaliths whose origins are lost in time – some say religious, some say astronomical – sinister rather than inspiring, and a short visit to the scrubland at the entrance to Carnac town, dotted with almost as many *meinherren* as *menhirs* (sorry), is enough, but it is certainly an excursion that everyone will want to try for themselves.

I made my own discovery in Carnac. Poking around the back streets behind the Office du Tourisme, I came across:

Le Marine
(HR)M *4 pl. de la Chapelle 97.52.07.33 Fax 97.52.85.7 Cl. 1/10–1/4 Sun. p.m.; Mon. o.o.s.*

A bright and cheerful modern hotel recommended by locals, with friendly management from the Gerière family. In the centre of the town, but with a nice terrace for outdoor eating and good food prepared by *père et fils*. Rooms from 310–556f, menus from 90f.

Lann-Roz
(HR)M *35 av. de la Poste 97.52.10.48 Cl. 31/12–1/2; rest. cl. Wed. o.o.s*

On the outskirts of the town, set in a particularly flowery garden, and usefully open for most of the winter. Unusually good food. Pretty flowery bedrooms are from 369f or from 620f for two people when there is a 12% reduction.

Le Ratelier
(R)M *4 Chemin du Douet. 97.52.05.04*

Not easy to find a 'real' French restaurant in this heavily touristed town, but one reader succeeded:
'After our fourth visit I feel this restaurant most certainly deserves a mention. The attractive old farmhouse-style building tucked away behind the main street, is full of true French ambiance. The clientele is almost exclusively French but we received a warm welcome on each occasion. On the 95f menu I had a beautifully presented salad with warm chicken livers followed by brochette de boeuf with potato gratin, spinach and salad, followed by chocolate charlotte. My husband's 130f menu produced stuffed clams, lamb and apple tart. Real value for money' Pamela Biles.

Map 6D   **CARNAC-PLAGE** 56340 (Morbihan) 3 km SE of Carnac

Only 3 km away, altogether another world. A smart little modern resort, with a beach that rivals La Baule's – pale fine sand curving round the vast bay. Not much of a heart to the place yet – shops and boutiques are still being built and you'd have to go to the other Carnac to find any Gallic atmosphere – but if its just wholesome sun and sand you're after, Carnac-Plage is probably one of the best bets in this area.

Lots of summer hotels, nearly all modern, functional. In June it was not easy to find a room with a sea view, and we ended up paying more than envisaged at:

Hotel Diana
(HR)L   *21 blvd de la Plage   97.52.05.38   Fax 97.52.87.91*

Here is a frankly sybaritic hotel that earns its keep. For 690f we got a spacious room, luxurious bathroom and large balcony overlooking that gorgeous beach.

No stinting with the extras. By the time we'd had the expensive chaises-longues and parasols carried down to the beach (name *Diana* prominent so that no-one should miss that here was the quality), washed off the sand in the kind of shower that gushes not trickles, hair protected by their bathcaps, soap by courtesy ditto, dried on blissfully dense white towels and descended refreshed to sip something long and cool on more expensive terrace furniture, we came to believe we were getting our money's worth. Pleasant efficient service and good breakfast reinforced the feeling.

The restaurant looked fairly international/boring and menus cost 220–300f, but there was no pressure to use it, so taken all around in this area, **Diana** is not a bad idea at all, especially in low season, when prices are reasonable. In August rooms start at 600f and so on to 1,200f.

Le Celtique
av. Kermario.   *97.52.11.49   Fax 97.52.71.10*

The third generation of Huons took the bold step of completely remodelling this old Carnac family hotel, 50 metres from the sea, in 1993; it now has 40 rooms, described as 'four-star comfort at three star prices', i.e. 385–660f. They are more functional than luxurious but well-equipped with good if compact bathrooms and a balcony a piece, all light and bright. Jacuzzi and gym are thrown in. Food is better than average for a seaside hotel and demi-pension, obligatory in high season, would not be a disaster here at 320–770f. Otherwise there are menus, with plenty of seafood included from 95f.

Map 3D   **CAUREL** 22530 (C. d'A.) 7 km NW of Mur-de-Bretagne; 27 km NW of Pontivy

---

On the N 164 between Gouarec and Mur.

Beau Rivage
(HR)M   *Lac de Guerlédan.   96.28.52.15   Fax 96.26.01.16   Cl. Mon. p.m. and Tue. o.o.s.; 5/1–15/2*

Inland Brittany can be somewhat boring – perhaps because the contrast with the spectacular coastline detracts from it. The Lac de

Guerlédan is one of its bonuses. Formed by the damming of the river Blavet, and of an interesting fjord-like shape, it makes a lovely peaceful resting place. The views over the lake from this simple modern hotel are the reason for its inclusion.

The restaurant is the main concern – no advantage taken here of the prime site. Menus start at 90f, and go up to a gastronomic 270f – all good value in their price bracket. Eight simple rooms cost between 225 and 350f.

Map 3G   **CESSON-SÉVIGNÉ** 35510 (I. et V.) 6 km E of Rennes – *Mkt: Sat.*

From Rennes take the Paris road, the N 157, and Cesson-Sévigné is signposted to the left. Although the autoroute is very near, the village character has somehow been retained.

Germinal
(HR)M   *9 cours de la Vilaine   99.83.11.01   Fax 99.83.45.16   Cl. 23/12–4/1; rest. cl. Sun.   P.   V*

A unique setting, on an island in the middle of the river Vilaine, qualifies this hotel as a member of the *Relais du Silence* chain. I think it may once have been a mill – the stone façade would suggest so, but the rear is modern, as are the majority of the rooms. Their styles therefore are in several distinct variations, those on the front being particularly pleasant. Most of them, back or front, look out over the surrounding water.

This takes care of two of my prime concerns, location and comfort, and I would rate it even more highly were not the other two – welcome and cuisine – sadly deficient. Distinct lack of welcome, with unsmiling manager watching us hump heavy cases unaided (wife very much more pleasant next day) and the worst food encountered so far in Brittany (chips soggily absorbing floury sauces, tinned beans, minute portions, canned fruit and commercial ices, and this on a 200f menu).

It does make a peaceful agreeable base, rooms 300–380f, from which to explore Rennes, which has plenty of restaurant choice.

Map 3G   **CHÂTEAUGIRON** 35410 (I. et V.) 16 km SE of Rennes, on the D 463 – *Mkt: Thurs.*

A pleasant little town, steeply sloping around its impressive castle. In the Middle Ages, Châteaugiron was one of the most important towns in Brittany, its lords having the right to serve as Grand Chamberlains to the Duke. Many of the houses date from that period, lining narrow streets, gabled, beamed, delightfully crooked. The castle was much-besieged, destroyed and re-built, with every century from the 13th to the 18th leaving its mark. The NE keep is the oldest part.

Auberge du Cheval Blanc
(HR)S   *99.37.40.27   Fax 99.37.59.68   Cl. Sun. p.m. rest. cl. Mon.*

A pleasant old hotel in the town's main street, which would make a useful overnight stop – not expensive and strategically placed on the N–S route, by-passing Rennes. A large twin-bedded room with its own bathroom at the back of the hotel, well away from any possible traffic noise costs 235f, but the cheapest double is only 150f. Wide range of menus starting at 68f, all perfectly adequate, but a happy combination would be an economical bed here and an extravagant dinner across the road:

'Mme Cottebrune was really very helpful. We enjoyed our dinner and had a very comfortable night. We thought that the hotel's inner courtyard was reassuring from a security point of view. The cost was very reasonable and we thought Chateaugiron a pleasant little town for an overnight stop, avoiding having to go into Rennes'. Michael Weir.

L'Aubergade
(R)M–L   *2 rue Comdel   99.37.41.35   Cl. 8/3–23/3; 16/8–2/9. Sun. p.m.; Mon.*

An old town house, heavily beamed and rough-cast, with accoutrements as elegant as the cooking. The Rennais drive out here for a better meal than any to be found in their city, and booking is wise. Chef Jean-Claude Barré, offers inventive variations on both the new and traditional cuisines. *Fricassée de gésiers* (giblets), *choux confits*, is recommended for the adventurous, or maybe smoked duck served with home made pasta, but for more conservative tastes the fillets of sole surrounded by a delicate green sauce contrived from the hearts of lettuce would be an equivalent treat. Superb wine list. Menus from 115f.

Map 3B   **CHÂTEAULIN** 29150 (Finistère), 31 km N of Quimper, 48 km S of Brest – *Mkt: Thurs.*

Astride the river Aulne and a great centre for salmon fishing. So important did the city fathers rate the noble fish that they included it in their coat of arms. Very pleasant to stroll along the wide sweep of the river on the tree-lined banks.

High above the town on the Quimper road, loftily looking down on the river's meanderings is:

Le Chrismas
(HR)S   *33 Grande rue   98.86.01.23   Fax 98.86.37.09   Cl. Sat. p.m.; Sun. Oct–Easter*

Mme Feillant represents the third generation to run this little Logis – a fact that speaks for itself. This is no fly-by-night establishment but a traditional, caring hostelry, where you can be sure of modest affordable comfort. Unfortunately the food does not match the high standard of the accommodation, but eating out is no problem around here. Doubles 140–235f.

'We recommend this hotel as a pleasant place from which to tour the Finistère peninsular. The accommodation, with en suite bathroom and t.v. was excellent value for money. We recommend eating at Au Bon Accueil at Port Launez just down the road, which is very good. Madame Feillant is extremely helpful and speaks excellent English'. Bernard Lloyd.

A reader with another recommendation: Le Perthuy du Roy on the Place de la Croix de Ville.

'No set menu but a la carte varied with predominance of sea food and reasonable prices. Staff most pleasant' Philip and Kathleen Gerrard.

Map 3C **CHÂTEAUNEUF DU FAOU** 29520 (Finistère) 35 kms NE of Quimper

---

In fact the town itself is rather disappointing, but its position, high above the banks of the Aulne at the foot of the Montagnes Noires is superb.

Make sure you detour down to the banks of the Nantes-Brest canal for a lovely walk or picnic on the towpath.

Le Relais de Cornouaiile
(HR)S *9 r. Paul Serusier 98.81.73.36*

One of those ordinary seeming hotels on the main road that you wouldn't look twice at unless you were briefed. Fortunately I was, and in any case I think the clues – the French cars, the hum of satisfied diners – would have alerted me to the fact that this is the kind of traditional solid-value that is fast disappearing from more tourist-ridden parts of Brittany.

Marie-Jo and Jean-Paul Gourtay share the cooking here and their menus at 60f and 75f are renowned. Specialities are seafood, but regional dishes are always featured on the four menus.

The 29 rooms are functional, clean, wholesome and cheap – 155–255f. I am convinced that French Entrée readers will love this one. Tell me I'm right.

Map 3A **CLÉDEN CAP SIZUN** 29113 (Finistère) 10 km NW of Audierne

---

A pleasant alternative to the tourist-crowded D 784 leading to the Pointe du Raz is to take the little D 43, running further north through hamlets and past grey farmsteads to the village of Cléden. It's worth it anyway to see the astonishing church, with strange carvings of lichened monsters on the main porch and fishing boats lovingly portrayed on the west wall and south porch. Face to face with the gargoyles across the narrow street is:

L'Étrave
(R)S   *98.70.66.87   Cl. 29/10–25/3; Wed. Oct.–April*

A shock in a sleepy little village to push open the door of this tiny restaurant and be met with a babble of local voices all vociferously appreciating their Sunday lunch outing. You step down into a dark little room, with a handful of tables, shake the hand of the *patronne* behind the bar and settle down, perhaps to a no-frills splendid *langouste* for 190f menu, or the 85f three courser. Wise to book.

Map 2G   **COMBOURG** 356270 (I. et V.) 24 km SW of Dinan, 37 km N of Rennes – *Mkt: Mon.*

At the hub of six roads, a strategic staging post for many a voyage.

The mediaeval pile of a castle, where Chateaubriand lived as a youth, dominates and gives considerable character to the town. As does the lake to the south, so that the best approach is from the Rennes road, where the castle can be seen, looking down on the water, from some distance away; the pleasant leafy square beneath it, where Chateaubriand's statue stands brooding, is a good place to abandon the car. Decision time – watch the car passengers dart across the square to consult the menus of the establishments on either side before the important choice is made. About the hotels I have no doubt:

➤ **Hôtel du Château**
(HR)M   *1 pl. Chateaubriand   99.73.00.38   Fax 99.73.25.79   Cl. 15/12–15/1, Sun. p.m.; Mon. o.o.s.*

I thought the rooms to go for here were those in the annexe, tucked away in a nice old stone building behind the hotel. Furnished with lots of character and good bathrooms, they are well worth 550f, but a reader who was there last year disagrees:

'We had a beautiful room for 230f with bath etc. – by far the largest bedroom we have had in any hotel. It was at the back, so no danger of noise. We could have paid more for a room leading out on to the garden, but why bother when Room 28 was such good value.' . . . Why indeed?

Very smart dining-room, with big log fire in winter and substantial menus at 87–270f.

I had spider crab and my husband chose *pâté,* then we had *porc à la crème* with a lovely sauce. A good cheeseboard, followed by *bavarois* and chocolate mousse.

There is also a boules pitch, terrace, children's games, so this represents a good-value comprehensive deal, and is arrowed accordingly.

'We stayed for a week and everything was right. The half-pension menu offered at least four different choices each day in both starters and main course and free choice of desserts and cheeses. The house wine we enjoyed was a very good claret. Mme Pele was a charming hostess and she has a happy and hard-working staff.'

Hôtel du Lac
(HR)S   *2 pl. Chateaubriand   99.73.05.65*

A cheaper and very pleasant alternative, 70–180f, is to eat here across the road, with a better view, right on the water's edge. Stick to the cheaper menus and you will be well pleased. I'd keep it simple – my *terrine de saumon de mer, sauce cressonière*, proved a bit too ambitious, with an offputting khaki sauce, but husband's more cautious choice – six oysters, generous *gigôt d'agneau* and an untraditional *crème caramel* (delicate egg custard served with separate toffee sauce) was voted excellent value. Some of the bedrooms are now good (310f). Some are awaiting improvement (90f).

'We took your advice, slept at du Château and ate at Le Lac, where we had an excellent dinner on the 80f menu. The salmon was so good I went out of my way to congratulate the staff and there was an immediate enquiry as to whether I liked the pasta; when I said I would have preferred a potato, a note was made. I would certainly go again.' H. Baskerville.

➤ L'Ecrivain
(R)S   *1 Plst. Gilduin   99.73.01.61   Cl. Thurs. and Wed. in winter. Four weeks Feb.– Mar.*

Praise continues to roll in for this delightful little restaurant opposite the church, named after the town's most famous writer. Pretty though it is, charming though the terrace and garden, excellent though the cooking of Gilles Menier, it is the welcome and enthusiasm of Gilles and his wife Nelly (who speaks English) that makes this a new arrow.

The cooking is unpretentious but interesting on menus from 68f (lunch from mon–Sat), then 98f to 158f.

'The food we had there on three occasions was superb. Gilles Menier is a splendid young chef and Nelly works the front of house in a calm and efficient manner'. Ronald Payne.

Map 2B   **COMMANA** (Finistère) 25 km SW of Morlaix

An isolated village in the foothills of the **Monts d'Arrée**, a strange wild region of rock and heather, rising abruptly from the surrounding flatness. Roc Travezel offers a rare panorama.

This is natural material for the Breton fondness for legends, and where else would you see a Will o'the Wisp or come across a *Kannerezed an noz*, a washerwoman condemned to spend eternity washing shrouds? If you should hear a strange tinkling, do not be tempted to investigate. It will be the Devil himself luring the avaricious by the clinking of coins.

The village is chiefly known for its fine *enclos paroissial* (see p. **000**) but there is another attraction:

Boutique du Bien-Manger
(R)S   *pl. de l'Église   98.78.90.68*

A row of dingy dwellings fronts the church; in one of them is my favourite Breton *crêperie*. Duck inside the door to find everything much as it must have been a hundred years ago; wood floors, scrubbed tables, benches, dressers, bunches of dried flowers and wicker baskets hanging from the rafters.

Their batter recipe is a secret – one I would dearly love to know – their fillings simple, the cost minimal. They also do other Breton specialities, like *Kig ha Fars* (a kind of *pot au feu*) and *poulet au cidre*, and sell rather upmarket preserves and honey.

Map 4B   **CONCARNEAU** 29900 (Finistère) 24 km SE of Quimper – *Mkt: Mon., Fri.*

A town of several faces: France's second fishing port, particularly concerned with tunny, so it's lively year-round, with lots of real fish restaurants that don't have to depend on tourists. Its west-facing aspects cross the bay are fringed with beaches and hotels, turning their backs on the industry going on behind them; its other completely self-contained attraction is the picturesque *ville-close*, a town within a town built on an island linked to the mainland only by two narrow bridges. Walk across them and enter a third altogether different world.

Deep inside the massive walls, built in the 14th century and completed in the 17th by the military architect Vauban, there is no feeling of a life outside those narrow twisting streets, old houses, souvenir shops and *crêperies* which cater for the snap-happy visitors, but take a walk round the ramparts (by ticket only, at Easter, then from May 1 to September 30) and the jig-saw slots together, with glimpses of channel, two harbours and town falling into place. Inside a former prison in the r. Vauban is the Fishery Museum, with a fascinating display of boats, marine creatures and 'preserved fish containers' (not always cans, since the first sardine preservers used glass not tin).

The Americans love the *ville-close*; they also love the restaurant that nestles so attractively at the end of the main street:

Le Galion

(R)L and Residence des Iles (H)M   *Ville-Close 15 r. St. Genole.   98.97.30.16   Fax 98.50.67.88   Cl. Sun. p.m., o.o.s. Mon.; mid Jan.–mid Mar.*

The obsessive cuisine nouvelle which spoiled my previous visit has been tempered somewhat but do not expect hefty hearty portions here. Presentation is still very important. The old granite house, with flowers cascading from every aperture, is enchantingly pretty, both inside and out. The restaurant has beamed ceilings, flagged floor, stone walls and bags of character. Menus from 150f and from Easter to September there is the option of a bistro, l'Assiette du Pecheur, with more modest prices. The five rooms are small but extremely comfortable, and at 350–430f a good choice for a quiet agreeable place to repose.

Le Chalut

(R)S   *20 quai Carnot   98.97.02.12   Cl. Wed.*

A change of name (ex La Pecherie), but not of character for this little fishy bistro behind the fishing quay. No-nonsense fishy menus at no-nonsense prices, i.e. from 75f. Another at 90f has a choice of two entrees, either fish or meat and a dessert, but for 150f you get a wonderful *assiette de fruits de mer*, *then* a little casserole of scallops, *then* a brochette of monkfish, *then* a dessert.

La Coquille

(R)M   *1 quai Moros   98.97.08.52   Cl. Jan.; Sun. p.m. o.o.s. and Mon.*

In the 'new' port, right in amongst the cargo ships, with a ferry to skip across from the *ville-close*. The classiest of Concarneau's fish restaurants, but still good value, with a lunch menu at 105f otherwise 150f. Tables outside and a terrace from which to watch all the harbour activity. Very pretty inside too, in a rustic kind of way, all beams and oil lamps.

Chez Armande

(R)S   *15 bis av. Dr. Nicolas   98.97.00.76   Cl. Sun. p.m.*

By the yacht harbour. Old-fashioned and trim navy blue with waiters in black jackets, and M. and Mme Dupais genial hosts to the many locals who regularly patronise this old reliable favourite. Good value straightforward dishes, mainly fish, all fresh and cheap. 85–180f.

I would rate this first choice in the town.

A reader contributes the following ideas:
'*The Ville-Close La Porte au Vin has superb 110f and 130f menus with tremendous plateaux de fruits de mer. Its neighbour, with the same owners, Le Penfret, has good value lunch menus including a creperie. Back in the market square facing the entrance to the Ville-Close is Le St. Patrick, with the option of sitting out in the sunny area at the front. We had a superb three course lunch there.*'

HOTELS

Nothing special in the town, so I made for the beaches. To the south is
Le Cabellou, with a choice of sands, facing towards the town (blowing
a gale) and out to sea (so sheltered that bikinis were feasible in May).
On the former stands the well-known **Belle Étoile,** which I thought
outrageously expensive even in its luxury bracket. An unexciting
double cost 530f, with breakfast a steep 40f each on top, and the
menus are just not worth the 150f starting price. Across the road in a
quiet garden is the much more modest **Bonne Auberge,** a Logis de
France, with rooms at 125–230f, but I stupidly missed the chance to
look round, so first-hand reports particularly welcome.

Right at the opposite end of the town, facing across the bay of
Concarneau on the Plage des Sables Blancs is:

Les Sables Blancs
(HR)M   *98.50.53.50   Fax 98.50.65.88   Cl. Nov.–Mar.*

The superb view is this modern hotel's greatest asset. It sits right on
the beach of Plage Sables-Blancs, the big windows of its dining-room
making the most of the watery proximity.

Bedrooms are on the small side but agreeably well-maintained, and
good value at 260–310f and – another big asset – the food is
immeasureably better than the norm in seaside hotels. Menus from
99f.

Map 5E   **CONLEAU** 56006 (Morbihan) 3 km S of Vannes, 109 km from
Rennes

Take the Arradon road, D 101, SW of Vannes, or follow Conleau signs
from the port, to arrive at a little promontory in the Bay of Morbihan.

You can catch the ferry boat from here to the **Ile d'Arz,** if you don't
have time to do the complete excursion round the bay – a very cheap
way of getting at least a glimpse of the fascinating scenery. Set among
the trees is a pretty chalet-like hotel:

The Roof
(HR)M   *97.63.47.47   Fax 97.63.48.10   Cl. 8/1–18/2; rest. cl. Tue. o.o.s.*

It takes its name not from the present building but from the original,
built at the turn of the century, whose multi-coloured roof was
eccentrically steeply pitched.

We were unlucky with our room – this is a popular little hotel and
even in late September it was full. Ours was hideously khaki/orange,
poorly furnished and expensive at 500f, but even so the view outside
redeemed the interior. When I managed to check the others, better
furnished, some with better views and balconies, and all cheaper (350f)
I realised we had paid for two extra unwanted beds. So ask for one on
the first floor with balcony and avoid No. 10.

Of course I don't know how over-crowded this might be in high summer – probably a favourite Vannois excursion, but I can heartily recommend it in the autumn. The food is particularly good – it really is more a restaurant with rooms than hotel – and you should certainly book a table in the pleasant dining-room overlooking the water. There is an adequate menu at 150f, but we ate oysters, bass, good cheese and puds on the 210f version and were well pleased.

Le Roof.

Map 2A   LE CONQUET 29217 (Finistère) 24 km W of Brest

There is always a feeling in exploring Brittany that one must go on to the ends of the earth until every corner, every promontory, every bay of its uniquely beautiful coastline is investigated. I am always nervous that I might be missing a gem if I don't pursue that last dead-end to its extremity. That is exactly what you must do if you wish to see Le Conquet. The Brest peninsula is a wild and secret place. Atlantic gales sweep in over tempestuous tides and stirring stories are relayed of shipwrecks and smugglers. Few hotels and restaurants find it appealing. It is therefore all the more welcome to find a little haven in Le Conquet, a quiet family resort, with wonderful sandy beaches. It has a nautical centre for sailing, windsurfing and scuba diving, you can hire dune buggies and bicycles, go fishing, take excursions to the remote offshore islands of Ouessant and Molène.

Pointe Sainte Barbe
(HR)M   *98.89.00.26   Fax 98.89.00.26   Cl. 12/11–17/12; rest. cl. Mon. o.o.s.*

The most westerly point in France, right on the end of the rocky promontory of Ste Barbe, surrounded by pounding seas, this is a popular tourist destination for a fishy treat. At weekends whole families sit in the vast panoramic dining-room consuming craggy piles of fruits de mer. The cooking is of a very high standard and predictably fishy. Chef Alain Floch keeps it mercifully simple but uses prime ingredients, so the prices are not cheap. 95f weekday menus jump to 143f at weekends, or 208f or even 422f (with lobster).

The hotel is a simpler affair, with nearly all the rooms having superb sea views. They cost from 150–350f. Demi-pension would be a good deal in this case – from 259f per person.

The hotel has stairs down to a sandy beach and there are stunning coastal walks to the lighthouse at Pointe St. Mathieu and a 13C abbey church.

Map 6E   LE CROISIC 44490 (Loire-Atl.) 10 km from La Baule –
Mkt: Thurs. Fish market every day except Thurs.

A favourite excursion from the beaches, casino, sophistication of La Baule, across the strange and eerie salt marshes, is to the little fishing port of Le Croisic, which has managed to retain a good deal of the character, if not the importance, of bygone ways. To the north of the spur of land that juts out from the Guérande peninsula is the busy harbour, divided by three islands into several basins. Sardines and crustaceans are the port's specialities but those with the will to be in the fish market before 10 a.m. will witness all manner of sea creatures being auctioned off.

A bustle of colourful fishing boats, a screech of scavenging gulls, and a promenade of holidaymakers is guaranteed, and very agreeable it all is too. At noon everyone crosses to the other side of the road to inspect the menus of the numerous restaurants and bars that face the water. One is spoiled for choice and indeed it is hard to go wrong, so obvious are the credentials of the fish served up fresh and simple all along the quays. By far the most enjoyable procedure is to stroll along with the crowd and make your own decisions, based on how much you are in the mood to pay for, décor, and at which end of the harbour you happen to be when the legs give in (quite a stroll from end to end).

We followed Michelin's recommendations and ate at **Filets Bleus** and **La Bretagne**, but I think we could have done just as well rather more cheaply had we followed the French families to any one of the more plebeian eateries. A biting wind was the cause of the best discovery, when at the extreme end of the harbour we turned in thankfully to the fug of:

L'Estacade
(HR)S   *4 quai du Lénigo   40.23.03.77   Cl. Tue. p.m.; Wed. 28/2–17/3; 28/11–3/12*

Unpretentiously old-fashioned in the brasserie genre, full of families all tucking in to mounds of *moules*, plates of steaming fish and teeming *plateaux de fruits de mer*. Excellent value menus from 85f. The rooms are clean and cheap, at 260f for a simple double, to 320f with bath.

Grand Hôtel de l'Océan, Port Lin
(HR)L   *40.42.90.03   Fax 40.23.38.03*

Generally thought of as a restaurant, and certainly an exceptionally attractive one with splendid ocean panorama and splendid ocean produce, but I discovered a bonus in 14 elegant and usually well furnished rooms, all with private baths for 460–580f.

I think the combination of such a comfortable base, superb food available in the restaurant, with a choice of alternative price-ranges nearby, the attractive site on the water's edge, with wild rocky coastline to explore, and the animation and local colour at Le Croisic, make a combination infinitely more attractive than La Baule's brassiness.

Map A3   **CROZON** 29160 (Finistère) 33 kms W of Châteaulin

See 'Morgat' for a description of the wild and wonderful western peninsula which takes its name from this little port.

La Pergola
(R)M–S   *25 r. Poulpatre.   98.27.04.01   Cl. sun. p.m.; and Mon. o.o.s.*

If you need cheering up when the weather is foul – which it has to be said it often is when there is nothing between you and America to soften the Atlantic gales, try a meal at this nice little restaurant, where good seafood-based menus start at 78f.

'Superb lunch on the cheapest menus. Nicely decorated, clean and smart with very helpful staff'. Angela Gardiner.

Map 5E **DAMGAN** 56750 (Morbihan) 9.5 km SW of Muzillac; 26 km SE of Vannes

On the southern side of yet another peninsula in this intricate and fascinating Morbihan jig-saw puzzle of promontories, bays, creeks and sea. The beaches here are some of the most spectacular, ideal for children.

L'Albatros
(HR)M–S *1 blvd de l'Ocean   97.41.16.85   Fax 97.41.21.34   Cl. Oct. 1–1/4   V*

A pretty little modern hotel on a gorgeous stretch of beach, perfect for the bucket-and-spade brigade. The 24 rooms are attractively furnished and will suit all pockets. If you want a bathroom en suite, and a balcony they cost 355f; if you can manage without, you'll get away with a mere 195f. Demi-pension is from 195f.

The two pleasant dining-rooms overlook the beach and are popular with day tourists as well as residents – always a good sign. Seafood platters are their speciality. Menus from 85f. Sitting on the terrace, sipping a reviver after the kids are tucked up, makes family holidays utterly bearable.

Map 2F **DINAN** 22100 (C. d'A.) 51 km from Rennes, 187 km from Cherbourg – *Mkt: Sat., Thurs.*

The 'Welcome to Dinan' sign on the approach road states firmly 'Ville médiévale, mérite une longue visite' and that's quite right. A gem of a town, one of the most attractive and interesting in Brittany, and not to be rushed through on any account. Not that it's easy to rush in Dinan – in the main thoroughfares too much traffic crawls helplessly, in the old town the uneven cobbles and narrow pavements enforce a leisurely pace, with irresistible frequent stops to stand back and admire.

I would put Dinan top of my list for an out of season break, when coastal hotels are desolate. Always lively, with plenty of restaurants, dozens of *crêperies*, it is ideal for a long weekend without too much driving, as it is of course as a staging post on a longer journey into Brittany.

From very first view (try to make it from the Rennes road across the suspension bridge), thanks to its unique hilltop site overlooking the Rance, 'impressive' is the word. Ten bulky towers and four gateways punctuate the mainly 14th-century ramparts. A two mile walk to complete the entire circuit is highly recommended but if that daunts, for views of the surrounding country, the port and the river far below, a

Dinan.

'must' is the section enclosing the English Garden; on the site of an old cemetery, it makes a cool and pleasant spot to picnic in summer and even in February the mimosa trees are in unseasonable bloom.

If time, extend the walk to the Promenades of the Grands and Petits Fosses – ditches built in the 12th century to protect the city walls. The Grands Fosses from the Porte St.-Malo to the Tour St.-Julien is the best preserved section with gardens in the moat, and the Petits Fosses from the Town Hall to the Castle is now a cool avenue of lime trees, with a view over the Val Cocherel.

Penetrate further into the heart of the old town with camera well-loaded, record the photogenic crooked gables, pillars, beams of the old houses built for 15th-century merchants, whose trades are echoed in the street names – *Cordeliers*, *Merciers*, *Lainerie*, *Poissonerie*. In the rue l'Apport you can see the three types of half-timbered houses typical of Dinan: *à porche*, with upper stories supported by pillars, *à vitrines* with high casement windows built by ships' carpenters and recalling the sterns of ancient sailing ships, and *á encorbellement* with stepped out upper stories. The rue d'Horloge is one of the most picturesque, with its strange 15th-century clock tower enclosing four bells, one of them a gift from the ubiquitous Duchesse Anne. Stallholders used to sell their wares in the shelter of the arcades formed by the stubby granite pillars supporting overhanging upper stories; nowadays the fish market is open every day in the narrow rue de la Chaux, part of tangle of little streets round the Old Market.

The main market takes place on Thursday on what used to be a mediaeval fairground, the Places du Champ and du Guesclin, full of parked cars on other days. Hard to imagine now that this was the site of a famous duel between the renowned local warrior Bernard du Guesclin and Thomas of Canterbury, representing the Duke of Lancaster who had treacherously captured du Guesclin's brother. Du Guesclin spent most of his career in combat with the invading English, nearly always successfully, as in this case. So popular was he that after his death in 1380 four different towns claimed parts of his corpse, but it is in Dinan's St. Sauveur's church that his heart lies. In the gruesome business of sharing out the mortal remains, he is one up on the kings of France whose members only get distributed three-ways.

When the delightful meandering round the old city is complete, take a closer look at the port (where the pleasure boats take off for a fascinating trip up the Rance to St.-Malo in summer), by walking down one of the most beguiling thoroughfares in Brittany. It leads from the English Garden, via the rues du Rempart and Michel, into the rue du Jerzual and its extension, the rue de Petit Port, winding through the 500-year-old Jerzual Gate, between elegant houses now owned and restored by craftsmen, right down to the water.

Here refreshment is at hand, supplied by one of several pleasant bars and restaurants:

Les Terrasses
(R)M *96.39.09.60 Cl. Nov.; Tues.*

The best position, with tables outside making the most of its water's edge site. In winter the bar is animated with vociferous locals and the 90f menu is good value in the cheapest of these short-seasoned restaurants, but service can be bad-tempered.

➤ **Le Relais des Corsaires**
(R)M–L and *Au Petit Corsaire* (R)M–S *3 r. du quai 96.39.40.17 Fax 96.39.34.75*

Madame Barbel Pauwels wrote to tell me the latest developments in this most popular combination, about which readers have been unanimously enthusiastic:

'My husband and I are running two different rooms, side by side, served by the same kitchen in the middle. My husband's side, Le Relais de Corsaires, a house from 1754, is the main dining-room with nice old stone walls and a fireplace which gives a beautiful warm and tender atmosphere. The first menu starts at 95f. The dining-room at my side, Le Petit Corsaire, is one of the oldest houses in the harbour, built in the 15th century. The front side is all of wood, the inside is with stonewall and decorated with big mirrors in the 1900 style. It has a nice family atmosphere and the first menu starts at 76f. In the summer we receive our customers on the terraces. I do not wish to say anymore about the quality of our kitchen, I prefer that your customers tell you how much they appreciate our table'.

They do, nice Madame Pauwels, they do repeatedly. Which accounts for the arrow.

Back in the town:

D'Avaugour
(H)M *1 pl. du Champ 96.39.07.49 Fax 96.85.43.04*

The rooms here have been renovated since my last report and readers have reproached me for describing them as shabby. Shabby no longer but light and bright, looking out over the ramparts and the garden, 410–490f. Thats the good news. The bad news is that M. Quinton, veteran hotelier, chef and well-known local figure, has died. His widow Gisele still keeps a maternal eye on the hotel but now sends her clients down to Le Corsaire to eat. Reports please.

Hotel Arvor
(H)M *5, r. A Pavie. 96.39.21.22 Fax 96.39.83.09*

I was delighted to find this addition to the very limited Dinan hotel scene, tucked away in the centre of the old town, in an ancient building that was once a Jacobin convent run by an English man and French wife. The rooms are comfortable and well-equipped, good value at 280–350f. I am sure this will be a favourite, and an arrow will follow.

'Most comfortably and tastefully equipped. Our room (No. 10) was large with a 5 ft. bed with excellent linen and the bathroom was

*equipped with fittings of a very high standard and plenty of good
towels. No restaurant but excellent Continental breakfast with plenty of
butter and jam without having to ask for extra supplies. Great joy was
the parking space in the grounds of the now disused abbey church. An
excellent meal was found in a restaurant only 100 yards away – the
Varangue, which claims to be Creole, but most dishes are regional
French.' D. Martin Cox.*

La Caravelle

H(S)R(M)   *14 pl. Duclos 96.39.00.11   Cl. Oct.; Wed. o.o.s.   AE, DC*

 H

 R

An unexpectedly attractive little restaurant on the busy Place Duclos.
The colours are warm tans and rusts, the beams are ancient, the
lighting subdued, and the food, cooked by patron M. Marmion,
straightforward and high quality. Go for the 125f menu – appetisers,
oysters, salmon, noisettes of lamb, cheese or dessert, or the 175f
version for more expensive items like a feuilleté of asparagus, ten
creuses oysters and fillet of beef.

Harlequin

(H)S   *8 r. du Quai Talard, Port de Dinan 22100 Lanvallay   96.39.50.30*

I was delighted to find this alternative to the hotels up in the town,
superbly sited overlooking the river across the bridge at Lanvallay. Its
an old stone house, with a little garden set to one side, with bedrooms
on three floors profiting from the entrancing aspect of first water then
the colourful quay on the other side, with all the café activity.

Its an English couple, Donald and Pamela Hargreaves, from Suffolk,
who are the patrons, deliberately keeping prices low in order to get
established. Friendly and helpful, they would provide the answer to
those whose French is minimal but who would like to know more
about the region from someone who lives there. Their rooms are good-
sized, comfortable, some with private bathroom, 190f ish.

Breakfast is served in the stone-flagged dining-room – pine tables
and chairs and red tablecloths – or on the terrace, and there is a lively
bar. A few more personal experiences for an arrow.
Reader's recommendation:

*'We had dinner at the Grill Room Duguesclin, 7 Rue Ste Claire. The
99f menu was excellent in all respects. Service was very pleasant and
with a smile. We were so pleased that we had a menu gastronomique
at 175f for lunch the following day. My starter of Fruits de Mer was
enough for both of us to tuck in.'*

Mère Pourcel

(R)M   *3 pl. Merciers 96.39.03.80   Cl. Feb. school hols. Sun. p.m. o.o.s.; Mon.*

Cannot be missed, in the centre of the old town, and worth visiting for
the unique old staircase, dark like a liquorice stick, that forms the
centrepiece of the elegant dining-room. It's a lovely old-fashioned
ambiance, with lots of service for your money and glowing displays of
tartes and fruit to whet the appetite. The cheapest menu is 99f lunch

weekdays, 160f otherwise. A lovely place to eat indoors or on the
terrace.

Map 1F **DINARD** 35800 (I. et V.) 22 km N of Dinan – *Mkt: Tues., Sat.*

A town of changing fortunes. Little over a century ago Dinard was a
simple fishing village, but its sheltered beaches, gentle climate and
magnificent natural setting at the mouth of the Rance enticed rich
Americans and English to build expensive villas there among the palm
trees and camellias, and it soon became the most fashionable resort
not only along the Emerald Coast but in the whole of Northern Europe.

The villas, a little faded perhaps, are still there, and the luxuriant
vegetation and the spectacular sands, but what would the Edwardians
have made of the Grande Plage now, with its hot dog and ice cream
stalls, plastic cafés and transistors? How unthinkable that the modesty
of bathing carriages should have given way to the (almost) ultimate
'topless'.

The town is still a favourite with the Brits and I heard more English
spoken here than anywhere else in Brittany. The cafés and souvenir
shop accommodate their requirements. Few luxury hotels remain, no
starred restaurants, but plenty of bars and more modest
accommodation.

The building of the dam over the Rance in 1967 made access from
St.-Malo by road a whole lot easier; an alternative is to take the ferry
across. For my taste this approach from the eastward side of the town
is the best, with the ramparts of St.-Malo and the old Solidor tower to
look back upon and the splendid beaches of le Prieuré and l'Écluse,
slightly less crowded than the one by the Casino, to view from the sea.
Arriving by car, park by the yacht club and take the utterly delightful
walk along the water's edge – the Promenade du Clair de Lune – to get
an idea of the past elegance and tranquillity of the place. Round a
sudden bend, the Pointe du Moulinet, lies unexpectedly a deep and
sheltered beach, the Plage de l'Écluse, unsophisticated and somehow
rural, in contrast to the brashness of the main Plage de St.-Énogart just
round the point. Not a lot there except:

Hôtel de la Vallée
(HR)M–S   *6 av. George V   99.46.94.00   Fax 99.88.22.47   Cl. 15/11–20/12; Tue.
o.o.s.*

An old-fashioned Logis de France, with good views of the water from
the dining-room and lots of expensive and very comfortable terrace
chairs. A good place for at least a drink, if not a meal. Rooms from
140–450f for one with bath and balcony. Menus from 100f.

→ Le Vieux Manoir
(H)M   *21 r. Gardiner.   99.46.14.69   Fax 99.46.87.87*

The best discovery for a long time. I had ignored le Vieux Manoir previously because of its situation. No sea view in Brittany seems a waste of raw materials. But there are other considerations. Like a stylish large house, a beautiful garden, cool trees, guaranteed peace and quiet, a friendly Madame Faisant, a big covered terrace, lovely large bedrooms decorated in fresh pastel colours, fresh paint everywhere, a price tag of 340–400f for a double with excellent bathroom. They all add up to an arrow and I am confident that FE readers will love this one.

In fact the rue Gardiner is five minutes walk from either the Plage de St. Enogat or the l'Ecluse or the port and the hotel is well signed from the town.

La Plage
(HR)M   *3 blvd Féart 99.46.14.87   Cl. Wed. Jan.–Feb.*

A pleasant middle-of-the-road Logis de France, modern, light cheerful, not far from the main beach. Some of the best rooms (395f) have sea views, all are well-equipped. It has the bonus of an unusually good restaurant **Le Trézen**, with menus from 80f, so demi-pension here would be a good bet. Good o.o.s. rates.

Altaïr
(HR)M   *18 blvd Féart   99.46.13.58   Fax 99.88.20.49   Cl. 15/12–15/1; Sun. p.m.; Mon.*

Yet another Logis, of very different character. This one is in a nice old town house, very French. It is best known for its restaurant. The food is simple but interesting – *flan de moules, truite rosé aux deux sauces* – on menus which start at 80f weekdays for three courses, up to a piggy 180f for six that includes half a lobster, but the 110f version is the one I would go for. All are served in a dining-room full of polished old furniture, with an apéritif perhaps on the sunny terrace.

The rooms, which I asked to look at as an afterthought, were a pleasant surprise. All very different, some modern, some (nos. 2 and 4) delightfully antique, 250 o.o.s. 380f in high season. Friendly and helpful chef-patron M. Leménager.

Not to everyone's liking, too eccentric perhaps. Don't go if you like a bland modern hotel.

Reader's recommendation: **Hotel Printania**.

'I can't enthuse enough about the Hotel Printania. Our 350f room had a balcony with superb views, two double beds, a large bathroom and nearly as much furniture as we've got in our living room at home. The whole hotel is fabulously furnished with Breton pieces. The breakfast was 32f and was the best of the trip'.

Map 2G   **DOL-DE-BRETAGNE** 35120 (I. et V.) 26 km NE of Dinan,
54 km N of Rennes, 175 km from Cherbourg – *Mkt: Sat.*

An ancient frontier town, where the severity of Breton architecture
mingles with the softer Norman influences. The oldest house in
Brittany is here, along with several other noteworthy mediaeval and
17th-century buildings, in the Grand'rue des Stuarts. St.-Samson,
named after a 6th-century Welsh saint, is a vast granite cathedral,
rather grim on a grey day with its blank western face and uncompleted
tower, but indicating the erstwhile importance of the town. John
Lackland burnt down the original cathedral in 1203, and, overcome
with remorse, paid for its reconstruction. Inside gets better, with its
Great Window of 13th-century glass and 14th-century choir stalls.

Locals say that an underground passage links one of its towers to
Mont Dol, the hump rising oddly out of the fertile polders below.
Prehistoric mammoth, elephant, and rhinoceros bones have been dug
up on this strange mound which was once an island, when the sea
lapped the escarpment on which Dol is built.

One of the most impressive dolmens in Brittany is to be found just a
mile or so south of Dol on the Epiniac road. It fell out of the sky, legend
has it, to divide the armies of two aggressive brothers, waging such
bloody war that the field is known as Champ Dolen, or the Field of
Suffering. They say it sinks one inch every 100 years and when it
disappears altogether the world will come to an end, so hurry hurry –
only another 31 ft to go.

Semi-pedestrianisation has worked wonders for Dol. Now you can sit
peacefully on a bench on the cobbles and take in the old beams and
turrets that give the main street so much character. Strategically this is
a valuable stop on the way south and I have always been anxious to
find a promising hotel. Now at least the two rivals have been
smartened up.

Hotel de Bretagne
(HR)S   *17 pl. Châteaubriand   99.48.02.03   rest. cl. Sat. o.o.s*

The town's most obvious hotel, in the main square since 1923, family-
run, Logis. The corridors, carpets and doors are still painted in gloomy
burgundy but the bedrooms have been renovated and now have good
bathrooms. At 150–290f they would be perfectly adequate for an over-
nighter. Menus from 65f.

La Brêsche Arthur
(H)S(R)M   *36 blvd Deminiac   99.48.01.44   Fax 99.48.16.32   Cl. Wed.; 15/11–
26/11; 1/2–11/2*

The downstairs of the hotel has recently undergone a considerable
facelift and is now very smart. Work is continuing on the bedrooms, so
this report may soon be out of date (keep me informed please). At
present those in the old style cost 180f and are functional rather than
luxurious, while those that have had the treatment rate 300f. But it is

69

the restaurant that makes this the preferred choice in the town. Catch it while the prices are still such a bargain. The locals do. It's an elegant charming room now opening out onto the garden, with inspired cooking by Philippe Martel. The 75f menu is a bargain but the 120f version is astonishing – I ate tartare of salmon and haddock in an oyster cream, then leg of rabbit imaginatively flavoured with coconut, good cheeses served with home-made nut and apricot bread and a range of chocolate desserts.

➤ **La Grabotais**
(R)S   *4 r. Ceinte   99.48.19.89   Cl. Mon. except for dinner in high season*

How *do* they do it? A smart little restaurant, with high backed tapestry chairs, elegant china and napery, stone walls, copper pans, wormy dark beams, huge high fireplace with comforting fire – in other words as charming as you could wish – and a menu for a mere 58f? In fact we couldn't tackle three courses and settled for two dishes off the carte – oysters and beef brochette for him and a rabbit and hazelnut terrine for me, but judging by the food presented on the plates around me, this is very good news indeed, and worthy of another arrow.

   'A venerable building where we had a very good lunch consisting of 6 oysters, followed by grilled halibut and decent house wine at 18f for a small pichet. One could choose any two courses from the three course menu, which suited us well and costs 56f each. We would definitely go again.' H. J. Brooks.

Map 3A   **DOUARNENEZ** 29100 (Finistère) 22 km NW of Quimper – *Mkt: Mon., Fri., Sat.*

Powerfully fishy. No doubt that its heart lies around the harbour; this part is vibrant and full of atmosphere, the rest of the town grey and drab. If, like me, you love watching fishing boats arrive, screeching gulls convoying, unloading their glistening heaving catch on the quays, or wandering round a busy fishmarket in the morning, wondering at the size and variety of the specimens, make for Rosmeur to the east of the town. Connected by a bridge to the west, narrow little Tréboul is for pleasure craft.

   In the beautiful bay of Douarnenez they say lies the drowned city of Ys. Listen hard when the air is still and you may hear its bells ringing after fifteen centuries of submersion! The King of Cornouaille, Gradlon, reigned here, over a debauched population, who modelled themselves on his licentious daughter Dahud. So incensed was God at the immoral goings-on that he handed over the town to the devil, who lost no time bedding the larky princess and persuading her to open the sluice gates which held back the tide. King Gradlon escaped on a galloping horse but Dahud got her come-uppance at last – she disappeared for ever beneath the foaming waters.

   The legend persists in many forms – when the tide is at its lowest you have only to look for yourself to see the remains of Ys buried in the sands. Which should work up an appetite:

Le Pourquoi Pas?
(R)M–S   *Port Musee 15 quai Port-Rhu*   *98.92.76.13*   *Cl. Mon. o.o.s.; Oct–April*

Very nautical – the decor is of an old sailing boat and its menu almost entirely of fish and seafood. Nothing wrong with that, especially as the fish, fresh from the market, is prepared without any fuss. Good plateau de f. de m. No menus but main courses on the carte run at around 85f. Unless you have lobster of course.

Le Tristan
(R)M   *25 bis r. du Rosmeur*   *98.92.20.17*   *Cl. Wed.*

Bag a table by the window for the best view over the harbour from this little restaurant by the port. Seafood of course, on a 90f menu. Popular and small, so booking advisable.
  'Delicious lunch. Restaurant very busy, full of local bon vivants. Family-run, small, exquisite seafood.' Shirin Court.

Interesting hotels found I none, but perhaps in any case Douarnenez is more a place to visit than to lodge in.

Map 4E   **ELVEN** 56250 (Morbihan) 14 km NE of Vannes

The N 166 now mercifully bypasses Elven and its 3000-odd inhabitants, making it an altogether more agreeable place to spend a night.

Hostellerie du Lion d'Or
(HR)S   *5 pl. le Franc*   *97.53.33.52*   *Fax 97.53.55.08*   *Cl. Sun. p.m.; Mon. 15 days in Oct.*

A little Logis de France with good cooking, by patron M. Brard, and comfortable beds. Ten rooms cost from 185–300f, depending on mod cons, and menus start at 75f for dinner or 60f for lunch.

Map 5D   **ERDEVEN** 56410 (Morbihan) 9 km NW of Carnac

Auberge du Sous-Bois
(HR)M   *97.55.66.11*   *Fax 97.55.68.82*   *Cl. 1/10–1/4; rest cl. lunch exc. Suns. and July/Aug.*

1 km on the Pont Lorois Road. A granite building set in the pine trees. Straightforward grills in the restaurant (from 90f) and clean functional rooms at 345–380f.

Voyageurs
(HR)S   r. Ocean   97.55.64.47   Fax 97.55.64.24   Cl. Tue. o.o.s.; 1/10–1/4

    'An excellent hotel restaurant; it is a modest establishment but extremely good value, the rooms are clean, overlooking an orchard. The only sound to disturb you is that of the nearby church bells calling the village to mass. The accueil of Mme Gouzerh makes you feel part of the family very rapidly, while M. Gouzerh buys fresh fish and shellfish at Etel or at Auray every day.' R. B. Cosgrave.

    Just what a family-run hotel should be in fact. Rooms cost 185–285f and meals start at 60f.

Map 1E   **ERQUY** 22430 (C. d'A.) 40 km NW on Dinan – *Mkt: Sat.*

A little fishing port, famous for its scallops, nestling under a spectacularly beautiful headland. Rather disappointing as a resort, but around it lie ten beaches to choose from, according to wind direction and inclination for fine sand, as at Caroual, or more private rocky coves. The best bit is around by the harbour, where lots of cheap cafés serve simple fresh fish.

L'Escurial
(R)M   *blvd de la Mer*   96.72.31.56   *Cl. Sun. p.m.; Mon. o.o.s.*

Most unpromising first impression – yellow plastic sign, in a block of flats by the dingy harbour, with a flashy mermaid to greet you at the door, but press on if you wish to eat the best scallops, straight from the boat. This is a serious gastronomic restaurant with inspired cooking by Veronique Bernard. In winter the seafood is reinforced with game. Good sea views.

    Menus start at 130f to 300f five courses including the lot, *via* apéritif, through lobster, best wines chosen to complement the food, coffee and *digestif*.

Relais St. Aubin
(R)M   *3 kms from Erquy on the D68 towards La Bouillie.*   96.72.13.22

A real find, combining atmosphere (ex 17C priory now an antique shop as well as a restaurant), with good welcome, straightforward cooking of prime ingredients, and reasonable prices. No wonder it is so popular that it would be folly not to book. House specialities are grills cooked on the open fire – langoustines, côte de beouf, lamb, chicken and fish dishes like monkfish in a shellfish coulis or warm scallop salads. Their plâteaux de fruits de mer and lobsters must be ordered ahead but are well worth the effort. Menus start at 90f. Some signs of approval please for an arrow.

Map 3B **LE FAOU** 29580 (Finistère) 19 km N of Châteaulin, on the
N 170 Brest Road – *Mkt: Sat.*

The little town is dominated by its wide market square with 16C
covered halles, in which, side by side, stand two very popular
establishments.

I always find it difficult to choose between these two. Here are two
recent reports so that you can make your own mind up:

Vieille Renommé
(HR)M *pl Mairie.   98.81.90.31   Fax 98.81.92.93   Cl. Sun. p.m.; Mon. o.o.s.*

> *'The 80f menu was one of the best meals I have had in over 30 years
> travel across France. The service was smiling and friendly, the
> restaurant full to capacity. Our room, the last available, was a very
> spacious twin, with shower and w.c. for 225f – very good value indeed
> for what is quite a large hotel. We would have liked to stay longer.'*
> Christopher Hall.
> 38 rooms for 245–320f.

Relais de la Place
(HR)M *pl. Mairie.   98.81.91   Fax 98.81.92.58   Cl. Sat.; two weeks in Oct. 21/12–
15/1*

> *'We were lucky to get in, after 8 p.m., and its popularity is well-
> founded. We went for the budget menu at 68f, which was delicious.
> There was a considerable choice of starters and main courses. The top
> of the range was the ultimate in seafood, at 225f. I have rarely seen
> such a spread of fish and shellfish and many people were ordering it. I
> have rarely enjoyed better.*
> *'I would thoroughly recommend the restaurant and believe that the
> quality extends to the hotel, which is very well run.'* Jacky Rattue.

Map 4B **LA FORÊT-FOUESNANT** 29940 (Finistère) 16 km SE of Quimper

A village at the head of La Forêt bay, busier nowadays because of the
vast yacht harbour opened up at Port-la-Forêt across the estuary.
Market day Tuesday.

Auberge St.-Laurent
(R)M *6 r. de Beg-Menez   98.56.98.07   Open all year*

2.5 km E of the village on the Concarneau road. Cosy with log fire, and
authentically beamed. Menus at 75–175f, more enterprising than most.
Good value (ten oysters for starters) and interesting *quenelles
d'homard.* Completely conflicting reactions – most readers approved
but one *hated* it. *'We were very cross with you for sending us there.'*

Hôtel de l'Espérance
(HR)S   *pl. de l'Eglise   98.56.96.58   Cl. 11/10–25/3*

> A little Logis set back from the road, behind a garden and terrace. It
> manages to retain a lot of character – white shutters, stone-walled
> dining-room – along with the mod. cons., and is popular with locals
> and regular tourists alike, so booking advisable. A simple double room
> costs 128f and the most expensive, with bath, 295f. Menus start at 50f.

Manoir du Stang
(HR)L   *98.56.97.37   Cl. mid-Sept.–mid-May; rest. cl. 10/10–20/6. No lunch and
dinner only for residents.*

> Signed off the D 783 heading north. A stunningly beautiful 16th-
> century manorhouse, set in a hundred acres of parkland. You can feel
> the green tranquillity settling as you approach through an avenue of
> ancient oaks. A *stang* is a large lake; here there are several and their
> watery vistas dominate the view from house and garden. Roses and
> hydrangeas abound, climbing round the house and set in formal, very
> French, flowerbeds. 'Idyllic' is the only word. When I did a sneak Easter
> preview the drive was carpeted with primroses, the trees in early bud
> and the birds noisily celebrating; I think it's a pity that the hotel doesn't
> open its doors to the public until so late in the year.
>
> The rooms vary enormously in size and aspect, as you would expect
> from a building not built as an hotel, but all those I saw were utterly
> charming, furnished with antiques and gentle colours, *toile de Jouy*
> curtains, good bathrooms. The food is unremarkable, but well-served,
> in a pleasant atmosphere from 160f.
>
> A lovely place to spend the odd couple of luxurious days, and with
> 26 rooms it is often surprisingly possible to get in on short notice.

Beauséjour
(HR)S   *98.56.97.18   Fax 98.51.40.77   Cl. 15/10–15/3*

> *'Greatly improved, as is shown by its increased popularity. Well-
> priced menus with most interesting choices'. Pamela Biles.*
> A reliable little hotel 25 rooms cost 160–310f and honest cooking
> comes on menus from 75f.

Map 4B   **FOUESNANT** 29170 (Finistère) 15 km SE of Quimper on the
D 44 – *Mkt: 3rd Fri.*

> The best Breton cider of all comes from Fouesnant, surrounded as the
> little town is by apple orchards. There is a festival of the apple trees on
> the first Sunday after July 14, which is a good time and place to see the
> traditional costumes of Fouesnant, as is the July 26, the *pardon* of
> Sainte-Anne.

➤ Hotel d'Armorique

(HR)S   *33 r. de Cornouaille   98.56.00.19   Fax 98.56.65.36   Cl. 30/10–1/5; Mon. o.o.s.;*   P.

A splendidly French little hotel in the main street, run by the famille Morvan. Go through the popular bar to an unexpectedly charming dining-room, giving on to a courtyard, with a great wall of hydrangeas, whose summer colour spills over into the room.

Comprehensive menus from 70f (lunch) or 90f (dinner) include plenty of shellfish. On the middle price we ate six oysters, two generous *rougets* crumbed and pan-fried in butter, and a home made *crème caramel*. M. Morvan cooks straightforward food and plenty of it, all excellent value, plus several Breton specialities, like a vast *cassoulet Breton*. Try the local cider, of course.

The bedrooms are fine; old-fashioned ones are in the main house and newer with all mod. cons. in the annexe in the garden, from 160 – 330f. Good for families.

I cannot fault this one in its modest class for value for money, good honest food and smiling welcome, and the arrow is well deserved.

Unanimous praise from many readers.

'Excellent in every way. Also visited by our daughter and family who commented on the good selection of starters and pleasant atmosphere.' Pamela Biles.

'We found it specially convenient to park in the shady garden and enjoyed our sunny balcony. We also found the most perfect beach just down the road at Cap Coz, and strolled across the road to the yachting inlet on the other side. The swimming was also delightful there.

'Delightfully friendly people, wonderfully good food and a lovely dining-room to eat it in. The fish soup was delicious but enough for two, as was the steak. However I have to mention that we could not get an en suite room.' Suzanne Nott.

'Definitely number 1. The children could have the plat du jour on the menu enfant but it was a full sized portion and they could have a proper dessert as well. The cassoulet remains superb. The service was excellent and they have some remarkably good wine in the cellar. I suspect they have not updated the prices of their older vintages for some years'. Andrew and Liz Bamji.

Two reader's recommendations:

Le Bistro de la Plage
Plage de Kesteven   95.56.90.87

'This little café is right on Kesteven beach and has recently changed hands. It is extremely good value – whole crab 48f, sardines 43f, moules mariniere 36f, steak frites 48f. There are also rooms at 200f with loo and shower but we did not see them.'

Fort Cigogne
(R)S *1 descente de Roz an Bars   98.56.53.36   Cl. Mon.*

*'We ate there on our last night and were delighted with the menu and
the whole atmosphere. Madame Scotet's husband was the chef and
when he had finished he came and played the guitar and sang. Their
children served and laid the tables'. Susan Maxwell Scott.*
　　　I hope the food was good too!

La Pointe de Mousterlin
(HR)M   *98.56.04.12   Fax 98.56.61.02   Cl. Oct.–10/4; rest. cl. Tue. in April and
May.   6 kms SW by D 145 and D 134*

Just 30 metres from an immense beach of fine sand – ideal for the
kids. You have the choice of rooms overlooking the sea or more
modern ones in a comfortable annexe facing on to a pleasant garden,
280–440f. Cooking makes full use of local seafood on menus from 92f.

Map 2H　　**FOUGÈRES** 35300 (I. et V.) 40 km S of Avranches – *Mkt: Sat.*

Even the 'new' Upper Town is dominated by the massive castle dating
from the 12th century down in the valley of the Nançon. Situated on
the border of Normandy, it was obviously an important mediaeval
fortress and it was the surrounding lakes and marsh land that secured
its impregnability.

It's a fair old puff up to the Upper Town, the centre of a shoe-making
industry. Some of the streets and houses here are old and interesting
too, with a colourful covered market in the rue Nationale, leading to
the best view of the mediaeval town and valley from the park, the Place
aux Arbres, a good place to get your breath back and perhaps enjoy a
picnic. You can complete the tour by taking the rue des Vallées and the
Escalier de la Duchesse Anne down the side of the valley, crossing the
bridge to the Place de Marchix, the town's oldest and most interesting
quarter.

All very fascinating and obviously well-sited for an overnight stop
but I have yet to discover a lodging possibility. The **Hotel des
Voyageurs** near the central parking could be noisy and one reader
points out that there is no sitting-room and only the bar to breakfast in.
　　　I could recommend its restaurant, however:

Restaurant Les Voyageurs
(R)M   *9 pl. Gambetta   99.99.14.17   Cl. 17/8–6/9; Sat. o.o.s.   AE, V*

Popular with the locals (but then there doesn't appear to be anywhere
else to go!) Menus from 92f.

Map 1F   **FRÉHEL** 22240 (C. d'A.) 50 km NW of Dinan

The highest point on the Emerald Coast, with probably the most
spectacular views in Northern Brittany. To approach it from Sables
d'Or at sunset is a never-to-be forgotten experience, since the colours
of the porphyry and red sandstone cliffs, towering 225 ft above the
water, glow with technicolour intensity; dark shapes of wheeling
migratory birds, for whom this is a natural sanctuary, punctuate the
brilliance. The coastal panorama stretches from the Cotentin peninsula
to the Ile de Bréhat, with the Channel Islands visible in particularly
clear weather. Round the Anse de Sévignés is the mightily impressive
fortress, the Fort la Latte, almost entirely sea-girt, mediaeval origins,
more wonderful views. Ten minutes walk away is:

Le Relais de Fréhel
(HR)M   *96.41.43.02   Cl. 3/11–1/3*

Originally an old Breton farmhouse, stone walls, mansard roof, into
which are set some of the rooms, none of them large, but offering
simple calm comfort. From 275–310f. The food concentrates on grills
and seafood; menus from 75f. The salon boasts a good log fire and
there is a pleasant garden.

La Fauconnière
(R)S   *Le Cap Fréhel   96.41.54.20   Cl. 1/10–1/4*

A simple restaurant and bar perched right at the end of the peninsula,
on the cliff edge. The views are, simply, stunning. You can take the
path down beside the restaurant to watch the cormorants and take
pictures of the seagulls nesting on the multi-coloured rocks.
   Clientèle is mostly sightseers and walkers, who come here for
simple tuck-ins of omelettes, fresh fish and seafood, on menus
from 85f.

La Pointe du Cap Coz
(HR)M   *153 av. Pointe, Cap Coz, (2.5 kms)   98.56.01.65   Cl. Wed.; Jan.–Feb.*
School hols.

A magic position, posed on a spit of sand and open to the waves on
two sides. The rooms have mostly been renovated; they are simple but
pleasant, 215–260f.
   The big bonus here is the restaurant, where the cheapest menu at
98f is a winner. Cooking is far more interesting than one would
anticipate – sea trout cooked with lentils and baked shellfish served on
roasted vegetables, apples on sable pastry, flavoured with honey.

L'Espérance
(HR)S   *6 r. Baie   98.56.96.58   Cl. Wed. lunch; Oct.–Mar.*

Behind a façade enveloped by wistaria there are 27 rooms, small but
well equipped and opening out onto gardens, good value at 210–285f.

But the main reason for staying here would be to stay in for dinner. In an unpretentious family atmosphere simple well-cooked food is served on an excellent menu of a mere 80f. Incredible value, it included fresh crab mayonnaise, chicken tarragon, and chocolate profiteroles.

Le Victorine
(R)S   *Placede la Mairie. Le Bourg.   96.41.55.55   Cl. Wed. and Sun. p.m. o.o.s.; 15/11–30/11; 15/1–15/2*

Because the Cap is so spectacular the actual town of Fréhel tends to be overlooked by tourists and prices are accordingly lower. Never mind that Le Victorine does not have a sea view – it still specialises in 'La Cuisine de la Mer'. Menus from 75f. This one was originally recommended to me by the owner of a nearby chambres d'hôtes that I was investigating and I always find that these recommendations are among the best – the bed and breakfast hosts get regular feed-back from their clients and know that they will suffer too if the meal is not good, so I was not surprised to find it a winner.

Map 4F   **LA GACILLY** 56200 (Morbihan) 58 km SW Rennes, 16 km N of Redon

---

We discovered La Gacilly by chance; some of the canals were shut for their winter clean-up and we were asked to return our boat not to Malestroit, whence we had first set off, but to La Gacilly. This enforced detour gave us one of the most attractive stretches of water to explore – the narrow, peaceful little river Aff. It also gave us the opportunity to spend a night in the basin by the falls in La Gacilly, a charmingly picturesque and flowery artists' town. Their workshops line the narrow streets – the woodworker, the jeweller, the weaver, the basket-maker and the leatherworker, all beavering away unselfconsciously in view of the perambulating visitors, for whom La Gacilly is obviously a favourite excursion. There are several bars and small restaurants to assuage the pangs brought on by all this exercise. The best is undoubtedly:

Hôtel France et Square
(HR)S   *15 r. Montaulon   99.08.11.15   Fax 99.08.25.88   Cl. Sun. p.m. o.o.s.; 24/12– 3/1*

A simple old-fashioned hotel in the main street, serving simple old-fashioned meals at 70f and with rooms here and in its smarter annexe at 115–250f.
   The fact that it stays open in the winter is a good indication that it caters for locals rather than tourists.

Map 3D   **GOUAREC** 22570 (C. d'A.) 118 km W of Rennes on the N 164 –
Mkt: 2nd Sat

Nothing special about this little town on the intersection of the Nantes–
Brest canal and the river Blavet, but if, following the Nationale, on the
way west, an overnight stop were required, here is the answer:

Hôtel du Blavet
(HR)S   *96.24.90.03   Fax 96.24.84.85   Cl. Feb.; Sun.; Mon. o.o.s.; 20/12–15/3*

A pleasant little hotel overlooking the Blavet, with friendly patronne,
Mme Le Loir. The bedrooms are all comfortable and well-furnished,
but no. 6 is a joy. Four-poster, bath, view over the river, all for 350f.
Cheaper rooms from 160f.
   The dining-room also enjoys the soothing water aspect and M. Le
Loir dishes up his traditional specialities – no skimping here – on
menus from 82–330f. Recommended and potential arrow.

Map 4B   **GOUESNACH** 29950 (Finistère) 6 km N of Bénodet

Aux Rives de l'Odet
(HR)S   *10 pl. de l'Odet   98.54.61.09   Cl. Oct. and 15 days in Feb.; Mon. o.o.s.*

First reaction was annoyance that this little Logis had misled me by its
name into expecting something pretty on the banks of the river Odet;
in fact it is a dull little building in a dull little village, with no riverbank
in sight. On reflection, though, I am including it as a rare example in
these parts of a really simple, really French hotel/restaurant, only ten
minutes away from gorgeous beaches. The fact that it stays open in
winter is significant – it feeds locals not tourists.
   I went back a second time to see what was on offer and found one of
the best value meals around, cooked by patron M. Le Nader. No choice
and different every day; 88f bought home-made soup, *langoustines
mayonnaise, foie de veau* and dessert. Simple rooms cost 150–290f.

Map 1G   **LA GOUESNIÈRE** 35350 (I. et V.) 12 km SW of St.-Malo

Hotel Tirel
(HR)M   *99.89.10.46   Fax 99.89.12.62   Cl. 17/12–17/1; rest. cl. Sun. p.m. o.o.s.   AE,
DC*

1½ km north of the village on the D 766 Cancale road, opposite the
station, this is the **Hotel Gare** but known to all the locals by the name
of its owners, the Tirels. Not sure I would have picked it without the
guidance of a Michelin star, but I'm very glad I did.
   The large dining-room is the kind of plush the French love, velvet

swags, tassels, awful oil paintings, tented draped ceiling, fake panelling, fake brick, fake marble, but definitely not fake food. Set in the middle of nowhere, it's a pleasant surprise to find it always full, warm and lively.

No need to look beyond the excellent 125f menu, but the most popular order around was undoubtedly the lobster, for which the hotel is renowned. As I can never work out how much the grams are going to cost me, I stuck to the menu and was delighted with my *terrine de trois poissons Guillaume Tirel, foie de veau de vieux vins*, superb cheeseboard and blackcurrant mousse with fresh raspberry sauce. Home-made bread full of nuts and the *feuilleté* nibbles arrived in great profusion, even though I was clearly not going to be the night's big spender. My modest bottle of Bourgueil cost 83f, but the elaborate wine list included bottles in the 900f range.

The hotel part, in another building at the back, is ultra-modern. Someone has gone mad with the wall-to-ceiling carpet, but it's all very comfortable and well equipped, with indoor swimming pool, sauna, tennis court, and good value at 390f with bathroom (cheaper rooms from 265f). The staff, mostly family, are friendly and efficient and the whole set-up is a pleasant experience, but it's all bigger than you'd think and 60 rooms means party bookings, so prior reservation for both hotel and restaurant is wise.

Map 6F   **LA GRANDE BRIÈRE** (Parc Régional) N. of La Baule

If any proof were needed of Brittany's infinite variety, I would point to the Regional Park of La Grande Brière. Within a few kilometres of La Baule's sophisticated sands, a mere half hour's drive from the wild cliffs of the Croisic peninsula, or St.-Nazaire's industry, or the popular yacht harbour of Roche Bernard to the north, lies this strange other world of marsh-canals; granite islands support whitewashed cottages whose peasant owners have cut reeds to thatch their own roofs and journey by flat-bottomed punts (*blains*), not automobiles.

The coming of spring and the draining of the flood waters are signals for myriads of wild flowers to cover the rich low-lying land. Fields of yellow iris precede the exotic waterlilies. All around there is an explosion of flora and teeming of wildlife. Birds and fish literally abound.

Since many of the young Brièrons are deserting to the towns, a problem facing the remaining inhabitants is how best to maintain the delicate balance between encouraging tourism and continuing their simple peasant-style existence, living off the land, carrying on traditional occupations of thatching, breeding ducks and geese, cutting peat. The natural charms of this unique area could so easily be swamped. Some of the residents are happy to take you for a boat ride and it's a time-warp experience to glide through the expanse of glittering water along labyrinthine routes known only to the locals, with just the plop of the puntpole and sometimes the whirring of powerful wings overhead to break the depth of the silence.

A few roads cross the marshes and one of them, the D 50, north from Montoir de Bretagne, leads to what is probably the best preserved village, Fédrun, entirely surrounded by water. You can visit a traditional Brièron cottage here, white and thatched, and engage a boatman guide.

Map 1G **GROUIN, POINTE DU** 35260 (I. et V.) 5 km N of Cancale

---

A finger pointing NE into the Bay of Mont St.-Michel, with the Mount swimming on the horizon to the right and a panorama of rocky headlands as far as **Cap Fréhel** to the left. The offshore **Île des Landes** is a bird sanctuary and the inhabitants can be well observed by the energetic who care to take the marvellous walk towards Cancale, *via* the beaches and sheltered bays of **Port-Mer** and **Port-Pican** down to the little cove of **Port-Briac.**

Hôtel Pointe du Grouin
(HR)M   *99.89.60.55   Fax 99.89.92.22   Cl. 30/9–Easter; rest. cl. Tues.*

The privileged position, with views from all its windows across the bay, brings this well-known Logis a steady stream of customers. The impression, I have to say, is that it is too steady, and not a lot of *accueil* need be extended to ensure a full house.

With those views, those beaches, those sheltered coves, I think I'd be happier with a picnic, but the hotel is all very well-groomed, with an elegant dining-room where excellent seafood menus start at 115f, rooms, are from 380f. Booking definitely advisable. Rooms smallish but pleasant.

Map 5F **GUENROUET** (Loire-Atl.) 21 km SW of Redon, 86 km from Rennes on the D 2

A very attractive section of the river/canal system that lattices Brittany is south of Redon on the wide river Isac. Dense foliage, writhing roots, a certain stillness, kingfishers blazing a shining darting trail, all confuse the senses. Tarzan-territory, Breton-style.

This is a favourite stretch for fishermen, who line the banks, hunched in silent contemplation, or sit back to back like bookends in ancient flat-bottomed boats.

The odd modern roof in the trees surprises by its incongruity – villages are rare in these parts and not particularly attractive. Guenrouet has a church, a *boulangerie*, a couple of *charcuteries*, a bar and a plastic restaurant, but down by the water, a step from our night's mooring we found a treasure:

Le Relais St Clair
R(M)   40.87.66.11   *Rte Mozay cl. Mon. p.m.; Tue. p.m.; Wed. o.o.s.*

Many changes in what was once a simple bistro, on the bridge on the D 2, into a gastronomic restaurant. There is a new 'salle panoramique' overlooking the river and the new pontoons, and in summer there will be an outdoor barbecue with buffet service for 70f. Mme Geffray has exceeded our fondest hopes and made this one of the most agreeable stops along the waterways. Menus from 110f. Arrowed for situation and good food.

Map 6E   **GUÉRANDE** 44350 (Loire-Atl.) 6 km N of La Baule – *Mkt: Sat.*

One of the most delightful aspects of Guérande is its unexpectedness. Rising unpredictably from the strange chequerboard of the salt pans is this encapsulated mediaeval town.

An unbroken coronet of 15th-century ramparts, ten towers, four gates, surrounds highly photogenic old streets, squares and churches. Stroll from the Place du Marché au Bois to St.-Aubin, *via* the rue St.-Michel, which leads into the heart of the mediaeval town. The church was founded in 852 but was rebuilt between the 14th and 16th centuries, with a strange exterior pulpit flanked by two angels' heads.

Not difficult to guess from a look at the map that Guérande must be a popular excursion for holidaymakers seeking diversion from sand and sea, and there are plenty of cafés and little restaurants to refresh the tourist. There is also a perfectly delightful little hotel:

Roc Maria
(H)M   *r. des Halles   40.24.90.51   Fax 40.62.13.03   Cl. Wed. p.m.; Thur. o.o.s.; 15/11–15/12*

Cross the square from the church and look left to find, tucked away in a cul de sac, the picturesque old house in a flowery courtyard. Simple rooms are 250–290f and there is no restaurant other than a crepêrie, but that should prove no problem.

'Run by a very friendly couple. We had a good sized family room with bath for the three of us for 260f in this lovely old house just behind the covered market. Plenty of atmosphere – strong fishy smell when we opened the front door! We ate out at Hotel des Voyageurs where we had a very adequate meal at only 52f in a restaurant which was full and appeared popular with locals.' Christopher Hall.

Les Remparts
(HR)M   *15 blvd Nord.   40.24.90.69   Rest. cl. Sun. p.m.; Mon. o.o.s.; 2/11–26/3 for dinner*

(New)

Not so immediately appealing as Roc Maria, since it is extra-muros, on the ring road, but the eight rooms have recently been renovated and the welcome is warm. Menus from 98f and demi-pension, obligatory in high season, would be no hardship at 258–295f per person.

La Collégiale
(R)M   *63 fg. Bizienne   40.24.97.29   Cl. Wed. lunch; Thurs. Feb.; 20/12–25/12*

A stunning garden is overlooked by a picturesque veranda in this attractive old house, once a seminary. Cooking by Christian Mimault is probably the best in the area – sophisticated and interesting on menus from 130f. Essential to book in high season, but I wouldn't go then anyway because prices leap, unjustifiably I consider, to 300f.

Map C2   **GUERLESQUIN** 29650 (Finistère) 15 kms SE of Morlaix

A typical ancient Breton village, set in wild desolate country where the Monts d'Arree meet the Mene Moor. In the centre of the huge square surrounded by old granite houses is the former courthouse, a square 17C building with a turret at each corner.

Mont d'Arrée
(HR)S   *98.72.80.44   Fax 98.72.81.50   Cl. Sun. p.m.*

Recommended primarily for its restaurant, a well-appreciated local meeting place, where good value is recognised. Book ahead if you intend eating there on Sunday, when both dining-rooms are bulging. 69f buys three courses of simply-cooked prime ingredients. Intrinsic generosity is evident – for starters on the cheapest menu a whole crab appears, served with home-made mayonnaise, or eight fat oysters instead of the usual six. Go mad and eat on the 99f version and you get a dozen!

There's nothing wrong with the rooms, simple they may be but they are quiet, clean and comfortable, most with en suite bathrooms, for 195–260f.

Map E4   **GUILLIERS** 56490 Morbihan 13 kms from Ploërmel by D 766 and D 13.

A small village in the heart of the Argoat interior, useful for a comfortable overnight stop.

Au Relais du Porhoët
(HR)S   *97.40.17   Fax 97.74.45.65*

A substantial white and granite building, rusticised inside with beams and huge brick fireplace in which a comforting fire burns at first chill. A reader first alerted me to the value to be found here, away from the

main tourist routes. Just 15 rooms, comfortable, some with brass beds, all decorated pleasantly in pastel shades, most with en suite bathrooms, 190–260f, but it is the restaurant which is the main reason for staying here. Outstanding value on its 85f menu. Three courses of high quality prepared by the chef-patron and served up with a smile. More reports please for a potential arrow.

Map B4   **GUILVINEC** 11.5 kms from Pont l'Abbé. 30 kms from Quimper

A busy commercial fishing port, interesting rather than attractive, particularly in the late afternoon when, one by one, the fishing boats return to unload their catch. Within walking distance are some good beaches and of course the whole area has fascinating possibilities, so this would be a reasonable base:

Centre
(HR)S   *r. Gen. de Gaulle.   98.58.10.44   Fax 98.58.31.05   Cl. Sun. p.m.; from Nov.–Mar.*

> *'Charming, well run and immaculate. The family speak some English. The rooms are lovely, the food very good indeed – predominantly sea food – and if you are British, you are sure of a great welcome'.*
> 17 rooms cost between 235 and 310f and excellent meals are from 70f.

Map 2D   **GUINGAMP** 22200 (C. d'A.) 32 km W of St.-Brieuc

On a steaming July Saturday, with the colour of the market stalls vibrant in the sun, there was more of an air of gaudy Provence than grey Brittany in the square; here were fountains, lime trees, awnings protecting great piles of Cavaillon melons and peaches limp in the airless heat, and plump farmers' wives fanning themselves with newspapers. Even the frightened rabbits forgot their trauma and dozed in their hutches.

Very pleasant was Guingamp then, with its cobbles, old houses, cathedral viewed from a café table complete with cool beer; it had looked altogether different in winter, or a non-market day, uniformly grey, with through-traffic clogging the square. The one constantly agreeable factor:

Relais du Roy
(H)M, (R)M–L   *42 pl. du Centre   96.43.76.62   Cl. 1/9–15/9; rest. cl. Sun. p.m. o.o.s.*

A 17th-century grey stone house facing the market square, with a wonderful Renaissance door inside its courtyard. Lots of other ancient features discovered in unexpected quarters, like the stone carved chimney breast in the corridor. Which leads to the seven rooms set in the quiet of the rear of the building. All are furnished elegantly and well equipped with modern bathrooms – good value at 450f. Some have been lavishly refurbished and now cost 800f.

The whole establishment is smart and well-run, with M. and Mme Mallégo very much in attendance in their attractive dining-room. They resolutely maintain that it is possible to serve traditional cuisine that is not boring, enlivened with a certain individual touch. This generosity of quantity and quality would make the **Relais** an ideal base out of season when heartier appetites need satisfying.

Lots of meat as well as seafood appear regularly on the menus, which leap from 125–290f. If the cheaper menu, no-choice, happens to suit, you'll get a bargain, but if you weaken towards the *carte* it will cost around 200f, so it's worth checking to see what's an offer. Certainly on my last visit the braised pork *plat du jour* would not have appealed on such a sultry day.

Map 2G   **HÉDÉ** 35630 (I. et V.) 23 km N of Rennes on the N 137 – *Mkt: Mon.*

It takes eleven locks for the Canal d'Ille et Rance to climb up to the hilltop village of Hédé, whose ruined castle, old houses and colourful gardens cling precariously to a rocky ridge. Below, the Valley of the Windmills makes a tranquil respite from the main road, with lovely walks along the canal banks.

Vieille Auberge
(R)M   *99.45.46.25*   *Cl. 26/8–3/9; 15/1–15/2; Feb.; Sun. p.m.; Mon.*

Tucked away from the Nationale among the popular trees, with a pleasant terrace where you can eat on fine days, is Marcel Leffondré's little inn. His cooking is skilled but unfussy, ingredients superbly fresh – red mullet served with a mousse of sorrel and a sharp blackcurrant ice cream melting imaginatively into warm apple slices. I recommend the 140f menu.

Hostellerie Vieux Moulin
(HR)M   *99.45.45.70*   *Cl. 20/12–1/2; Sun. p.m.; Mon. o.o.s*

  H

     R

You'd think, wouldn't you, that two inns in the same community would see to it that they didn't close on the same days, but no – the dreaded dead Sun. p.m. and Mon. prevail. For the rest of the week this one is also old, also very picturesque, with attractive dining-room serving less-upmarket, cheaper menus than the **Auberge**, starting at 90f for lunch or 150f. It does have fourteen rooms, from 230–260f, but reports on them are not good.

'I went off the main road into the village before I discovered it was very conveniently on the main road itself. Exactly as you said, rooms are adequate in a rather gloomy decorative style.

'Since there were few guests at this time of year Madame said I could only stay if I ate in. Naturally dubious of such restrictions I reluctantly agreed. I was glad I did; the meal was extremely good. I went à la carte when I saw what was on offer. The dining-room in that French baronial style that looks overdone, but not so the food.' Barry Russell.

Map 5D   **HENNEBONT** 56700 (Morbihan) 10 km NE of Lorient

Château de Locguénolé
(HR)L   *97.76.29.04   Fax 97.76.39.47   Cl. 16/11–1/4; rest. cl. Mon.*

R   Outrageously over-priced accommodation. Our modest back room cost 650f, a bad buy only surpassed by that of our friends, whose attic walls were livid with vinyl flowers of species unknown to nature – a far cry from the classy French wallpapers and elegant bedchamber they had

H   been looking forward to. An absence of hot water at bath time and holes in the stair carpets made us even more convinced that a stay here was not a good idea. (Other rooms up to 1,400f.)

A pity, because the setting is magnificent. The squat bulk of the not-very-ancient château, more impressive than beautiful, commands a striking view through the wooded hills, down the rough-cut lawns to a wide sweep of the river Blavet. Little boats and water-skiers animate the view in many an American lens. The grounds otherwise are a disappointment to English gardeners, all unpruned rosebeds and straggly grass, with the swimming pool's temperature uninvitingly chilly.

So forget the bed and concentrate on the board. Altogether another story. Here is money well-spent indeed. The two cheapest menus at 190f and 280f looked only moderately interesting, and the 490f version is designed for those on a restricted international diet – *foie gras*, lobster, fillet steak and out of season strawberries. So we felt entitled to eat *à la carte*. The four hours from eight to midnight passed ecstatically, the 'oos' following the 'aahs', preceding the 'mms'. Will those who feel ill/disgusted/jealous please turn the page:

Amuses-bouche (gratis) – almond-shaped mounds of salmon mousse, pigmy shrimps of a translucent coral petalled daisy-style round the (porcelain) plate, a baby galantine of cubed ham, flecked with sweet peppers and herbs, set in an aspic gentle of texture, rich in flavour, a wine glass of minted melon balls, peach-coloured, wine. And more to come one might well ask? Ah yes . . . a cold *entrée* of sole fillets, swiss-rolled around a fishy/herby mousse, garnished with crayfish, sharpened with a crunchy tomato *coulis*, or a palette of white and green turbot in a sorrel sauce, artichoke hearts and stuffed baby lettuce parcels. Then a great flourish to remove the silver domes protecting the main course – a whole shoulder of pink baby lamb between the two of us, coated with herby crumbs, stuffed with black olives, whose smokiness permeated right through the tender slices.

The sweet trolley! Our unstinted selection of chocolate *marquise*, wild strawberry tart, *fromage blanc* mousse and nectarines coated with apricot sauce was arranged with such consummate artistry that we felt not greedily guilty but self-congratulatory at our clever selection.

The bill was astronomical and worth every penny.

Map 3C   HUELGOAT 29690 (Finistère) 24 km S of Morlaix

The most popular inland tourist attraction in Brittany, as the lines of coaches and parked cars testify. They come to this area of mammoth mossy rocks, cool beechwoods, rushing streams heard not seen between the piled boulders, not only for the beauty of the place but for its atmosphere. The tourist authorities have taken full advantage of the legends that have proliferated since the days of King Arthur, and there are well-signed routes to follow to the Devil's Grotto, the Trembling Rock, the Rock Chaos, the Virgin's Kitchen, the Chasm, and many more attractions. Maps and ideas from the tourist bureau for short strolls or more ambitious hikes, all fascinating but populous.

The town centres on a lake, which used to be more romantic before someone built a housing development on its banks. The wide main street is charming and very Breton, with its old grey houses and colourful market stalls most days of the year.

I didn't think much of the restaurant and hotel scene – so often disappointing in tourist centres. **Ty Douz** has a good setting overlooking the lake, but the food was banal and the service harassed, and the **Hôtel du Lac** looked very tired indeed. There is a little hotel, **An Triskell**, up the hill on the Plében road, but the orange vinyl wallpaper and the weedy garden put me off.

I suggest a day visit only, with a picnic to eat in the woods.

Map 4B   ILE TUDY 29980 (Finistère) 10 km SE of Pont l'Abbé

A narrow spit of land that juts out into the estuary of the Pont l'Abbé river, with a good view of all Loctudy's fishing boats opposite and of the Anse de Bénodet to the right. The *haute marée* is most impressive from this vantage point, when the spring tides flood the narrow winding alleys of the little village – with a magnificent beach.

This is a real fishing village, not an instant holiday resort, and is correspondingly picturesque. It tolerates the tourists at summer weekends, accepting that some of its residents gain their livelihood through them, but once the parking lot is empty, it settles back happily to the serious business of putting the world to rights in the bar of:

Hôtel Moderne
(HR)S   *9 pl. de la Cale   98.56.43 34   Fax 98.51.90.70.   Cl. Sat. o.o.s.*

A Logis de France in a splendid position overlooking the water. Tables outside from which to observe all the fishermen coming and going. The locals drink in the bar and it's all very friendly and un-trippery.

Rooms with shower and loo cost 200f and menus are from 75f, but I would settle for an omelette at 38f.

There are several other bars and a *crêperie* to choose from but the **Moderne** is the friendliest and liveliest. A reader's letter sums up the atmosphere:

'I walked along the peaceful seashore while my daughter sat outside the Hotel Moderne writing her postcards with a cup of hot chocolate, surrounded by the locals and the friendly owner who said he could remember you. It was Sunday and the bar was crowded and alive with French chatter; families out for Sunday lunch in the restaurant made a real French atmosphere prevail.' Suzanne Nott

---

Map 4E   **JOSSELIN** 56120 (Morbihan) 72 km E of Rennes on the N 24 – *Mkt: Sat.*

A more attractive approach from Ploërmel than the main road is to take the D 122 and D 123, which follow the canal through pleasant wooded countryside. Josselin is a delightful little town, familiar from many a poster showing the turrets of the Rohan family's home, half palace, half fortress, reflected in the river Oust. Josselin de Rohan-Chabot, the 14th Duke de Rohan, has been the town's mayor for over twenty years.

josselin

They say the best viewpoint is from the Redon road but I can assure you that it's only from the pit of a small boat tied up in the castle's shadow that its full immensity can be realised. Those towers rear up for ever.

From the river they make an impressive example of mediaeval military architecture, but the façade over the main courtyard is altogether different, extremely elegant, ornamented with lacy stonework on balustrades and window frames. Look for the letter 'A', crowned and surmounted by the emblem of Queen Anne – a girdle – and accompanied by the royal fleur de lys. The castle is open 2–5 p.m. in summer every day, and on Thursdays, Sundays and fêtes from April to June.

Old slate-roofed houses climb the steep hill to the basilica of Notre Dame de Roncier – Our Lady of the Bramble. Legend has it that eleven hundred or so years ago a peasant found a glowing statue of the Virgin in a bramble bush that never lost its leaves, winter or summer. He carried his prize away but the next day it was back in the bramble bush. Twice more he removed it, twice more it returned, to indicate firmly the place where the Virgin wished a chapel to be built in her name. The present basilica is mostly Flamboyant Gothic; it is renowned locally for the great *pardon* which centres on it on September 8, and whose strange name of the Procession of the Barkers also concerns the Virgin Mary. It seems she once asked, in the guise of a beggarwoman, for a glass of water from some Josselin housewives, who turned her away. As a punishment she condemned them to bark like mad dogs at Whitsun and on September 8. Their barking and frothing only ceased when they were brought into the basilica and made to kiss the holy relics. Since then many epileptics are said to have been cured by similar tactics.

For the less spiritual refreshment, Josselin is well equipped. Following local recommendations, we bypassed the more obvious claim of the **Hôtel Château** and climbed the main street, to find a little Logis:

Hôtel du Commerce
(R)M   *9 r. Glatinier   97.22.22.08   Cl. Mar.; Tues.; Wed.*

Big changes here. The hotel part is now closed and M. Blot is concentrating on his restaurant. The dining-room is delightful and surprisingly elegant, high above the river. In winter it is cheered by a big log fire whose flames are reflected in polished copper pans. Menus now start at 82f but I would go for the 140f which includes a dozen oysters followed by a whole sole or filet of beef, goats cheese salad and dessert carte. A reader reported recently that the dining-room was empty (winter admittedly) which is odd, since it used to be the most popular place in town, so any other experiences would be welcome.

Hotel de France
(HR)M   *6 pl. Norte Dame   97.22.23.06   Fax 97.22.35.78   Cl. Sun. p.m.; Mon. 15/1–31/1*

Up and coming – now my first choice in Josselin, and the locals, whether they are using the lively bar or the dining-room, agree with me. The 20 rooms are comfortable enough, at 230–330f, and the menus excellent value. 75f (not Sundays) buys a salmon terrine, a gigôt of lamb, cheese and home-made desserts, and the 97f Sunday version is equally to be recommended, but you will have to book for that.

Hotel du Château
1 r. Général de Gaulle   97.22.20.11   Cl. Feb.; Sun. p.m.; Mon. o.o.s.   P.   V

The **Château** has the prime position, right opposite the castle, dining-room overlooking the river, but this of course makes it the obvious tourist attraction. If you get a table in the window you do get a good view, but the aspect is north and no sunlight penetrates into the vast and gloomy room. The welcome is just as cold. Rooms from 200f. Readers have enjoyed menus from 80f.

Map 1F   **LA JOUVENTE** 35730 (I. et V.) 7 km S of Dinard

Take the D 114 immediately after crossing the barrage, signposted La Richardais. La Jouvente is a hamlet well marked to the left.

➤ **Manoir de la Rance**
(H)M–L   *99.88.53.76   Fax 99.88.63.03   Cl. 5/1–10/3*

Madame Jasselin was very unhappy. *Les tempêtes* had cruelly decapitated the 300 tulips that had been such a feature of her spring garden. She is very proud of that garden, as well she might be. Ivy-covered chains, spattered with roses, loop between pillars either side of the path to the château door. Lily of the valley are densely packed in one bed, velvet wallflowers glow in another. The gravel paths lead down between laurel hedges to the little jetty and a bizarre outpost of GB – the Jersey Lilly pub.

Mme J., waiting for a hip operation, can no longer tend her precious garden herself, but like the rest of her establishment it is under her strict control. The bay-windowed sitting room, overflows with cushions, lace cloths, artificial flowers, plump furniture, but even the stuffed Babar is sitting up straight in his armchair.

There are many excellent qualities about Le Manoir but prime among them must be the situation. High above the river Rance, its windows look back to the *barrage* and the roofs at St. Mâlo, across to a series of bays and inlets, a little sandy beach, Devon-like wooded hills, and on to the winding river past a rocky island towards Dinan. Masts cluster in every shelter. This is not a shallow, straight river, like the

Manoir de la Rance.

Loire – the Rance curves and flirts with the imagination, hiding inlets and river villages until another viewpoint reveals their charm. Tourist boats invite further discoveries.

Since my last visit a new conservatory has been added on beyond the bar so that during the excellent breakfast you don't have to miss a single marine coming or going. Pale green and pink and pretty, it is a light and cheerful contrast to the older-style furnishing elsewhere.

The two bedrooms that best exploit the astonishing view are the largest, No. 1., with a bay window, and my old favourite of the blue Toile de Jouy, No. 2. Both have modern bathrooms. Prices, alas, have escalated, and these two are the most expensive at 950f. However there is a wide choice of cheaper accommodation – you get what you pay for. Of the smaller rooms (400f) No. 5 or No. 9 are the best.

I am pleased that readers have shared my enthusiasm for this very individual hotel and the arrow stays.

*'It was everything you said, very personal and an extraordinary view
of the Rance with and without mist. A delightful garden and afternoon
tea on the terrace.' Barry Russell.*
*'All that you say. But you should warn people off room 10, the
smallest and largely taken up by its king-sized bed. Too small for
breakfast in room, no view – overlooking kitchen yard, dark. 380f is
way over the top. I shall return but not to room 10.'*

Map 2E **LAMBALLE** 22400 (C. d'A.) 40 km W of Dinan by N 176 – *Mkt:
Thurs*

The Tourist Office now occupies the 16th-century executioner's house
facing on to the Place du Martray (Graveyard Square) in the centre of
this important livestock market town. Horse lovers will no doubt wish
to visit the National Stud, from 12.30 to 4.30 p.m. 'except during the
covering season', which I am informed is from 10/2–15/7, when the
stallions go off on a prolonged orgy all round Brittany.

Not far away from the Stud the Gothic-Romanesque church of Notre-
Dame de Puissance stands on the promontory once occupied by the
castle, with a fine view over the valley of the Gouessant.

The popular old **Hotel Angleterre** is now part of a chain but still
retaining a lot of individuality is:

La Tour d'Argent
(HR)S *2 r. Dr. Lavergne   96.31.01.37   Fax 96.31.37.59   Rest. cl. Sat. o.o.s.*

The hotel part is in a side street off the main square, away from traffic
noise. Bedrooms from 210–360f, some renovated and now very
comfortable indeed. Some 500 yards away down the hill by the
roundabout is the black-and-white restaurant. Once inside the ancient
building, though, the picture changes; through the cheerful bar there's
a smart new dining-room and menus, popular with the locals, from 85f.

Map 2B **LAMPAUL GUIMILIAU** 29230 (Finistère) 4 km S of Landivisiau

---

I had not intended to write at length about the *enclos paroissiaux* and
churches of this region, and indeed could not as far as those of
Lampaul Guimiliau are concerned, since no words of mine could do
them justice. If you wish to see but one example, I can only urge you
not to miss this little village, buy a guide in the ossuary-turned-
bookshop, and prepare for a very special experience inside the church.
Allow plenty of time to take in all its treasures, from the first blast of
colour to the detailed craftsmanship of the font, rood beam,
astoundingly beautiful reredos, Entombment, and Pietà, whose six
faces I guarantee will stick in your mind long after any gastronomic
experience I can lead you to.

De l'Enclos
(HR)S *98.68.77.08 Fax 98.68.61.06 Cl. Fri. p.m.; Sun. p.m.; Sat. lunch o.o.s.*

It must be lovely to wake up in Lampaul-G and visit the church
privately. You could do so after a night at de l'Enclos, Mme Caucino's
modern little Logis, in the centre of things. The 36 rooms cost from
225–260f and menus start at 70f.

'We had an excellent diner here en route to Roscoff. Excellent whole
crab was served as a second course before the main course.' Pamela
Biles.

Map 2B   LANDERNEAU 29800 (Finistère) 44 km SW of Morlaix

The estuary of the Élorn narrows here and is crossed by the
picturesque 16th-century Rohan Bridge, one of the few in Europe on
which there are occupied houses. It takes its name from the ubiquitous
Rohan family who held the town in fief, and joins two bishoprics, Léon
to the north, and Cornouaille to the south. The quays are named after
them.

It's an agreeable town, with a lively Saturday market and many old
houses, especially around the church dedicated to St. Thomas of
Canterbury, a reminder of the trading links with England. Take a stroll
along the quayside and perhaps some refreshment at the bar built out
over the water, all most civilised on a fine sunny day.

Le Clos du Pontic
(HR)M *r. Pontic 98.21.50.91 Fax 98.21.34.33 Rest. cl. Sat. lunch; Sun. p.m.;*
Mon.

An odd turreted house set peacefully in a shady garden some ten
minutes walk (uphill!) from the town centre. Unexpectedly at the rear is
an uncompromisingly modern wing with 32 bedrooms each with all
mod. cons. and bath, at 260–340f. Pleasant restaurant and interesting
meals from 160f (lunch 100f).

Map 3B   LANDÉVENNEC (Finistère) 33 km NW of Chateaulin

To the north of the Crozon Peninsula take the D 60 off the D 791. Well
worth making this diversion to the little hooked peninsula to appreciate
the contrast of its soft greenness and freak Mediterranean climate,
which allows even palm trees to flourish, with the harsh greyness of
the rest of the area. But that's not the only reason; Landévennec is an
instantly charming village, starting on a hill above the bend of the wide
and gentle river Aulne, and flowing down past the old lichened church
to the little landing stage, with pleasant vistas of estuary and trees all
the way. Good walking country, with suggested routes well
signposted. Thee's an old ruined abbey there, with the tomb of the

once bawdy King Gradlon, converted to Christianity and a life of sobriety here by St. Guenolé, son of a 5th-century British nobleman. It was Guenolé who founded the monastery that was to become Landévennec.

A reader's recommendation:

Langast
Auberge St Gal   96.28.77.50   Cl. Mon. o.o.s.

'Langast is a hamlet between Moncontour and Loudeac on the D76 near Plouguenast. Here we found a wonderful little auberge in the middle of nowhere, where we had a superbly presented and cooked lunch prepared by the young chef patron. It was well patronised by locals and every table was full. The whole family was serving.'

Map 1C   **LANNION** 22300 (C. d'A.) 63 km NW of St.-Brieuc – *Mkt: Thurs.*

A most agreeable town on the river Léguer, with a wonderful Thursday market, that spills over from the river banks and extends up the steeply climbing old streets. Worth arranging your holiday schedule around this weekly burst of colour. At any time it is a pleasure to explore the pedestrianised area, lined with old houses, that leads up to the pl. Général Leclerc. Not particularly worth the effort, except for the masochist is to climb the 142 steps (I counted 'em all out and I counted 'em all back) to the church of Brélévenez, a Templars' church, remodelled in the Gothic period, where the promised view doesn't include, as I had hoped, a panorama of river and estuary, but only the more recent roofing of this ancient town.

Park by the river and discover **Jean-Yves Bordier**, the cheese shop *par excellence*. Allow at least fifteen minutes to wait while the young and knowledgeable owner shakes each customer's hands and discusses his needs. Tell him when you want to eat your favourite cheese and he will select it for you accordingly. Light worlds away from picking up a hunk of Irish Cheddar in the local Co-op.

Just opposite is:

Le Serpolet
(R)M   *1 r. Félix le Dantec   96.46.50.23   Cl. Mon.; Sat. lunch*

A charming old stone restaurant in a quiet street just by the parking on the Quai de Viarmes. Small, dark, cosy, with charcoal fire – just the thing for a gloomy day.

Much appreciated by the local clientèle. The 75f menu is lunchtime only – chicken terrine with fresh herbs, steak with mustard cream sauce, and a wonderful French item – tarte chaude aux pommes grany. Evening menus include a good cheese course and cost 110 or 170f.

> **La Ville Blanche**
> (R)M   *96.37.04.28   Cl. Sun. p.m.; Mon. o.o.s.; 10/1–11/2 (4 kms E of Lannion on the D 786)*

Local appreciation is well in evidence. It took all the forceful persuasion of the aristocratic château chatelaine with whom we were spending a blissful night (see chambre d'h. book!) to squeeze in an extra table for us and that was mid-week o.o.s., so don't court disappointment by failing to book.

It's a smart little restaurant on the main road to Lannion with particularly agreeable owners. The two sons, Jean-Yves and Daniel Jaguin, are joint chefs and their mother, nice Mme Jaquin, is front of house. Decor is fairly nondescript but fresh and bright, with good china and fresh apricot roses on the tables. Nothing so far to get excited about. But the 180f menu (could have been 95f) offered an *embarras de richesses*. I could have happily eaten my way through every item. Lacking that capacity, it had to be a warm salad of scallops, then sole with asparagus, then hot Brie with rhubarb(!) The unusually interesting dessert menu presented the same dilemma of choice. Reluctantly eliminating a strawberry sable with strawberry sorbet, I took Madame's advice to sample the tarte au fromage, especially as it came with a *sorbe* of *melisses*, which for all Madame's explanation of '*citronelle*' I had never hitherto experienced. (Think lemon balm.) Every mouthful was memorable. As for the melted Brie with rhubarb and pine kernels – O.K. I won't try and convince you, just try it and tell me if it isn't the most natural combination in all the culinary world.

Husband went for the day's specialities – terrine of hare with garden herbs and oxtail stew with red wine. How I wish I knew the secret of producing an oxtail like this, dark, dark, dark, meltingly tender, rich wine sauce, no residue of fat. Wonderful country cooking with creamy potatoes and other root vegetables all beautifully arranged in little turrets.

Best Breton meal of the year. Arrowed accordingly.

Hotels are dismal. Better make for Le Yaudet (see p. 192).

Map 6D   **LARMOR BADEN** 56790 (Morbihan) 16 km SW of Vannes

---

A little fishing village on a promontory, facing south, with splendid views towards the entrance of the Gulf of Morbihan. From here you can take the boat to the **Gavrinis** tumulus, said by Michelin to be 'The most interesting megalithic monument in Brittany and perhaps in the world.'

Auberge Parc Fétan
(HR)S   *17 r. de Berder   97.57.04.38   Fax 97.57.21.55*

An uncompromisingly modern Logis on the road out of Larmor-B and so without the spectacular position of Les Isles, but with a good deal else going for it. Mme Berster keeps her 31 rooms spotless and they cost a modest 160–370f. Menus are from 100f and there is private parking.

Map 5C   **LARMOR-PLAGE** 56100 Lorient (Morbihan) 6 km S of Lorient

The seaside escape for the Lorientais and fast becoming their dormitory suburb. However the village still has a pleasantly unsophisticated air about it, with a large market place centring on a Gothic church, with some remarkable 16th-century polychrome Apostle statues in its side porch. A charming ancient custom is still respected: whenever a warship leaves Lorient on a long tour of duty, it salutes Our Lady of Larmor by guns, and Our Lady replies by hoisting a tricolour and saluting the ship with bells.

A pleasant beach curves round the bay facing across to the citadel at Port Louis.

The above was written seven years ago, when I awarded an arrow to the delightfully old-fashioned Beau Rivage hotel, overlooking the water. The intervening years have not dealt kindly with the former charmingly sleepy fishing town. True there is now a pleasant promenade connecting the old town to the beach of St. Malia, true there is now a row of south-facing bars and restaurants that serve a very pleasant and useful purpose for those who like sun worshipping with food and drink readily to hand, (on the first fine spring day, not yet Easter, their tables were full; I favour the Big Ben pub,) but what, oh what, have they done with my long-cherished Toulhars bay? I looked for the friendly Hotel Beau Rivage, where I used to bag a room at the front and lie in bed watching the sails passing the fort opposite and where in the goldfish bowl of a dining-room little old ladies in black dresses and white pinnies used to dish up pristinely fresh fish. I found the steps leading up, here was the road, but surely they wouldn't have dared pull down what was patently the heart and stomach of the town and substitute that bland apartment building, would they? They would and they have. And now I take off my rose-coloured specs and look more closely at my favourite walk around the bay, I see that the infilling between the small French seaside villa architecture is cruel.

To be more positive . . . if you never knew l'Armor-Plage before, you will never miss the gone-forevers. The beaches are still sunny, the view fascinating and they haven't pulled the church down. Yet.

The nearest hotel I can suggest is at Anse de Kerguélen, 1 km W:

Les Mouettes
(HR)M   *97.65.50.30   Fax 97.33.65.33*

A lovely position, 21 rooms from 350–430f, menus from 85f. More reports needed.

Map D1   **LEZARDRIEUX** (C. d'A.) 5 km W of Paimpol

Here is the bridge that crosses the wide estuary of the river Trieux.
How pleased we used to be to tie up the boat at the end of a long sail,
at the safe anchorage in the river, knowing that we had only to puff up
the hill into the wide market square to find a good meal. Alas, today's
seafarers will not be so lucky. I failed to find anything recommendable
up there, but at least there is a good crêperie now:

La Moulin de la Galette
(R)S   *96.20.18.36   Cl. Mon.*

Opposite the Port de Plaisance. Very pretty inside, with lots of yellow
chintz. The owners, M. and Mme Julien, own another restaurant, La
Ferme de Kerroc'h at Ploubazlanec, so if you like one, you might like to
head for t'other. Here you will find simple meals – omelettes, crêpes,
and salads mainly – attractively served.

Hotel du Pont
(HR)S   *r. St. Christophe   96.20.10.59   Fax 96.22.17.38*

Fine for the odd night stop, just 100 metres from the estuary. 15 rooms,
well-maintained, from 150–275f.

Map D6   **LOCMARIAQUER** (Morbihan) 25 km SW of Vannes

Anyone with a car in the Gulf of Morbihan is going to find it irresistible
to explore the arms, inlets, bays and headlands which beckon so
appealingly from the map of this unique region, where water is never
far away. Locmariaquer lies on the western peninsula which stretches
out towards Port Navalo, almost succeeding in enclosing the bay
altogether. It has a delightful harbour, around whose narrow streets it
is most agreeable to stroll, before settling down to a meal at one of the
many restaurants, many of them specialising in oysters. But its
principle claim to fame is that it is one of the world's foremost centres
of megalith monuments. Most of the more interesting stones are on
the east side of the peninsula and are well signed. By the cemetery
stands the Great Menhir, which was the tallest known menhir (65ft)
before it smashed into four parts, probably felled by an earthquake.
After this the Roman remains and pleasing Romanesque church seem
parvenus.

Hotel Lautram
(HR)S   *Cl. Oct.–Apr.*

A simple little hotel with rooms from 180–330f and good fishy menus
from 70f.

Service somewhat lacking in enthusiasm, but the short opening dates indicate that might be because it caters principally for tourists not critical locals.

'My room, no. 12 was at the front. A good room, even though those facing front can be woken by light traffic in the morning. Little effect in late evening. Menus are fish and shellfish-orientated and are very good, with reasonably priced wines. Our overall impression is good and the place has moved up in the rankings since our first stay here in 1982. Our bill – 552f was the cheapest of our holiday.' Richard and Charlotte Bass.

Map 3B   **LOCRONAN** 29186 (Finistère) 22 km NW of Quimper on the D 63 – *Mkt: 1st Tues.*

A living museum of a town, almost too picturesque to be true. The large paved square, featuring an old well, is surrounded by a stage setting of grey Renaissance houses, built at a time when the canvas industry brought prosperity to the town. Nowadays the textile tradition has been revived in the shape of weaving and knitting; nearly all the old buildings house craft centres.

The town took its name from a 9th-century Irish monk, Ronan, after whom is named the imposing church on the square. Take in the best view of it from the cemetery, with a calvary in which St.-Ronan and the Virgin flank the crucified Christ, before going inside to see the stone-vaulted roof, rare in Brittany, added in the 16th century to the 1420 origins. The ten medallions round the pulpit relate the story of St.-Ronan's adventures. The saint's tomb is in the adjoining chapel, Le Pénity, which, sadly, is increasingly being eroded by the underground springs.

The Grand Troménie, an eight-mile procession through the countryside, following St.-Ronan's supposed route, takes place on the third Sunday in July every six years, to the solemn sound of drums, stopping at 44 resting places where arched branches shelter statues from the local parishes. The faithful process up the mountain to a block of granite known as St.-Ronan's chair, which the locals have no doubt is the boat in which the saint sailed from Ireland to Armorica. In other years, on the same day, is the Minor Troménie, a mere three miles long.

Locronan has more than its share of tourists to feed and water and caters for them with several bars, a *crêperie* and two restaurants. Right in the square is:

Au Fer à Cheval
(R)M   *98.91.70.74   Cl. 11/11–15/12*

Well-known and popular restaurant; if you bag a window seat on the first-floor dining-room you get an elevated view of that stunning square. Don't be put off by the noisy bar down below. Menus from 65f.

The management runs a hotel by the same name, a kilometre or so outside the village signposted off the D 63, but the best I can say for it is that it is certainly functional and (excruciatingly) modern. 35 plastic rooms cost from 200–300f.

Much more to my taste is:

Le Prieuré
(HR)S   *98.91.70.89   Fax 98.91.77.60   Cl. Nov.–mid Mar.*

A pretty old granite Logis at the entrance to the village, with a nice dining-room and attractive country-style bedrooms. Some in an annexe. Good value at 270–300f for a double with bath. Menus at 65–250f. Readers have thoroughly approved.

Manoir de Moëllien
(HR)M   *29550 Plonévez-Porzay   98.92.50.40.   Fax 98.92.55.21   Rest. cl. Wed. o.o.s.; Jan.–Mar.*

3 km N on the C 10, well signposted. The grey 17th-century manor house was the home of Chateaubriand's lover, Thérèse de Moëllien. Very impressive is the approach down a tree-lined drive to caved stone gateway guarded by two lions, as is the manor itself, and particularly appealing in the summer when banks of hydrangeas soften the harshness.

Good value for money in what could easily be a tourist trap, since the manoir features in many guidebooks and is a Château Hotel and a Relais du Silence. The dining-room is lovely – beamed, log fire, elegant *couverts*. Menus from 130f (not Sun.)

The bedrooms are very quiet and comfortable, in an annexe contrived from the old stables. French windows are the only ventilation, which might prove a hazard in summer for stiff-upper-lip Englishmen like us who like to sleep with some air around. As it was blowing a south-westerly straight from America when we were there, that particular problem didn't arise, but I felt extremely sorry for the poor girl who had to brave the weather to carry out our breakfast trays, under an umbrella. Good breakfast, good bathroom, good value at 340f a double.

Map 4B   **LOCTUDY** (Finistère) 6 km SE of Pont-l'Abbé – *Mkt: Tues.*

A fishing port, most interesting because it has the best-preserved Romanesque church in Brittany, whose first prior was St.-Tudy who landed on the coast of Armorica in the 5th century from Britain. There are those who will make the journey specially to look at the barrel-vaulted chancel and there are those who will seek out the rather rude carvings on the base of the capitals!

Another reason for visiting Loctudy is the splendid view from the port towards Ile Tudy (see p. 87), no distance at all away across the

Manoir de Moëllien

water but a fair drive round the soft and gentle river Odet, lined to waters' edge with pine trees.

 There is a good bar and grill by the port, **Le Rafiot**, and a recommended *créperie* in the village.

Map D1   **LOGUIVY DE LA MER** 22620 Ploubazlanex. (C. d.'A.) 5 km N of Paimpol by D15

 A little fishing village, right on the point of the estuary of the river Trieux, with predictably splendid outlook over water and islands.

Au Grande Large
(R)M   *96.20.90.18   Cl. Sun.; 1 Wed.; Mon. p.m. o.o.s.; 10/1–10/2*

 An incongruously modern building right in the port, whose large plate glass windows and terrace make the most of the view. Fishing of course, especially notable for its plâteaux de f. de m. Surprising to find bedrooms attached, but there are six of them, well-equipped and comfortable, with that fabulous view. 300–320f.

Unless you care to drive 7 kms to Locmaria Berrien:

Auberge de la Truite
(HR)M   *98.19.73.05   Cl. Sun. p.m.; and Mon. o.o.s.; 2/1 Mar.*

In what used to be the old station of Huelgoat-Locmaria, facing the valley, is this pretty rustic dining-room in which is served country food – trout, quails, and gâteau breton, with a surprisingly grand wine list. The hotel has six rooms from 105–180f, as yet uninspected.

Map 5C   **LOMENER** 56270 Ploemeur (Morbihan) 5.5. km SW of Lorient; 3 km S of Ploemeur

---

Continue on the D 163 over the D 152 to hit the coast at this village in an area of rocky coves and small sandy beaches. It is predictably popular with Lorientais looking for a gulp of sea air. The views across to the Ile de Groix add to the appeal.

Le Vivier
(HR)S   *97.82.99.60   Fax 97.82.88.89   Cl. Sun. p.m. o.o.s.; 2/1–21/1*

A modern hotel built into the very sea-wall to make the most of the views. Bag a table by the window to capitalise on them. The rooms, at 285–3800f are basic – you look out of the window rather than at the decor – and there are none with baths (showers though). The cooking is good solid Breton fishy stuff, on menus from 98f (not Suns.).

Map 2D   **LOUARGAT** 22540 (C. d'A.) 13 km W of Guincamp

Now by-passed off the N 12. The Manoir is 4 km NW by the D 33a.

Manoir du Cleuziou
(HR)M   *96.43.14.90   Fax 96.43.52.59   Cl. Feb.*

M. Bizen's ensemble is very popular with the English, who are attracted to the lovely 16C building used as the restaurant and the de luxe 'camping' of the hotel section, in various outbuildings. Swimming pool and tennis make this a good family centre, and there is a general atmosphere of good humour and intent to enjoy the holiday. 28 rooms cost from 325–430f.

Various readers have approved of the food, fairly sophisticated menus start at 98f.

Map 3E   LOUDÉAC 22600 (C. d'A.) 85 km W of Rennes – *Mkt: Sat.*

Included only as a useful stopping place on the axis of several roads, including St.-Brieuc-Vannes, and Rennes-Morlaix.

Les Voyageurs
(HR)S   *r. Cadelac   96.28.00.47   Fax 96.28.22.30   Cl. Sat.; 23/12–6/1*

All the rooms in this little hotel have been renovated in 1994 and are now peaceful and comfortable, at 165–300f. But it is the food that is special. There is an excellent 90f menu, but I was lured on to the 145f version which supplied wonderful home-made duck pâte de foie gras scallops *à la provençale*, cheese and dessert. It is seafood and grills that are the backbone of the cuisine and all very good too. Reports for an arrow.

Map 1F   MATIGNON 22550 (C. d'A.) 6 km SW of St.-Cast

La Musardière
(R)S   *96.41.12.43   Cl. Mon. p.m.; Tues. o.o.s.*

Go more for the setting than the food, which is acceptable but in no way outstanding. Wood-fired grills are the speciality.
    Very rural. An old stone and slate farmhouse down a country lane, with only the scuttering of bantams and the swishing of cows' tails to disturb the deep calm. Pleasantly rustic inside – beams and log fire – and a few tables with umbrellas outside, from which to keep an eye on the kids working hard at their '*amusements*' – swings etc.

Map 3F   MAURON 56430 (Morbihan) 49 km W of Rennes

Nothing special about this little town, with Friday market, and I note it only because it lies at the hub of six roads, between Dinan and Vannes, on the D 766, and it might be appropriate for a traveller's rest.

Brambily
(HR)S   *pl. Mairie   97.22.61.67   Cl. 15/9–15/10; Sun. p.m.; Mon.*

Central, noisy, but cheap, with a good (45f menu a '*repas de famille*'). There are 29 rooms from 160–190f, all with bath or shower.

Map 5F   **MISSILAC** 44780 (Loire-Atl.) Half-way between Nantes and
Vannes, 1 km off the N 165

Make the détour anyway, even if you have no intention of staying, just
for the experience of seeing:

Hôtel du Golf de la Bretesche
(HR)M   *40.88.30.05   Fax 40.66.99.47   Cl. 4/1–3/3*

A stunning castle reflected, fairytale-wise, in the water of the immense
lake on whose very edge it stands. The 14th-century original was
successively burned and pillaged over the centuries, but the 19th-
century restoration has been a clever one, and now the Renaissance
towers, sharply pinnacled, set in mellow grey stone, cannot fail to
impress.

The setting is truly magnificent; 500 acres of surrounding parkland
include an 18-hole championship golf course, and package holiday
golfers ensure that even out of season this hotel is never dead. Old
stables round a flowery courtyard have been harmoniously converted
into self-catering accommodation (details from hotel) and the 25
bedrooms in the hotel proper are all light and cheerful; an overnight
stop here (370–630f a double) would be a comfortable one.

If you can stand the golfing chat, make full use of the spacious
lounges and terraces, enjoy the calm of the outstandingly beautiful
surrounds, then plan to eat out – the menus looked expensive and
boring.

MORBIHAN (the Gulf)

Morbihan means 'little sea' in Breton, and the gulf is just that – an
inland sea almost landlocked by the two arms of Quiberon and the
Presqu'île du Rhuys. With 58 km of water and 200 km of coastline,
there is a very special, enclosed, world-apart feeling to this most magic
seascape.

They say there are as many islands in the gulf as days of the year,
some inhabited, some mere reefs, but the two biggest are **Ile d'Arz** and
Ile aux Moines; both are connected to the mainland by ferries, a cheap
way of getting a view of the gulf.

The Ile d'Arz has the best restaurant, **l'Escale**, open from April to
October, at the landing stage. Lunch there on a fine day is a very good
idea. The food is excellent and not as expensive as one would expect
in a short-season, tourist-orientated spot. You can stay at **l'Escale** too I
believe.

The Ile aux Moines is the most beautiful island of them all. Three
miles long, with Mediterranean vegetation, mimosas, eucalyptus, palm
trees, and even a few fig trees. There are beaches and cliffs, woods
with romantic names like Forêt d'Amour, heaths and pines, and a steep
path up to the old village from whose terrace you can identify
bearings. Several nothing-special restaurants, bars, *crêperies* to deal
with hunger/thirst pangs.

Hôtel Du Golf de la Bretesche

The best way to enjoy the panorama, of course, is by boat and the possibilities and permutations of excursions are many. Vannes is the main departure point for the *Vedettes Vertes* – vast plate-glass palaces of pleasure steamers with excellent vision from within but not much aesthetic appeal from the shore. You can pick one up from Locmariaquer, Port-Navolo or Auray, combine a bus-trip one way, have dinner and board, or lunch, and so on. The schedule is drastically depleted after the high season and it is best to make enquiries at the depot on the Promenade de la Rabine (Vannes 66.10.78) at the port in Auray, on the jetty in Port Navalo or at the *tabac* in Locmariaquer.

The round trip to and from Vannes takes several hours and is quite expensive. Our recipe for a perfect day was to drive to Port Blanc to catch the ferry across to the Ile aux Moines, picnic there under the pines before a swim from the sandy beach, and then to pick up the round-the-islands boat for the last 1½ hours of its tour. This called in at Port Navalo and Locmariaquer and returned us, gratifyingly tanned, to the island. A highly recommended tourist treat.

Forty of the islands are inhabited, many are pleasantly wooded, some have beaches and landing stages for dinghies to land picnickers. There are few prettier sights than the bay on a sunny day, water glittering, little boats bobbing, yachts burgeoning, windsurfers queening. Take any turning south off the N 101, which loops along the bay between Auray and Vannes, and it will end in a little harbour with a few houses, often a simple hotel, and a different aspect of island and water.

The two main towns take their names from the rivers on whose estuaries they stand – the Auray and the Vannes. Both are charmers (see p. 31 and p. 185). In fact the whole area is one delight after another, especially given a particularly good climate – the flora is similar to that in the South of France.

A reader's recommendation:

Montfort-sur-Meu
Le Relais de la Cane r. Gare

'It is a pity that this delightful establishment is in such an unattractive town, to the west of Rennes, which we were bypassing. It is near the Forest of Broceliande. We had the menu du jour which included a carafe of red wine for 45f! It turned out to be fantastic value with superb food. The whole place is most attractively decorated and furnished. There are 13 rooms and we shall probably stay there next time'.

Map 3A   **MORGAT** 29160 Crozon (Finistère) 37 km W of Chateaulin

---

The trident of the Crozon Peninsula jutting out into the Atlantic, next stop America, bounded by the Rade de Brest to the north and the Baie de Douarnenez to the south, encompasses a whole secret world of spectacular seascapes, coves, creeks, rocks, cliffs and pounding waves.

Impressive, sometimes awesome, this is no gentle green country but rather an expression of nature at its most untamed.

Best taken at a leisurely pace, with time to explore whatever lane looks promising, invariably ending by the water's edge. Particularly stunning sea views are to the south-west between the Pointe de Dinan and the Cap de la Chèvre; between these points lie a succession of little rocky coves, headlands, indented with caves and beaches.

Don't miss the 68m (227ft) high Pointe de Pen-Hir, a bird sanctuary with fantastic views of a panorama of headlands and islands, or the Pointe des Espagnols to the north, whose telescope, pointing eastward, will reveal a totally different aspect – the whole of the Plougastel peninsula from the harbour of Brest, with the bridge across the estuary of the Élorn.

This is no area to explore unaided though – its treasures are revealed reluctantly; buy a local guide if you intend to penetrate the Fairy Grotto – *les Grottes des Korrigans* – whose colours are as remarkable as their lofty roofs, and don't even try to explore the secrets of the Ile Longue – the finger pointing towards Brest – it's a nuclear submarine base!

Better look elsewhere for undemanding family holiday resorts – this is not carricot country. Even harbours are few – **Camaret**, a little lobster and crayfish port, and **le Fret**, a popular day excursion away from Brest. The only resort is **Morgat**, to the south, curving round a bay sheltered from the prevailing westerlies. You can take a boat trip from here to the caves, Les Grandes Grottes, lie on the sandy beach or watch the fishing boats unload their catch, and that's about it.

I found the hotel and restaurant scene disappointing, with never a sign of the little fishy bistro I had hoped to discover near the port. Plenty of bars and *crêperies*. The main hotels, overlooking the water, are unremarkable, but tucked away behind the town, alas with no seaview but still no distance from the beach, I found one nice little hotel:

Hotel Julia
(HR)M   *43 r. du Trèfle   98.27.05.89   Cl. 15/11–30/12; rest. cl. Fri.   V*

Good value bedrooms, all full of regulars at Easter-time when I called, are from 160–330f for a well furnished double with bath. The dining-room is super – surprisingly elegant. Menus from 80–270f offer safe but dull choices, with lurid desserts, but you can always stick to the seafood, which is irreproachable, and the grilled lobster is a treat.

Map 2C   **MORLAIX** 29600 (Finistère) 85 km W of St.-Brieuc – *Mkt: Sat*

Set in a steep-sided valley, where the rivers Jarlot and Queffleut join, and dominated by a giant viaduct, built in 1864 for the Paris–Brest railway – the object of an unsuccessful British air raid in 1943.

The English had also unsuccessfully attacked Morlaix in 1552 when the massacre of the would-be invaders led to the strange town motto: 'If they bite you, bite back'! (*S'ils te mordent, mords-les*).

Best approached from the north, via the D 76 which follows the river past the many yachts tied up at the entrance to the town. Some of the river has been covered in and many of the old houses demolished but traces of antiquity remain in steep cobbled streets, now pedestrianised, like the Grand' rue. Duchesse Anne's house, a tall 16th-century mansion, is one of the town's showpieces. It was built in 1505 when Queen Anne made a pilgrimage to all the saints of her duchy, to give thanks for the recovery of the King from a serious illness. The façade is decorated with statues of the saints.

Hotel del'Europe
(HR)M   *1 r. Aiguillon   98.62.11.99   Fax 98.88.38*

Don't be put off, as I was originally, by the elephantine size of this central hotel. The main reason for staying here is not the rooms (spacious, re-fitted recently, 220–35f); these are just for falling into after a magnificent meal at either the brasserie Le Foc, or in the restaurant. Chef Olivier Brignou goes from strength to strength, concentrating on prime ingredients rather than fussy sauces. Menus from 140f.

La Marée Bleue
(R)M   *3 rampe Ste.-Mélanie   98.63.24.21   Cl. Sun. p.m. o.o.s.; Mon. 17/10–27/10*

An old stone house, up an alleyway that leads to the Flamboyant Gothic church of Ste.-Mélanie.

Pretty and smart inside, with a nice atmosphere generated by friendly patrons M. and Mme Coquart. They make a speciality of traditional cooking, so this is the place to make for if you're sick of *noove*, but the locals say the standard varies. Can be expensive if you don't stick to the very good menus from 70f, with a superior wine list.

Map 3D   **MUR-DE-BRETAGNE** 22530 (C. d'A.) on the N164, 45 km S of St.-Brieuc, 100 km W of Rennes

Mur is one of inland Brittany's busiest tourist centres, thanks mainly to the proximity, to the west, of the artificial Guerlédan Lake, and the forest of Quénécan, both offering peaceful countryside diversions. The barrage is a fearsome ugly grey sprawl and I wouldn't bother to take the signposted D 18 to it, but you can do a tour right round the lake, catching glimpses from different viewpoints of the water far below in the Blavet Gorges.

Auberge Grand' Maison
(R)M   *1 r. Léon le Cerf   96.28.51.10   Fax 96.28.52.30   Cl. 15/2–3/3 & Oct.*

H
R

A large house in the centre of the village, where the cooking of patron Jacques Guillo is much acclaimed (Michelin star). He seems to have modified the excesses of nouvelle cuisine that I grumbled about previously and now one can appreciate the finesse and pungency of his marvellous sauces without going away hungry. If you are feeling fishy, extravagant (though there is good value on offer here in his menus) and in the mood for a pampered meal with a warm welcome from Madame Guillo, this is the place to make for. Menus start at 170f for lunch or 220f.

There are twelve rooms from 260–600f, which are on the small side but well furnished with antiques. An accessory really for the restaurant.

Map 6G   **NANTES** 44000 (Loire-Altantique.)

Reluctantly I have to give way and concede that, whatever the Bretons and I say about this being a Breton city, it is now firmly affiliated to the region of the Western Loire. It's one of my favourite French destinations, no matter what region is designated by bureaucracy to include it, and I shall look forward to re-investigating it thoroughly for the next Loire edition, but not for Brittany Encore, alas.

Map 1F   **NOTRE DAME DE GUILDO** 22380 (C. d'A.) 10 kms SE of St. Cast on the main road just where it crosses the river.

Le Gilles de Bretagne
(HR)S   *96.41.07.08   Cl. Tues.*

So obvious, with a large terrace overlooking the water, that I thought it could not be any good, until it was recommended locally. Then we found it represented good old-fashioned value and was full not of nasty trippers but of French. The 88f menu is to be particularly recommended. Rooms at 180f uninspected.

Map 3G   **NOYAL-SUR-VILAINE** (I. et V.) 12 km E of Rennes, N off the N 157 – *Mkt: Tues.*

Les Forges
(HR)M   *99.00.51.08   Cl. Sun. p.m.; fête p.m's.; 13/2–26/2*

A little modern building, with fairly ordinary rooms at 235–335f, but a pleasant dining-room with excellent cooking on the 125f menus by chef patron M. André Pilard, particularly strong on fish, cooked often in seaweed – *à la vapeur d'algues*. Useful perhaps as a peaceful, hassle-free base from which to explore Rennes.

Map 3G **PACÉ** 35740 (I. et V.) 7 km NW of Rennes

Turn off the N 12 very conveniently before getting embroiled in the Rennes agglomeration, to find a haven of non-motorway calm, where the Pont de Pacy crosses the river Flume. No less than four restaurants and a hotel to choose from:

➤ **La Griotte**
(R)M   *43 r. du Dr Léon   99.60.62.48   Cl. Tue.; Wed. p.m.; 26/2–6/3 Aug.*

> Q. What is the most reliable guide to a good restaurant? – *Michelin? Gault-Millau? French Entrée?*
> A. None of them. Look for a car park overflowing with French cars.

A not-to-be ignored crowd of parked cars outside **La Griotte** diverted my lunch intention from the recommended **Hôtel du Pont**, and I could not have wished for a better guide.

Inside the din was prodigious, both in the large bar area, cherry-red as the restaurant's namesake, and in the light garden extension. Regulars arrived, were greated warmly by Mme Morand and with much chat on the way escorted to their tables; the telephone rang with insistent bookings, the rattle of a busy lunchtime's cutlery and plattery necessitated an even higher decibel count for animated conversation throughout, and it was all very bright, cheerful, efficient and exactly what was needed to enliven a grey November day.

Not hard to see why **La Griotte** is so popular – the 97f menu was a comfortable three courses of excellent value choices – *soupe d'etrilles* or *pâté de foie maison* or perhaps six oysters, then *brochettes* of pork, rumpsteak, etc; but there was even more interest on the next one up at 120f lunch only, like *pâté de brochet aux crevettes*, *fricassé de gesiers d'oie*, with walnuts, *brochettes de poissons*. With four veg, an excellent cheese board and super desserts, including a good range of interesting home-made sorbets, I find this one hard to beat in the area for value and atmosphere. Arrowed too for its strategic position.

Map 1D **PAIMPOL** 22500 (C. d'A.) 45 km NW of St.-Brieuc

The harbour is not as appealing as are many along this stretch, but the little town behind, with pedestrianised shopping area, is attractive enough, with a few bars in the main square that catch the evening sun better than those on the quay.

Repaire de Kerroc'h
(HR)L   *quai Moraud   96.20.50.13   Cl. Jan.   AE, DC, V*

An old stone 'malouiniere', overlooking the harbour, with most agreeable new dining terrace. Unfortunately the restaurant seems to have more downs than ups and on my last visit it was definitely the former, a view reinforced by the locals and an empty room. Menus start at 135f. The hotel side has extended too, annexing the house next door. There are now twelve rooms, very comfortable, at 200—480f.

There always seems to be a certain something lacking in this potential gem. Perhaps it is because the welcome is less than warm?

La Cotriade
(R)S   *16 quai Armand Dargot   96.20.81.08   Open all year*

The antidote perhaps for the chi-chis. Simple fish restaurant on opposite side of the quay, serving straightforward fish and grills, in a pleasant jovial atmosphere, on menus from 75–120f.

Vieille Tour
(R)M   *13 r. Église   96.20.83.18   Cl. Mon. lunch in July & Aug. Sun p.m.; Wed. o.o.s.*

Climb up the steep cobbled main street towards the church to find this most attractive old stone restaurant, predominantly fishy but with some interesting alternatives. Stray from the menus (110f–300f) and the *à la carte* could be expensive, but altogether good value in pleasant surroundings.

Hotel de la Marne
(HR)S   *30 r. de la Marne   96.20.82.16   Cl. 31/10–1/1; Sun. and Mon. o.o.s.*

A little Logis de France, attractive enough but possibly with noise problems for the rooms on the front. Rooms from 290–310f. The cooking is the big attraction here. Excellent menus from 99f.

l'Escale
(R)S   *quai Morand   96.20.81.88*

A newish very upmarket crêperie/bar, much smarter than most, with much better food. Particularly good in bad weather when the green leather banquets and cosy decor seem especially welcoming. Very pleasant obliging owners. On the first floor, overlooking the harbour, there is a salon for fruits de mer sampling. I was cross that we had already eaten before we discovered this welcome newcomer. Reports please for a possible arrow.

Map 3F   **THE FOREST OF PAIMPONT** 35380 (I. et V.) 40 km SW of Rennes on the N 24 and D 38

Centre of Arthurian legends and still, I wouldn't be at all surprised, capable of practising all manner of magic on those who seek to discover its secrets. Many give up trying to make map references tie up with road signs, and although locals readily hand over brochures describing the charms of Brocéliande, they never seem at all upset to see you back again after a frustrating hour's abortive circuit. Are these the natural heirs to Merlin's wizardry, conniving to keep their prisoners inside the ancient forest's bounds?

I never did find Merlin's tomb, criss-cross though I might through the shaded tracks of the eastern side of the forest where it purports to lie. The largest of the fourteen lakes is here, the Pas du Houx, 212 acres of silent water, presided over by Brocéliande Manor. A good place to park the car, abandon a set plan of campaign, get out the picnic basket and let the faery kingdom weave its spell.

To the west, near the village of **Tréhorenteuc**, the forest paths lead to the Val Sans Rétour, which features in many a legend. Here, Morgane La Fée, King Arthur's sister, in a fine piece of mediaeval women's lib (her morals were distinctly flexible), lured all the lovers who had been unfaithful to her into the enchanted valley from which there was no escape. Go inside the church to see an odd juxtaposition of symbols pagan (a voluptuous Morgane) and Christian (the 9th station of the Cross) or King Arthur's knights experiencing a vision of the Holy Grail, in a strange set of paintings (1946-ish).

Take the D 141 a few km north of here to stop at the hamlet of Folle-Pensée, and walk down to the Barenton Fountain, a rather insignificant trickle whose medicinal properties nevertheless are said to have rid Merlin of some of his more disturbing fantasies. They say if you pour water from the fountain on to Merlin Steps you can conjure up a storm, but someone had been there before me – it was already blowing, raining, howling.

The Arthurian ladies were a wily bunch. Poor Merlin himself fell victim to the lovely fairy Viviane, when she practised one of his own spells on him – how to charm men. By this very fountain he fell asleep one day and Viviane recited the words he had taught her, imprisoning him forever in an enchanted castle. A shame really. Half devil, half Christian, he sounds a far more interesting character than any of those goody goody knights.

Comper Castle lies 3 km E of **Concoret**, in the middle of a bleak moorland, overlooking another lake. Only the ramparts and moat remain of the original castle, where Viviane is said to have been born, but another Comper Castle built by Merlin lies submerged beneath the waters of the lake, or so they say.

Les Forges de Paimpont is one of the most attractive sections of the forest and since it is easily accessible, via the N 24 and D 773, make for this spot if time is limited and map-reading doubtful. Iron was smelted here in Renaissance times until about the last century. Now the ancient cottages, mills and fountains lie silently in a picturesque huddle beside a gorgeous lake.

Paimpont

This little market town attracts most tourists, with invariably a coach pulled up outside the intriguing abbey church, restored from the 13th-century original. Well worth going inside to see the 17th-century wooden statue of Our Lady of Paimpont, jauntily painted.

The setting is most attractive out of season, when footsteps echo in the single street of the *bourg*, approached through a stone archway, and the anachronistic *crêperie* and souvenir shops are unobtrusive. The lake is vast, altogether a delightful spot at any season, lively with pedalos and windsurfers in summer, always good for walking round or sitting by. Refreshment is at hand.

Relais de Brocéliande
(HR)S   *99.07.81.07   Cl. Mon. o.o.s.   All credit cards*

Stone-walled, slate-roofed, geraniumed, with surprisingly comfy and spacious bedrooms in the adjoining annexe, where a large well-furnished room with bath costs 285f and the cheapest, 180f. The well-patronised bar is decorated with stuffed creatures of the forest and has a log fire to comfort chilled fishermen. Good value simple meals from 70f (not Suns.)

An inexpensive base in a most attractive area, strategically placed as an overnight staging post, near Rennes, and well on the way to coastal destinations.

Map 5E   **PENESTIN** 56760 (Morbihan) 16 km W of Roche-Bernard; 32 km NW of La Baule

---

A westward-facing peninsula at the mouth of the river Vilaine. The Pointe de Loscolo is 2.5 km SW of Penestin, a narrow peninsula surrounded by lovely sandy beaches. Good coastal walking.

Loscolo
(HR)M   *Pointe de Roscolo 99.90.31.90   Cl. Nov.–Easter; rest. cl. Tue. lunch and Wed. lunch o.o.s.*

An unpretentious little hotel of sixteen rooms, peacefully set right on the beach. It has recently been renovated and prices have accordingly risen for some of the better rooms, which share a terrace. These cost 460f but there are others at 290f. The restaurant has a good local reputation for its seafood. Menus from 125f.

Map 5E   **PEN-LAN** 56190 (Morbihan) 4.5 km S of Muzillac, 37 km SW of Redon

---

Muzillac the coastline north of the Vilaine estuary is imposingly wild and rocky. A thin neck of sand straggles out from Billiers to bulge into the granite headland of the Pointe de Pen-Lan, with a stunning bay on either side, and dominated by:

Domaine de Rochevilaine
(HR)L   *97.41.69.27   Fax 97.41.44.85   Cl. Feb. 15/3*

Recent reports indicate that the management now smiles and that the cooking is polished and full of flavour. The bedrooms too have been improved. As for the setting, that could hardly be improved since it was already superb. The hotel is literally at the edge of the sea, with a very impressive approach – a sprawl of white, more village than hotel,

built out on to the Atlantic rocks. Guests can recline on the terrace encircling the hotel and I doubt if there's a finer situation in the whole of France. There is a swimming pool too, all making the price of 750–1,150f for a room and menus from 190f seem justified. I should welcome a favourable report or two, just to give me a good reason to go back.
Reader's Recommendation:

Map D6   **PENVINS** 56370 (Morbihan), 7kms SE of Sarzeau by D1198.

Mur du Roy
(HR)S   *97.67.34.08.*

'Rooms are not large but pleasant, many with sea views. The food was very good indeed, with fish and shellfish predominating. We would return for the food alone.' Richard and Charlott Bass.
Rooms 295f. Menus from 98f.

Map 1C   **PERROS GUIREC** 22700 (C. d'A.) 12 km N of Lannion – *Mkt: Fri*

The largest resort along the pink granite coast and used to be the smartest but has lately succumbed to the souvenir and ice cream stalls. The town is a lively modern one, with a good Friday market.

Several beautiful bays edge the point, fringed with pines. Trestraou, the biggest, has the harbour from which the *Vedettes Blanches* chug away on an excursion to the **Sept Îles** off the coast, thrice daily in season but book ahead – very popular.

And deservedly so – the memorable trip starts with a visit to the **Ile des Oiseaux**, white with seagulls, the haunt of little penguins and guillemots. I thought our boat would sink with the weight of the expensive and expansive equipment its passengers required to photo and observe the wild life. Then on to the **Ile aux Moines** for a hour's visit ashore – not a minute too long to climb to the summit for the most remarkable panorama of the coastline as far as Roscoff and the Ile de Batz. One would have thought the formidable surrounding reefs would have deterred invaders, but the island was fortified by Vauban, and his fort remains, with the odd canon still in position. Flat warm grass, closely cropped by the rabbit population, makes for ideal picnicking in a unique site.

The boat's homeward route follows the coast from **Ploumanach**, a little fishing village facing south in the lee of a hook of land, with the commentator pointing out the extraordinary rocks along the way. Sure enough, if you try hard enough, you too can make out the turtle, the scallop shell, the old man, the elephant, formed by the creasing and crumpling of these strange phenomena, more like Spitting Image puppets than real rocks or real anything else.

The grassy cliff edge is dotted with walkers, following the Douaniers' path – another wonderful (and cheaper) way to view the coastline.

In the centre of Trestraou is:

Le Sphinx
(HR)M   *67 ch. de la Messe   96.23.25.42   Fax 96.91.26.13   Cl. 5/1–5/2; rest. cl. Mon. lunch*

An eccentric, tall, thin, turn-of-the-century building, recommended particularly for its position overlooking the rocks far below. Views from the bedrooms towards Ile Tôme are spectacular. The eleven bedrooms are vast but oddly furnished, in keeping with the overall nonconformity. They are comfortable and clean however and, for my taste, preferable to plasticity. 450–580f.

Grab a table at the window at all costs – the view of the ocean is infinitely preferable to the decor within. Fresh, generous, if uninspired cooking on menus from 110f. Good breakfasts.

Les Feux des Iles
(HR)M   *rte. de la Corniche   96.23.22.94   Cl. 10/1–30/1; 14/10–12/11; Sun. p.m.; Mon. o.o.s.*

It says in the brochure *Mme Le Roux pour votre accueil*. On the day I was there Mme Le Roux knew she had all her rooms fully booked and wasn't worrying too much about the '*accueil*', but it was July and rare is the French hotel bird who smiles much then.

When I did extract a key from her for a nosey, I found the rooms were smallish but very pleasant, some with a view of the sea beyond the large sloping garden and not expensive, at 315–600f with bath.

So, in spite of its *patronne*, I include this one for good value in a quiet position near the town and beaches, and particularly for its restaurant. I did not meet M. Le Roux but no doubt he was busy preparing lunch for the *pensionnaires*. I'm told the food is very good indeed and in fact this is more a restaurant with rooms than vice versa. All of which is good news, since demi-pension is compulsory in season at 330–390f. Non-residents would also do very well in the pleasant dining-room whose bay windows take in the view, and excellent menus start at 125f.

Printania
(HR)M   *12 r. des Bons Enfants   96.23.21.00   Fax 96.46.01.10   Cl. 15/12–10/1; Sun. o.o.s.   V*

The smartest hotel nowadays in Perros, whose era of grandeur between the wars has been left far behind. A lot of charm in this large white balconied house, with a superb position overlooking the bay and Les Sept Îles. Well-tended garden and tennis court.

Most of the rooms overlook the sea and are comfortable enough; everything is a bit plastic, but expensive plastic, for 520–650f. Demi-pension obligatory in season from 490f but I know nothing about the restaurant.

➤ Les Vieux Gréements
(R)S   *19 r. Anatole Bras.   96.91.14.99*

So picturesque, so central, so obvious, that I almost missed it. In this somewhat over-priced town, more and more dedicated to tourists, what a pleasant surprise it was to find this exceptionally good crêperie. The building it occupies on the quay by the port de plaisance is exceptional – very olde-worlde with worm-riddled beams and lots of galleon models to emphasise the marine theme. The service is young, friendly and efficient and the food the best of its kind. I had an excellent salad before my crêpe, husband chose something grilled and we looked at other peoples' plates and reckoned that you couldn't have gone wrong. Arrowed as one of the best crêperies discovered.

Map 2F   **PLANCOËT** 22130 (C. d'A.) 17 km NW Dinan on the D 794 – *Mkt: Sat.*

The river Arguegnon rushes surprisingly through the centre of this undistinguished little town, with a bridge just opposite:

➤ **Chez Crouzil**
(HR)M   *les Quais   96.84.10.24   Cl. 15/1–15/2; Sun. p.m.; Mon.*

A little restaurant in front of the station but not at all the English concept of a station caff. Named after its patron of the past 36 years, Jean-Pierre Crouzil, here is an attractive comfortable stop, well worth making a considerable détour, by road or rail. Jean-Pierre believes, however (how wise), that the less travelling his ingredients do the better, so his refreshingly regional menus feature fish from Erquy, oysters from Cancale, strawberries from Jugon. Traditional cooking, but never heavy, unlike the *carte* which is too ponderous by half, the line of least resistance is to settle for the menus and the 195f one is no hardship whatsoever, 125f lunch a splendid alternative. Good, reasonable wine list.

Attached to the restaurant is a small hotel of seven bedrooms, known as l'Ecrin. The rooms, named after gems – Emeraude, Onyx, Opale, etc. are well-fitted and very comfortable, from 350f with shower to 700f, apartment with bath. Half pension here, with an excellent dinner guaranteed, would be a good idea (from 400–550f per person) but you have to stay three days to qualify. Breakfasts are a treat. An arrow for good food, comfort and welcome.

Le Petit Bignon
(R)S   *rte du Cap Fréhel   96.84.15.37*

Lovely warm atmosphere in this old stone farmhouse, well endowed window boxes and tubs full of flowers. Inside is simple, cosy, with red tablecloths and log fire in winter, which we greatly appreciated. Its basically a grill/crêperie, but everything is of a high quality, making it a wise lunch stop.

Map 2G   PLEUDIHEN-SUR-RANCE 22690 (C. d'A.) 15 km NE of Dinan on the D 29

La Petite Touche
(R)S   *rte Mordreuc.   96.83.25.57   Cl. Sat. lunch and Sun.*

A reader's recommendation states that this little restaurant in an insignificant village is a good stop. They specialise in charcoal grills, both meat and fish, including lobster and all the desserts are home made. 68f (not weekends) or 90f with lots of seafood. Pleasant atmosphere with candles and roaring log fire. Mme Desvaux presides.

Map 2G   PLEUGUENEUC 35720 (I. et V.) 12 km SE of Dinan 14 km W of Combourg on the N 137

➤ **Château de la Motte Beaumanoir**
(HR)L   *99.69.46.01   Fax 99.69.42.49   Cl. 23/12–2/1*

One of a recent breed of châteaux. Owner Eric Bernard offers six stunning rooms and two suites in his beautiful 15th–18th century home. They all look over the vast lake, where the trout leap, into the 2,400 hectares of surrounding woodland.

The decorations have been achieved with a good deal of taste as well as expense and I would find it hard to choose between them. Maybe the one with the little tower sitting room. They all have luxurious bathrooms and would certainly make a wonderful sybaritic retreat, for 700–900f a double. Honeymoon perhaps?

La Motte Beaumanoir used to be a chambre d'hôte and the meal I ate there was a simple one with the family. Now it is all much more professional and a new young chef has brought the cooking up to the standard of the rooms. Service in the lovely blue and grey dining-room is suitably smooth. Menus start at 140f. Other agreeable innovations are a swimming pool and tennis court.

All the news is good and so, although the arrow was originally awarded for an outstanding bed and breakfast, it is still justified in an outstanding luxury hotel.

Map 4E   PLOËRMEL (Morbihan) 46 km NE of Vannes, 68 km SW of Dinan, 60 km SW of Rennes

A useful stop at the hub of several main roads.

Named after St. Armel, who arrived from Britain in the 6th century and promptly took on the local dragons. In this church you can see him leading away a very subdued specimen and making practical use of his stole as a halter. The 1944 air raids damaged nearly all the Renaissance stained glass in the church, but there remains one 16th-century window, featuring the Rod of Jesse.

Otherwise, apart from its ruined 12th-century ramparts, not a particularly interesting town. I would probably drive on for a picnic 2 km NW on the Loudéac road to the huge lake, the Étang du Duc, but if more substantial refreshment were required, try:

Le Cobh
(HR)M   *10 rudes Forges   97.74.00.49*

A very welcome addition to the town's facilities. The family Cruaud have worked hard to do justice to this old Breton house in the main street, extending the restaurants capacity, so that one is now in the old stables and one on the first floor. They have named the hotel after the Irish town which is twinned with Ploërmel, upgrading its standard to three stars.

Their chef, Philippe Guilloche has won many medals for his culinary achievements and his cooking on menus from 58–220f adds considerably to the pleasure of staying here, as several readers have testified. Thirteen refurbished rooms cost from 150–385f. A few more reports please for an arrow.

Map 4A   **PLOGOFF** 29770 (Finistère) 4 km E of the Pointe du Raz, on the D 784

Ker-Moor
(HR)S   *98.70.62.06   Fax 98.70.32.69   Rest. cl. Wed. o.o.s.*

On the Plage du Loch, a simple family hotel, with just a road between it and the gorgeous sandy beach. Very basic but everywhere clean, friendly and cheap at 170–270f for a double room overlooking the sea. Menus from 70f and lobsters always available from the wicker pots manufactured by M. Curzon, the patron. The cheapest base I found from which to explore this area of Finistère.

Map 4A   **PLOMEUR** 29120 (Finistère) 5 km SW of Pont-l'Abbé

I find the south coast of the **Bigouden peninsula** disappointing, **Lesconil** and **Lechigat** lack the usual charm of little fishing ports, and **Guilvinec** and **St.-Guénolé** are plain grim; but still very near the delights of the rest of the area is:

Ferme du Relais Bigouden
(HR)M   *rte. de Guilvinec   98.58.01.32   Fax 98.82.09.62   Cl. Jan.*

A smart Logis, Breton-style farmhouse, grey stone, slate roof. The combination of the appeal of the rustic with the practicalities of the

modern should please many people. Friendly proprietor, anxious to please.

Bright cheerful well-equipped bedrooms cost 255–295f; there are bar, lounge, garden, terrace and tennis court. It has no dining-room but there is a sister establishment, **Le Relais Bigouden**, in the town of Plomeur itself and with rooms from 220f, and menus from 70f. As both establishments are open o.o.s., there's a good deal going for them.

Map 3B   **PLOMODIERNE** 29550 (Finistère) 20 km N of Douarnenez

---

Turn off the D 65, 3 km E of the village on the C 4, well-signposted.

Relais Pors-Morvan
(H)M   *98.81.53.23   Cl. weekends o.o.s.; 1/11–1/4*

An old stone farmhouse restored to provide eight motel-style rooms in the utterly peaceful depths of the rolling countryside. The bedrooms, unfortunately orange vinyled, are uncomfortable only to the eye, being well equipped with excellent bathrooms apiece, at 295–315f, which includes, unusually, breakfast.

No restaurant, apart from a *crêperie*, open in summer only, and a pleasant terrace on which to sit in the sun and have a tea-break.

With the sea only 6 km away and a tennis court available, I think this could make a convenient and agreeable stop in the winter when seaside hotels are closed and in summer when they're full and expensive.

Map 4A   **PLONÉOUR-LANVERN** 29167 (Finistère) 8 km NW of Pont-l'Abbé, 18 km from Quimper on the D 2

In the heart of the **Bigouden** area, an unremarkable village. In its centre:

➤ **La Mairie**
(HR)S   *3 r. Jules Ferry   98.87.61.34   Cl. 20/12–20/1   V*

A spic and span little Logis, comfortable, friendly and inexpensive. The bedrooms are pretty and cheerful, and good value at 180–290f, and nice Mme Dilosquer aims to please.

Her husband is chef and his cooking of local produce (the kitchen was seething with *langoustes* when I was there) has made his restaurant popular with tourists and Bretons alike. Good menus from 65f.

Everyone agrees that La Mairie offers splendid value, so an arrow.

Map 2F   **PLOUER-SUR-RANCE** 22490 (C. d'A.) 8 kms N of Dinan by N
176 and a right turn towards Hisse, or even better by turning
right onto the D 57 at Carheil and then left onto the D 61. The
Manoir is actually 3 kms from Plouer village.

This is one of my favourite areas, blissfully little-known. The high
banks offer fabulous views over the wide and wonderful river Rance
and there are good walks on both sides. At Plouer there is a marina
down by the river and a superb little restaurant in the village centre
(see below); at La Hisse you can hire boats for river excursions.
Because the tourists stick to the coast or Dinan, there is little in the way
of accommodation here, so I was delighted to find:

➤ **Le Manoir de Bigourdaine**
(H)M   *96.86.96.96   Fax 96.86.92.46   Cl. 15/11–Easter*

In the summer of 1993 Patrick Valenberg fell in love with this old
manor house, crumbling and neglected, and decided that, with its
glorious situation high above the river, and loads of space, it would
make a perfect hotel. He set about most of the enormous amount of
necessary work himself and has now achieved a comfortable attractive
result, retaining the character by use of old materials while installing
all the desirable mod cons.

The buildings enclose on three sides a large open courtyard. Most
distinguished is the central one, where Patrick has incorporated a huge
glass window which floods the interior with sunshine. The dining-room
and sitting-room are vast, opening up to a high beamed ceiling, with
another sitting area on the landing. When I visited in the spring we sat
around a huge raised log fire in the salon. Old furniture has been
acquired gradually, from the local Depots à Vente, helping the place to
lose its initial rawness. The rooms are painted in pastel colours with
bright rather mediaeval looking print bedspreads, and high sloping
windows; some have showers, some have baths, for 280–350f. The
last six, in a side wing, were almost ready and looked as though they
would be very good news indeed. They have a small sitting-room and
kitchenette along with bathroom and bedroom and their own terrace –
350f with shower, 400f with bath. These are ideal for self-catering, and
you can order frozen food ahead to cook in the microwaves.

I loved staying here, with Patrick a thoughtful (English-speaking)
host, who will do everything possible to make his guests enjoy their
stay. The fact that there is no restaurant is no problem, since I should
be happy to eat every night at one of the most successful finds of my
tour (see below) just a few minutes away.

Arrowed for comfortable, well-priced accommodation in a prime
position. I know this one will be a great success.

➤ **The French Connection**
(R)S–M   *Le Bourg   96.86.87.87*

Why is it that when the Brits decide to open a restaurant in France,
they beat the French at their own game? Why can't people like Jennifer

Donaldson, with her front-of-house friend Victoria Sharp, come and cook back home, dishing up top quality for bottom prices? Never mind, it's a good excuse to go back and back to Plouer.

The ladies have acquired this old stone house tucked away in an alleyway off the main square, and livened it up with red and white bistro-like cloths and fresh red and white flowers. A touch of whimsy is provided by a huge shiny blackamoor holding up a lantern. So far so good – its really *very* pretty, especially by candlelight in the evenings, and equally in summer when everyone eats outdoors in the unsuspected rear walled garden – but of course it's the food that counts most.

We tested two menus – I on the 85f version – loved every mouthful of gratinéed artichoke hearts and haddock with perfect hollandaise, topped up with a lovely sharp lemon tart and husband was equally pleased with his croustade de prosciutto, which turned out to be like a frilly pizza-ette, then baby chicken with rosemary and ginger. For 120f he got a cheese course too. House specialities are marinated salmon sushi, large prawns with a light curry sauce, and generous charcoal grills.

Can't fault this one. Arrow. Keep up the good work girls!

A reader's recommendation:

Ploubazlanec
(R)S   *La Ferme de Kerroc'h. Rte de Brehat.   96.55.81.75   Cl. Sun. p.m.; Mon. o.o.s.*

'Attractive situation with charcoal specialities'.

Map 1B   **PLOUESCAT** 29430 (Finistère) 15 km W of St.-Pol-de-Leon

Westwards and northwards the coast lies low, sand-duney, windswept. Plouescat, inside the bay of Kernic, is a fishing and market garden centre, with a 16th-century covered market.

L'Azou
(HR)S   *r. Gen. Leclerc   98.69.60.16   Cl. 24/9–18/10, 23/2–3/3,   Wed. lunch & Tues. o.o.s.*

A simple hotel with a rear courtyard, popular locally for its surprisingly smart restaurant, presided over by patron-chef M. Azou. His cheapest menu at 76f, with lots of seafood, is recommended, but you can go up to 340f if you want lobster.

Five simple rooms for 210f with shower, loo in corridor.

Map 2A   **PLOUGUERNEAU** 29880 (Finistère) 29 km N of Brest, by D13
31 km NW of Landerneau

In the little-explored NW territory of windswept dunes and farming country. Take the D 71 for 5 km to find the Plage de Lilia.

Castel Ac'h
(HR)S   98.04.70.11   Open all year   Rest. cl. Christmas and Jan. 31   AE, EC, V

A modern hotel set beside a beautiful beach of fine sand, an excellent family holiday base. There are rooms for four at 250f, or doubles for 180f. None of them is large but they are more cheerfully decorated than in most French hotels, and the plumbing works.

The views from the restaurant across the bay merit the journey alone. Menus from 80f and cheap carafe wine.

Map 5D   **PLOUHARNEL** 56720 (Morbihan) 3 km NW of Carnac

Auberge de Kerank
(R)M   97.52.35.36   rte. de Quiberon   Cl. Sun.; Mon. in Dec.–Jan.

Anyone driving along the coast road is bound to be lured by this attractive old building right on the water's edge. Inside is quite lovely, with shining copper antiques, and waitresses in Breton costumes but when you get down to the real business of the day – eating – it's a bit of a let-down. *Andouillettes* may be a house speciality but they should never feature on a no-choice 140f menu in mid-June. À la carte is OK but not cheap. Perhaps on a beautiful day it might be worthwhile having a meal on the terrace, say with just one fish dish or charcoal grilled *brochettes*, and it is usefully open every day, so might serve as a desperation resort in this area of few good eateries, but otherwise – drive on.

Les Ajoncs d'Or
(HR)M   97.52.32.02   Fax 97.52.40.36   Cl. 2/11–1/3

A picturesque old granite farmhouse, set in a pretty garden, just a few minutes from the sea. Furniture is solid, Breton antiques, including a wonderful grandfather clock, dining-room has rough stone walls, big fireplace and Breton plates as decoration. 20 bedrooms are quiet and comfortable – good value at 280–320f for one with shower and 350f with bath. Menus start at 98f – nothing elaborate; for instance 8 oysters, rib of beef, salad and Brie and dessert choice. More reports welcome.

Map 2C   **PLOUNÉRIN** 22780 (C. d'A.) 30 km W of Guincamp. Take the old RN 12

Patrick Jeffroy
(R)L   96.38.61.80   Cl. Sun. p.m.; Mon. CB, AE

Used to be Le Bon Voyage, now an extremely smart, Michelin-starred restaurant, owned by chef Patrick Jeffroy, who used to cook at the Hotel de l'Europe in Morlaix. His menus – from 190f – are all highly commendable and good value for the quality, but I need more reports, please.

There are three comfortable rooms at 330–380f, so the whole combination is affordable luxury and could well be an arrow.

Map 6D   **LE PÔ** (Morbihan) 15 km SW of Avray

Follow the coast road west of Carnac for a couple of kilometres to find the strange little village of Le Pô, entirely dedicated to the raising and selling of molluscs and crustaceans, with primitive flat-bottomed boats pulled up all along the shore. If you're self-catering, this is the place to buy a lobster or oysters or mussels.

Here is that rare Carnac breed – a genuine little restaurant – with the inappropriate name of:

Le Calypso
(R)M   *97.52.06.14   Cl. 3/11–20/12; 20/2–28/2; Tues. p.m. o.o.s., Wed. lunch o.o.s.*

Very different from the conventional hotel meals and tourist menus of the town. This offers simple *fruits de mer*, prime grilled fish and meat, and very good too. Menus from 90f, to 190f including a whole lobster from their vivier.

'Don't let the name put you off. We enjoyed an excellent meal with pleasant service and good fish'. Howard Angliss.

Map 4A   **POINTE DU RAZ** 29113 Audierne (Finistère)

There's something alluring about extremities. Land's End and Raz attract the tourists not only because they are spectacular but because they are ultimates. The vast car parks at Raz testify to the numbers expected in summer, from whom the *crêperies* and souvenir shops will no doubt exact a second toll (parking 8f).

But forget the matazz and concentrate on the Raz; there's a lot of it to go round and it's hard not to be impressed with the power of the wind, the waves and the knowledge that the race below the dizzying cliffs is one of the most dangerous in the world. Beyond the lighthouse of the Old Lady, 10 km offshore, is the Island of Sein, reef encircled. The druids were rowed out to their burial ground here from the Baie des Trépassés, or so they say. Another theory is that the bay derived its name (a *trépassé* is a dead man) from the bodies of shipwrecked mariners washed ashore here. All stirring stuff, imbuing a certain thoughtfulness in those, vertigo-free, who walk over the scattered rocks to the edge of France and ponder for a moment on the fury of the forces unleashed below.

Serious climbers can take a guide for a 1½ hour tour of the point round l'Enfer de Plogoff (the Plogoff Inferno) where a sheer chasm and the untiring waves meet like battering rams; their clash is deafening, orchestrated by an odd moaning, said to be the souls of the dead!

For more relaxed appreciation there is still plenty to see and wonder at; Notre-Dame des Naufragés (Our Lady of the Shipwrecked) stands a comfortable distance away from the precipice, reassuringly calm and untroubled; walk past her to one of the less adventurous paths and you will still enjoy a memorable panorama.

I wouldn't suggest eating seriously at any of the tourist restaurants up here, but recommend doubling back, *via* the D 784 and V 0 to:

➤ **Hotel de la Baie des Trépassés**
(HR)M   *98.70.61.34   Cl. 15/1–15/2*

Standing centrally, in the wide sweep of the bay, with its marvellous sands and treacherous tides, is the large white hotel. Here one Easter Monday I ate the best Bank Holiday lunch I remember – a Gargantua of a crab.

It so happened that the previous week I'd ordered 'fresh crab salad' at an English seaside town. Poking dubiously at the cotton wool blob dumped on the vinegary beetroot that bled on to the hothouse lettuce limpness, and avoiding the dreaded word 'freezer' I commented that the specimen was very – er cold? 'Oh *yes* Madam', came the righteous reply, 'we keep all our shellfish in a cold cabinet.' *Keep*? The *Trépassé* monster had been kept only as long as it took to heave him off the boat into the pan and was still steaming from his immolatory immersion.

No genteel English 'dressing' for him, with breadcrumbs and colouring and chemical mayonnaise. Cleavered in half was all his presentation. Not even the unreasonable doubt that the customer couldn't work out for himself which bits tasted good – you just heaved out the dead mens' fingers and enjoyed the rest. (Query – another theory for the name of the bay – did the poisoned ones never come back?) The wicked pincers alone yielded several freezer-packs-worth of delectable, juicy, pearly flesh. Along with a bowl of home made mayonnaise, quantities of *baguette* and fresh butter, all washed down with Muscadet sur Lie, I could not ask for better. The cost – £5.

Had smaller portions of more courses been the mood, there is an excellent and sensible 85f menu – crab mayonnaise, six oysters, mussels etc., followed by three kinds of fish with a choice of three kinds of sauces (or chicken or pork) and a splendid *tarte aux myrtilles.* Lobster, bass and sole feature on the more expensive menus, but no doubt that the general favourite was the *plâteau de fruits de mer.* All round it was heads-down, with a cracking, and a spitting, and a mopping, and every table a battlefield of débris, from *langoustines*, oysters, mussels, clams and whelks. Not much conversation until the coffee stage, and then what a patting of stomachs and loosening of napkins!

Some very attractive new rooms have been built on recently, making full use of the view over the bay. At 170–350f for a double with bath, they are as good value as the food and the combination gets an undoubted arrow.

A new hotel, under the same management, has appeared. The **Baie des Trépassés** no longer stands solitary in the wide sweep of the bay. 200

metres away is the **Relais de la Pointe du Van** (29113 Cléden, Cap Sizun: 98.70.62.79), adding another 25 rooms to the original 27.

Rooms now cost from 218 to 320f, all are modern with good 'facilities' and all offer the opportunity to sample the beautifully fresh seafood, so much appreciated by readers. Demi-pension obligatory in season.

The Baie des Trépassés has proved one of the most popular entries in *F.E.5*, and the arrow is well deserved. Reports on the Relais would be welcome.

Map 4C   **PONT-AVEN** 29936 (Finistère) 15 km W of Concarneau – *Mkt: Tues.*

The wide tidal estuary of the river Aven probes deep inland to this little town, where it becomes narrow enough for a bridge to cross it.

Here was the meeting place for the followers of Paul Gauguin at the end of the last century. 'I love Brittany,' he wrote. 'I find wildness and primitiveness there; when my wooden shoes ring on the gravel, I hear the muffled dull powerful tone I seek in my painting.' He often stayed and painted in the town and along the river banks and was a founder member of the Pont-Aven school. One of his favourite themes was the simple faith and apparently trouble-free life of the Breton peasants and he used the Pont-Aven ladies in their distinctive *coiffes* to illustrate his point. 'Jacob Wrestling with the Angel' is one of the best-known, painted in the town in 1888.

The town is still full of art galleries but I found no works of genius there.

The bridge is the centre of the town but don't omit to follow the river to the 'port', an extremely pretty walk or drive along the banks, by water dotted with sailing boats, with green parks providing perfect picnicking space.

Some intelligent town-planning has resulted in an enchanting new walk along the stream that flows through the town centre, crisscrossing the water by picturesque bridges. Its an altogether charming place to stay.

Its charm and artistic connections, however, bring it a guaranteed supply of visitors, which perhaps make the hoteliers a shade complacent. There are plenty of them to choose from. I looked at:

Roz Aven
(HR)   *11 quai Theodore Botrel   98.06.13.16*

Absurdly pretty – thatched, 18th century, overlooking the river – sounds ideal, but I thought the rooms were too cramped to justify the tag of 350–610f.

Moulin de Rosmadec
(HR)L   *98.06.00.22   Fax 98.06.18.00   Rest. cl. Sun p.m.; o.o.s.; Wed. Feb. 2nd fortnight in Oct.*

A hundred years ago they claimed that Pont Aven had fourteen mills and fifteen houses. One of the mills has been converted into a luxury hotel in the prettiest imaginable setting, on a loop of the river, in a garden full of roses.

This one is a favourite with the Americans and you have to be very quick off the mark to bag one of the four rooms, which are reasonably priced but a bit disappointing in decor – 410–480f. The famous restaurant, in the old beamed dining-room, has been in the hands of the Sebilleau family for two generations. Menus start at 150f.

Hotel des Mimosas
(H)M   *22 sq. Th. Botrel   98.06.00.30*

This one, with an old-fashioned look, not quite so central but still just a short walk along the river bank, is better value. The rooms are spacious and look out over the water, some with a private terrace. 260–360f. I found the reception somewhat bored though.

In the end we settled for the obvious:

Ajoncs d'Or
(HR)M   *pl. Hotel de Ville   98.06.02.06   Fax 98.06.18.91   Cl. 1–20/123–20/1. rest. cl. Sun. p.m.; Mon. o.o.s.*

Bang in the centre of town, the kind of faded typically French hotel that you suspect will have vanished from the scene next time you visit. I was surprised to find it has only 23 rooms – in a building this size that can't be cost-effective. They are nothing special, with a variety of furnishings and fittings, but we negotiated for a suite for 315f at the rear, which we thought splendid value. Others cost from 240–375f.

Auberge La Taupinière
(R)L   *98.06.03.12   Cl. 26/9–19/10; Mon. p.m. o.o.s.; Tues.*

4 km on the Concarneau road. This is the one the locals recommend for a real gastro-treat. Chef Guy Guilloux takes the usual prime regional ingredients and conjures up his own-style miracles, without relying slavishly on either traditional or *noove cuis.* No-one does giant grilled *langoustines* as well as he, and his *soupe de moules en croute* at the other end of the price range is a different and delicious variation on an old theme. Good lamb and Breton ham too if fish palls.

Elegant décor, with big fireplace put to good effect for winter grills, and super efficient service. Menu at 260f. Book.

Map 4D **PONTIVY** 56300 (Morbihan) 107 km W of Rennes – *Mkt: Mon. p.m.*

The main market town in central Brittany, bustling and lively, Pontivy straddles the river Blavet. One look at the map will show how today it is the hub of a wheel of roads, river and canal. Napoleon recognised its strategic importance and laid out a formal town plan, with barracks, town hall, law courts; he made it a junction of the Nantes–Brest canal, with the intention of setting up his administrative centre for the whole area. It was actually called Napoléonville three times: 1802–14, during his One Hundred Days in 1815, and again during the Second Empire.

But the origins of the town's current name hark back to a Welsh monk, St. Ivy, who built the first mediaeval bridge over the river, and in the 15th century it became the seat of the powerful Rohan family, who built the mighty castle there.

Its history gives the town two distinct characters – the imperial to the south and the mediaeval to the north huddling round the picturesque pl. du Martray, with the Rohans' old hunting lodge still there.

The **Bar Central** here is the central meeting place for the townsfolk, always full, always lively.

Porhouet
(H)S   *41 r. Gén. de Gaulle   97.25.34.88   Fax 92.25.57.17   Open year round   EC, V*

28 rooms from 200–280f.

Map 4B **PONT-L'ABBÉ** 29120 (Finistère) 20 km SW of Quimper

The monks of Loctudy (see p. 99) built the original bridge that gave the town its name. Capital of the **Bigouden** area, formed by a chunky peninsula, Pont-l'Abbé centres on a vast market square, taken over on Thursdays by a real French country market. Here, and indeed on other days and especially on fêtes, you can see the black-dressed old ladies going unselfconsciously about their business in their amazing *coiffes*. Hard not to stare. The Pont-l'Abbé version used to be small and neat, but within the present century it has shot skywards and now, tall and narrow with streamers behind, it is probably the most spectacular in Brittany. If you don't hit lucky in the streets, you can always see a fine array of local *coiffes* in the Bigouden museum, housed in the 13th and 18th-century Town Hall.

In 1857 Flaubert described Pont-l'Abbé as a quiet little town and, market days apart, it still is, with a peaceful walks along the river bank.

➤ **Hotel Bretagne**
(HR)M   *24 pl. de la République   98.87.17.22   Fax 98.83.39.31   Cl. 15/1– 15/2;   rest. cl. Mon. o.o.s.   AE, CB, EC*

Marcel Cossec, once a fisherman, is a natural cook. Recognising a fellow foodie, he proudly produced, at the end of a memorable

La Bretagne

meal, a plastic bucket, inelegant true, but full of the most wonderful fish *fumet*, reduced and jellied, ready to enrich tomorrow's fish dishes. In this area of abundant fresh seafood, it is all too easy to get a reputation as a good chef simply by poaching or grilling the stuff and dishing it up to tolerant customers. Nothing wrong with that, but here is the little extra that sorts out the stars.

His *langoustines grillées à la crème* are the best I have ever tasted His poached turbot is not only pearly fresh, generously sized, but comes accompanied with a perfect *sauce au beurre blanc*, served instinctively, without any *nouvelle cuisine* dicta, underneath the fish, so as to enhance not disguise.

And what value! The *langoustine* evening was hardly a test; we had eaten there with local friends and advisers, the Coatalens, who had no hesitation in directing us to the **Bretagne** as simply 'the best'; we sat down very late, in high spirits induced by several glasses and much chat with the fishermen in the bar on Île Tudy, and we ate just those (providently ordered ahead *NB*) washed down with several more glasses, declared it was the perfect meal and remembered very little else next day. So several months later we arrived alone and ate on the menus 75f for lunch, then from 110f and they were just as good.

Super professional service, unfussy but attentive, in a charming dining-room that looks out onto a little terrace full of flowers and with an old well, all very romantic for summer eating. Fresh flowers everywhere and all the little touches that show the owners care.

I certainly care for their bedrooms, which are among the most comfortable and attractive encountered in Brittany. Bargains all the way, from the simple to the worth-every-penny with twin beds and super bathroom, 240f with shower up to 360f.

Marcel and Marie-José Cossec are the friendliest of hosts and are obviously proud of what they have achieved from what could have been an everyday tale of country folk. Their individual style of retaining the best of the old (the **Bretagne** lives up to its name and is no tourist pub; on Thursdays it is full of stallholders from the market and local shoppers) with willingness to add the best of the new is totally admirable.

Three innovations: a *crêperie* with terrace, open from 15/6–15/9 every day – what a good idea for lunch – and studios with kitchenette for rent by the week at 2900 to 3500f for two people, or 3300 to 3900 for four people. (The hotel takes care of the linen and cleaning.) And nephew Frank Even in the kitchen as 'second' to Marcel. Free parking.

'Quite delightful. The first two nights we had a quiet cosy room right at the back, with a shower, for 250f and on the third night, when our son joined us, a large family room at the front for 300f. Lovely food, pleasant staff and a friendly lady running everything. I found Pont l'Abbé an attractive place to wander in, less guant and grey than a lot of Breton towns and the hotel's position in the market place is just right. On the Sunday we attended the annual pilgrimage to the pardon at Tromoëor. Very colourful, attended by vast crowd'. Christopher Hall.

Still well deserving the arrow.

Chateau de Kernuz

(HR)M–L   *rte. de Penmar'h.   98.87.01.59   Fax 98.66.02.36   Cl. Oct.–Mar. Demi-pension oblig. in season.*

Impressive 16C mansion in its own extensive grounds. The nineteen rooms, which have all been recently attractively re-decorated and equipped, are good value at 335–455f.

Le Relais de Ty Boutic
3 km SW of the Plomeur Road.   98.87.03.09   Cl. Tue. p.m.; Thurs. lunch and Mon in July and Aug.

A choice here between the well-known restaurant, looking out on to a delightful garden, with Pierre Courrot cooking superb fish on menus from 70f (not Suns.), or the simpler buffet, ideal for a lighter, cheaper lunch.

Map 5D   **PONT-LOROIS** (Morbihan) 16 km S of Hennebont

The D 781 crosses the wide river Étel and on the Belz side, is:

Les Parcs de Navihan. *Downstairs is devoted to the oyster and mussel trade but upstairs is a Scandinavian style wood panelled dining-room overlooking the river. The restaurant only serves shellfish but was voted the best ever Fruits de mer by our two families. Everything straight from the holding pools to table in moments. A second visit confirmed first opinions. The fruits de mer comes in a series of huge platters, the oysters etc. being eaten while the crayfish and langoustines are being cooked. Only open in summer and only accept cash. Highly recommended'. Howard R. Anglish.*

Sounds just my kind of place. Thank you Mr Anglish.

Map 1D   **PORS EVEN** 22620 (C. d'A.) Ploubazlanec 5 km NE of Paimpol

---

A typically Breton little fishing port, all lobster pots and oyster trays, with no concessions to tourists except the **Café du Port** for drinks, *dégustations* and a good view, and:

Pension Bocher
(HR)S   *96.55.84.16   Cl. 5/11–27/3   AE*

A charming low grey stone house, covered in creeper, set sideways onto the road leading down to the port. More a restaurant with rooms, which is always a good sign, although here there are in fact surprisingly 16 bedrooms, all spic and span, four with sea views, from 170–295f, and a lounge to relax in with log fire after a **Bocher**-style substantial meal. Predictably, seafood is the house speciality, and for 115f you get expensive varieties like *langoustines* and *lotte* on your menu. Unpretentious good value.

Map 1D   **PORT BLANC** 22710 (C. d'A.) 17 km E of Perros-Guirec

A little fishing port which gets its name for the white(ish) pebbles on its beach; to be sure there's not a lot of sand there but nearby are some relatively unknown stretches of coastline, with practically untenanted beaches and plenty of sands to choose from, backed by pine trees for picnickers.

To the right of the little harbour is a statue of the Virgin in a rock top shelter and before the village is a well-known and much photographed chapel, whose pitched roof reaches down to the grass; Gothic nave, with wooden rafters.

➤ Hotel des Îles
(HR)S   *96.92.66.49*   *Cl. 30/9–26/2*

This little hotel just across the road from the beach, seems to me to embody all the virtues of a modest seaside establishment. Most important is the food – way above the usual one-star hotel offering. Do use the restaurant even if you do not plan to stay. Seafood is the star of course, lavishly served here on menus from 80f, which are worth double. Book well ahead if a Sunday or fete is involved – this is the locals' favourite. A simple room costs 190f and a good-sized one with bath is 290f. Sea view thrown in. Hectic flowered decor, good bathroom.

There's a good atmosphere here and readers have approved of the welcome. An arrow for unpretentious quality.

Map 5C   **PORT-LOUIS** 52690 (Morbihan) 145 km SE of Rennes

At the mouth of the river Blavet, opposite Lorient. Nowadays a small fishing port and beach resort, once an important fortress. A trading centre from mediaeval times but developed in the time of Louis XIII, from whom the town took its name. Richelieu completed its fortification in 1636; his sea-pounded granite citadel still stands guard on the entrance to Lorient which has long since superseded Port-Louis as a port. Even the sardine fishing industry has declined but the fishing fleet in the harbour inside the headland still brings in the giant tunny.

Pass through a gap in the ramparts to find the gorgeous beach – fine sand and lots going on, with a view across the estuary to Larmor Plage and the Ile de Groix lying a pleasureboat-trip away. All very seasonal though; on a beautiful early September day the beach cafés were shuttered.

The little town lies between port and beach, preoccupied on Saturday with its market which straggles along the main street and fills the market place, completely surrounding:

Hotel du Commerce
(HR)S   *pl. Marché   98.82.46.06   Fax 97.82.11.02   Cl. 20/10–15/11. Mon. o.o.s.*   P.

> Nothing special – just a cheap base from which to explore the area;
> good for the kids, with a pleasant green garden and only 200 metres
> from that beach. A double is from 115–255f and good fishy menus
> start at 78f (lunch). Popularity with locals augurs well.

Map 4A   **POULDREUZIC** 29710 (Finistère) 16 km N of Pont-l'Abbé

> Take the D 2 NW of the village of Lababan, to find:

Ker Ansquer
(HR)M   *98.54.41.83   Cl. 1/10 to Easter; rest. cl. weekends. Reservation only.*

> A solidly comfortable stone-walled, slate-roofed hotel of eleven rooms,
> 310f or 330f in season with bath. Modern, but very Breton in flavour.
> Mme Ansquer greeted me in *sabots* and the end wall of the charming
> dining-room is elaborately carved and painted in traditional designs by
> local craftsmen. Near the beach of Penhors but probably more suitable
> for those in search of a rural rest than for young families. Menus 190f.

Hotel Ker Ansquer

Moulin de Brenizenec
(H)M   *98.58.30.33   Cl. 15/9–Easter*

> On the main road to Audierne, between Pouldreuzic and Plozevet. A lovely old stone mill set back in its utterly delightful shady gardens, stream running through small lake, lots of flowers. Ten most attractive bedrooms have been contrived, all individually furnished with 'real' furniture at 355–435f a double, including breakfast. No restaurant but a nice *salon* to relax in when the garden's too damp.
>
> Peaceful situation, helpful owner, anxious to make his guests comfortable. Would make a most agreeable base from which to explore the area and be free to try the local restaurants.

Breiz-Armor
(HR)M   *plage de Penhors   98.54.40.41   Fax 98.51.52.30   Cl. mid-Oct–1/4; Mon. o.o.s*

> A modern motel-type Logis in the middle of the bay of Audierne right on the vast windswept beach of Penhors. Good views from the bedroom balconies of the spectacular rollers.
>
> It's all a bit plastic and predictable, but the beach is good, the swimming under surveillance, and best of all it has an unusually good restaurant. At Easter it was solid with locals, who know a good *plateau de fruits de mer* when they see one. Menus from 95–230f with a huge *langouste*. All rooms with bath at 360f.

Map 5C   **LE POULDU** (Finistère) 14 km S of Quimperlé

> In 1890 Gauguin painted the stunning 'Farm at Pouldu' here in the village he came to prefer to Pont Aven. His lodging is now the **Hôtel de la Plage.**
>
> Pouldu is a seaside resort with two distinct faces. The one with the beaches looking out to sea has big hotels, with names like **Les Bains**, **Les Dunes**, all with superb views over the water; the port, which I prefer, looking in the opposite direction over the river Laïta, has a nice old-fashioned hotel, **Le Pouldu**, with balconied bedrooms, a seafood restaurant and a bar with terrace from which to contemplate the odd small fishing boat.

Map 5E   **QUESTEMBERT** 56230 (Morbihan) 88 km from Rennes

> *Kistin* is the Breton name for the chestnuts from which 'Questembert' derives and which feature on its coat of arms. A splendid 17th-century covered market hall dominates and gives a lot of character to the little town, and there is a carved calvary to inspect in the cemetery of St. Michael's chapel.

Georges Paineau
(R)L **and Le Bretagne** (H)L–M   *13 r. St. Michel 97.26.11.12   Fax 97.26.12.37   Cl.
Sun. p.m.; Mon.*

Many changes here, always onward and upward, with Georges
Paineau now sufficiently well-known and confident to name the
Bretagne's old restaurant after himself, and to conclude a programme
of extension and refurbishment that makes this a top Morbihan
combination.

His cooking is faultless – heavily weighted by local ingredients,
dictated by the best the morning market can offer, but cooked with
unique flair and imagination. Predictably seafood triumphs. From a list
of exceptional dishes I would pick out his cockles with coriander and
cumin, or his mixture of humble and exalted in a cabbage dish stuffed
with lobster. He loves cooking with old-fashioned traditional
ingredients like pigs trotters, shin of beef and oxtail. The style is more
Gary Rhodes than Marco Pierre White.

Ah yes you may well say, but a double Michelin star must involve
loadsamoney. Not if you sample this food for the Gods at lunchtime,
when his first menu is an incredible 140f. The next one up at 250f
makes an equal bargain for dinner. The dining-room, oak panelled, is a
bit serious perhaps, so if its a fine night bag a table on the verandah
overlooking the pretty garden.

The 13 rooms in the hotel section are also modestly priced,
considering their spaciousness and luxury fittings. They start at 480f up
to 980f, with special out of season rates. It would be well worth asking
about demi-pension here for a special treat, and in any case it is
obligatory in high season at 580–1,100f per person.

Map 6D   **QUIBERON** 56170 (Morbihan) 46 km SW of Vannes

Once an island, now joined to the mainland by a narrow strip of land,
the Quiberon peninsula is fairly boring centrally, but has great variety
of coastal interest. The Côte Sauvage to the west is the more
interesting, with wild rollers crashing into little coves. Good walking,
with spectacular views, along the stretch between **Pontivy** and **Port
Maria**. For safe bathing it must be the sheltered bay facing eastwards.

You can take the ferry from Quiberon to the well-named **Belle Île**. I
long to go and explore and in fact got as far as making a hotel booking,
but the mainland proved so rich in discoveries that it had to take
precedence. I believe there are several good hotels and restaurants in
the island – **La Forge** is the name that cropped up most often – and one
day I'll get there for what I'm sure will be a delightful visit.

The town of Quiberon is a busy seaside resort with dozens of hotels.
Personally if a beach holiday were indicated I would prefer Carnac –
even better sands, quieter and more accessible – and I found the
Quiberon hoteliers too over-confident to want to please much, but here
are one or two ideas:

The hotels all looked the same to me – **Ker Noyal, Bellevue, Ty Breiz** probably the best, all perfectly adequate but all insisting on demi-pension, which means that you need to know a lot more about the chef than I can tell you before deciding where to stay.

My hunch would be to make for **St. Julien**, 2 km N.

Au Vieux Logis
(HR)S   *97.50.12.20   Cl. 2/10–1/4; rest. cl. 25/9–29/4*

In the centre of the village, an enchantingly pretty old stone house covered in roses, with green views from its windows. Flowery terrace, shady garden, all very different from the razzamatazz down the road.

The bedrooms are simple country-style at 170–260f. Dinner (menus from 70–165f) tends to end up round the piano or sitting round the big log fire, so it's all very sociable.

Back in Quiberon:

Ancienne Forge
(R)M   *20 r. Verdun   97.50.18.64   Cl. 7/1–31/1; Wed. o.o.s.*

Tucked away in a cul de sac off the main road it is unexpectedly tranquil and pretty. Interesting but no-choice menus start at 85f. Probably at its best in the evening.

Up the same alley is nice little tea place, **Ty Cup**, for a range of teas and home ices.

Map 4B   **QUIMPER** 29000 (Finistère) 204 km from Rennes – *Mkt: Tues., Sat.*

The capital of **Cornouaille** is a delightful place to spend more than a few hours. Its natural blessings include the wide river Odet, that flows through its centre to meet the river Steir, and its setting, encircled by gentle hills and dales. Man has added his enhancements – the fascinating old streets around the cathedral, like the rue Keréon (the shoemakers' street), the squares with intriguing names like pl. au Beurre, the r. du Salle with what must be the most elegantly housed *crêperie* anywhere, with beams and corbels and carved fireplaces, and the Terre au duc, all alleyways and timbered houses.

The Gothic cathedral was started in the 13th century and took five more to complete. It takes its name from St.-Corentin, first bishop of Quimper. On the west side stands an equestrian statue of the king of Cornouaille, Gradlon, who retreated to Quimper when his daughter Dahud succumbed to the Devil and opened the sluice gates to drown his kingdom of Ys (see Douarnenez).

The old Bishop's palace overlooking the river is a good place to spend a grey day. Here is the Breton museum of pottery, costumes and furniture.

For a fine day, a tour of the river Odet down to its enchanting estuary is a good idea.

A more modern attraction is the new market, not far from the cathedral, a splendid conception of a vast wooden hall, ceiling-lighted, with all the treasures of a traditional marketplace under cover. Every day, year round.

The faïence of Quimper is charming, well-known, and unfortunately quite expensive. However, a brightly coloured plate, lively with the little stylised Breton figures, makes the perfect holiday souvenir and this is the place to buy it. Wherever you wander, through the pedestrianised shopping area or along the quays, you will find enticing pottery shops. The other take-home trophy from Quimper is its teatime speciality, whose name – *dentelles* – describes the laciness of these crisp little sweet pancakes, rolled like cigars and packed into painted tin boxes.

For such an obviously attractive town, ideally placed for the tourist geographically, particularly out of season when the coastal hotels are shut, I find it strange that Quimper has so few hotels. The old **Tour d'Auvergne** (13 r. Réguaires, 95.08.70) has lost most of its old charm for me and is now more of a businessmens' hotel than a discerning traveller's; the **Griffon** (rte. Bénodet, 90.33.33) is a vast modern pile outside the town, expensive and boring, and I personally didn't like the atmosphere of **La Sapinière** (rte. Bénodet, 90.39.63) which was full of smoke and commercial travellers when I was there (but I am told I was unlucky).

I generally would stay outside and come in for shopping, especially on Wednesday and Saturday, when the square outside the cathedral is full of peasant ladies sitting engulfed in bunchy black skirts and shawls, occasionally coiffed, selling a bunch of wild daffodils or a dozen speckled eggs.

Gradlon
(HR)M   *30 r. de Brest   98.95.04.39   Fax 98.95.61.25*

But occasionally I feel an urgent desire to break away from my usual preference for staying in the countryside and to make for a metropolis. Especially in bad weather it seems a good idea to exchange dripping trees and sodden paths for animation and hard pavements. So it was one dreadful April week when it rained for days and even Brittany's charms were blurred. We headed for the cathedral, the heart of Quimper, and looked for a hotel that would combine calm and convenience.

The Gradlon's exterior does not encourage such hopes. It is on a busy dusty main road, clogged with rush hour traffic. Pass through the reception area, however and an oasis materialises. Here is an unsuspected courtyard where breakfasts no doubt could be enjoyed on finer days. Part of it is glassed-in, providing a bright alternative for my kind of weather. The rooms, set well back from the traffic, come in various combinations of twin/double, bath/shower, conventionally furnished. Most of them cost 380f (but negotiate), up to 600f for one luxurious ground floor suite with jacuzzi. We wavered but decided on economy and were well satisfied. Friendly management helps to make this a good bet.

What is the matter with Quimper? We tried three restaurants and were severely disappointed with them all; even the old trusty brasserie formula at the Bretagne didn't seem to be at the top of that particular tree. I can only suggest creperies, of which the town is well endowed. Suggestions?

Map 4C   **QUIMPERLÉ** 29300 (Finistère) 34 km E of Concarneau – *Mkt: Fri.*

Kemper Ellé = confluence of the Ellé, and here that river joins the Isole to form the Laïta, with the town set in its narrow valley. The old part in the lower town centres on the curiously shaped Ste.-Croix, modelled on the Church of the Holy Sepulchre in Jerusalem; the lovely apse and crypt are Romanesque but the rest of the church had to be rebuilt 100 years ago after the belfry collapsed. Across the river climb up the rue Savéry to reach the beautiful Gothic church of St.-Michel.

The road from Le Pouldu, the D 49, cuts through the cool and peaceful forest of Carnouet. 3 km south of Quimperlé is:

Auberge de Toulfoën
(H)S (R)M   *98.96.00.29   Cl. 25/9–31/10; Mon. o.o.s.; rest. cl. 25/9–1/4; Mon.   AE, DC, V*

Just a simple erstwhile coaching-inn but with a high standard of country cooking – the 100f menu kicks off with eight oysters and for 250f you get five courses. Nine rooms at 180f for one with a shower or 375f with bath.

➤ **Bistro le la Tour**
(R)M   *2 r. Dom Morice.   98.39.29.58   Cl. Sun. p.m.; o.o.s.; Sat. lunch.*

A real find, tucked away in the tortuous streets of old Quimperlé, behind the market halls. Bernard Carious is patron/chef/sommelier in charge of the twelve tables in his charming little restaurant, but he is also an '*antiquaire*' and the front room is packed with treasures, many accentuating the 1930s flavour of the establishment. His cooking is of the style dubbed '*grand-mère*' and newly fashionable oxtail, casseroles, roasts. Superb wine list, not all expensive. Menus from 99f. Arrowed for good value, good cooking, in exceptionally attractive surroundings.

Map 5C   **RAGUENÈS PLAGE** 29139 (Finistère) 12 km SW of Pont Aven

---

Raguenès in argoat means 'opposite the island'. Here the islet is joined to the mainland, except at high water, by a causeway of fine sand, which curves out from the little harbour, bolstered by rocks, making

Men-Du at Raguènès Plage.

the kind of picturebook combination that has the photographers readily clicking.

Magnificent is the only word for the main beach just below the hotel **Men Du**. It sweeps around the bay, firm sands inviting walkers. Even on a cold blustery day there is usually the odd stalwart bent against the wind but enjoying the kilometre or so of splendid scenery. You can walk along the cliff edge too in either direction, fields, poppies, nightingales to one side, breakers, seaweed and gulls to the other.

The **Nevez Peninsula** of which Raguenès forms the tip, is remarkably unspoiled. **Kerascoët** is a tiny village said to be 'typically' Breton but rare in its attractiveness. All its small granite cottages have thatched roofs, flowers tumble, chickens cluck, dogs doze.

Drive through it, down green honeysuckled lanes, to **Rospico**, a deep sheltered inlet with fine sands and a bar/*crêpérie*, and then on to **Port Manec'h**, a popular little seaside resort set in the pines on the estuary of the Aven – sands, beach huts, fishing harbour. I didn't care much for any of the hotels but there is a very attractive bar, in a large old stone house covered in wisteria, with a good terrace overlooking the sandy bay, so an excursion and light lunch should be no problem.

If it's peak season and you hanker for solitude you could find it by following the signs to Kerantré and bumping down a spectacular drive of chestnuts to a little inlet called **Poulguin**, with a small shingly beach and a few boats, all completely sheltered from the west. Then on to **Kerdruc**, whose little harbour is full of yachts and fishing boats, with a bar and picnic seats overlooking the water. From here the old road crosses an ancient narrow bridge and leads to Pont Aven.

But there's no doubt that the star of the peninsula is Raguenès, with two hotels to choose from:

➤ Men Du
(H)M   r. des Îles   98.06.84.22 in season, out of season 98.06.81.60   Cl. 1/10–1/4

A lonely little white building standing solitary above the beach. It looked so windswept that we were somewhat dejected that our stay there should have coincided with bad weather, but there is a large glassed-in bar/terrace from which to catch the view in inclement times, and a cosy bar. No restaurant but the place is always animated with locals and tourists. M. Ollivier, the patron, finds nothing too much trouble to serve his customers and Mme Ollivier ditto, with lots of excellent ideas for excursions and local restaurants.

The rooms all claim to have views of the sea but it has to be said that the windows are small and set high, so a splendid opportunity to lie in bed and enjoy the fabulous surroundings has been lost. They're on the small side too but immaculately presented, extremely comfortable and well furnished with a good bathroom, at 270–310f.

Everything about the hotel is on a small scale but of a high quality, the management is particularly friendly, the site supreme and no restaurant means freedom to eat out. One of my favourites.

Chez Pierre
(HR)M   98.06.81.06   Cl. 27/9–2/4; rest. cl. Wed. from 1/6–14/9

In the village but still no great distance from the sea; very popular with the Brits, who congregate happily in the pleasant bar and garden and greet old friends from previous years. They come primarily for the food, which used to be outstandingly good; recently there have been grumbles that chef, patron Xavier Guillou, is perhaps cashing in on his popularity, and certainly the waiting time is appalling. Menus at 110f. Rooms are very pleasant, at 199–395f with bath.

Map 5F   **REDON** 35600 (I. et V.) 65 kms SW of Rennes on the D 177

The Nantes–Brest canal crosses the river Vilaine here, making the town a natural centre for the Brittany water network. It is a very agreeable exercise to stroll along the quays, especially the quay St-Jacques, with its fine 18th-century houses, and peer down inquisitively on the canal boats invariably tied up there.

Their occupants have only a short walk up the delightful Grand'rue to the market place, brimming over with outside stalls on Mondays, but always a good place to stock up the boats with fresh vegetables, cheeses, terrines and fish from the excellent covered market hall.

The largest romanesque tower in Brittany looms over the square, seven centuries old, detached from St.-Sauveur, the old abbey. Some of the frescoes being restored inside are just as old.

One wet and windy night it was only a scamper from our little boat tied up by the lock to:

La Bogue
(R)M   *3 r. des États   99.71.12.95   Cl. Sun. p.m.*

We could not have chanced upon better. A delightful little restaurant, warm and welcoming. The four course 95f menu was not only a bargain but at least as good as those of some of the starred and vaunted restaurants sampled on the same holiday. (There is a cheaper menu at 72f.) The twelve oysters alone for a first course made my husband's evening when he reflected what they would have cost back home. I ate *rillette de saumon* – tiny almond-shaped moulds of a flavoursome salmon pâté, sitting in a delicate cream and chive sauce. The *steak marchand du vin*, generous and well sauced, and the *côte de veau fermière* – tender veal garnished with lardons of bacon, mushrooms and buttery potatoes, were both prime, but for me the most interesting dish was a *râgout* of snails, beautifully presented out of their shells, artichoke heart slices fanned around, in a memorable cream and basil sauce.

An enterprising use of the local speciality – chestnuts – is made in a *gâteau de châtaignes*, but if you wish to try my favourite – the hot *feuilleté de pommes* – you must remember to order it at the beginning of your meal. Its crisp flakiness, caramelised apples, dollops of *crème fraîche* really should not be missed.

'We confirm your view about this restaurant. The ambience and service excellent. The four course meal at 98f was memorable as was the excellent vin de la maison'. Bernard Lloyd.

La Belle Anguille
(HR)S   *rte. de Ste-Marie   99.72.31.02   2 km from Redon*

An establishment that lives up to its name. Eels feature prominently on its menus, along with pike and perch from the river Vilaine that flows past its door. It is a stone-faced typically Breton house, converted by the Robert family into a small unpretentious hotel. The setting is idyllic, on a particularly peaceful stretch of the river; in summer you can actually sit on the river bank to eat and drink.

The rooms are freshly decorated and excellent value at 195f. Menus from 80f.

'A real hideaway, much patronised by fishermen and boating people who moor on the river bank ten yards from the hotel. We occupied three spacious single rooms, each with bath and w.c. at a special price of 150f each. The rooms are bare but spotless and the menu simple but adequate'. Susan Zivkovic.

'Well decorated room with en suite shower room for 185f. Good value, with beautiful view overlooking the river. The only problem was that there was nowhere to hang our clothes. Food at 78f was good value. Recommened'. Bernard Lloyd.

Map 3G **RENNES** 35000 (I. et V.) – *Mkt: Every day in Les Halles*

The administrative and cultural capital of Brittany, lacking the immediate charm of its long-term rival, Nantes, but, thanks to its two universities, a lively city, always animated by a population of chattering students. Parking is diabolical; best make for the section of the Vilaine now covered over and used as a car park. Ask for Le Parking Nouvelles Galeries and you will be within walking distance of all the action.

Until the early 18th century here was a city of mediaeval black-and-white timbered houses, separated by narrow winding streets, but a fire that blazed for six days in 1720 changed all that. Most of the centre was razed and nowadays only the 'Vieux Rennes' area round the cathedral gives any feeling of an old Breton town. Here there are cobbled streets, narrow crooked houses, over-hanging gables, beams galore, to activate the sentimental tourist's Kodak, but of the Rennais in this quarter there are few – for them the heart of their city is a few blocks eastwards, the spacious pl. de la Mairie, where the students and the pigeons foregather and the flowers festoon the baroque town hall, designed by the architect Gabriel, appointed by Louis XV to build a new city.

But the most noteworthy building of all (pity about the lumpish cathedral) is undoubtedly the former Breton Houses of Parliament, now the law courts, which dominate the pl. du Palais with their elegant 17th-century ensemble, designed by the Palais de Luxembourg's architect. You can visit its Hall of the Great Pillars, *via* a series of impressively decorated rooms culminating in the panelled Grand' Chambre, which used to be the parliamentary debating chamber.

A short walk from here, in a north-eastern direction, leads to the Thabor Gardens, an unusually calm retreat in the heart of a city, good for a picnic or restorative. It used to be the garden of the Benedictine abbey and some of the cloistered serenity seems to have endured in its 1,080 hectares of park, flower beds and shrubberies.

Most of the hotels are in the newer area, south of the river, centering on the pl. de la Gare. The old **Du Guesclin** is here, but alas, the colourful façade is more interesting than the interior, now distressingly plasticised under its Minimote owners. However the new Salad Bar might be useful for a cheap light lunch – 65f menu, open every day.

Assessing the number of Michelin stars and Gault-Millau toques gives a useful idea of the character of the city. In Rennes single stars and toques are liberally dotted about, but no more than that. This I take to mean that here is no great gastronomic centre but no shortage of reasonably affluent residents and businessmen. The students are beginning to make their presence felt, encouraging the opening of several new bistros, *crêperies*, pizza parlours, but generally eating here is a reliable, but unexciting and expensive experience.

Le Président
(H)M   *27 av. Janvier   99.65.42.22   Garage   AE, DC, V*

Undoubtedly my first choice. Central, quiet, thanks to sound-proofing, no parking problems, efficient friendly staff and most attractively

furnished and well-equipped rooms and bathrooms. No plastic here.
Worth every penny of 325–375f for a double.

Le Sévigné
(H)M   *47 av. Janvier   99.67.27.55   AE, EC, V*

Nothing like as stylish as **Le Président** but cheaper, equally central, and
useful as a fall-back. It also has the advantage of a restaurant next door
with the same name but different management, which specialises in
Alsation food, and very good too. Allow around 90f for the *à la carte*
consumption of *choucroute*, or excellent beef steaks, followed by
splendid desserts, but note that the restaurant is closed on Saturday
lunch and Sunday. The hotel rooms are modern and efficient and cost
from 230–295f.

Anne de Bretagne
(H)M   *4 r. Tronjolly*

A large insistently modern hotel in a new section of the city, south of
the river, but still within walking distance of the centre. 390–480f.
   *'New, clean and comfortable. Twin bedded rooms excellently
furnished with modern bathrooms; staff courteous and friendly. Would
certainly stay there again.' – C. Comley.*

Le Corsaire
(R)M   *52 r. d'Antrain   99.36.33.69   Cl. Sun. p.m.; 1/8–15/8*

The r. d'Antrain runs north of the pl. Ste.-Anne, in a straight line from
the pl. de la Mairie. A smart little navy-blue lacquered restaurant,
whose chef has also become patron. Stick to the 108f weekdays 150f
otherwise menu and you can't grumble at the value. Good wine list,
with Touraine wines especially recommendable.

Le Palais
(R)M   *7 pl. du Parlement   99.79.45.01   Cl. Sun. p.m.; Mon.   CB, AE, DC*

Chef M. Tizon, has made all the difference to what I slated as a disaster
in the first edition. Michelin thinks so too and has awarded a rosette for
his cooking. Seafood is No 1. priority, but his duck – fed for three
weeks on honey and figs prior to despatch – is a miracle of delicate
flavourings, as is his chicken with coriander. Desserts are something
special too, particularly the millefeuille.
   Catch this one while you can – a menu at 100–125f (weekdays) from
a Michelin-starred chef is not easy to track down. The 160f version
includes wine and is wonderfully good value. Reports please for an
arrow.

Chouin
(R)M   *12 r. d'Isly   99.30.87.86   Cl. Aug.; two weeks in Dec./Jan.; Sun. Mon.*

Listen to the locals and eat here. **Chouin** is a splendid fish shop,
proffering all manner of marine creatures, in glistening colourful

heaps, on marble slabs. Next door is a little black and white restaurant, with portholes and lifebelts in case you hadn't got the message. But high quality fish doesn't come cheap anywhere, and if you take, say, a dozen prime oysters and a helping of perfectly grilled pearly white turbot, expect a bill of around 200f. Mercifully the white wines here are not expensive, and there is a lunchtime menu of three courses for 99f. Or, of course, you could settle, as I did, for just a steaming bowl of *moules à la crème*, with bread mopper-up, for 35f. In any case you will get value for money.

Ti-Koz
(R)M-L   *3 r. St.-Guillaume   99.79.33.89   Cl. Aug.; Sun.   DC, EC*

Du Guesclin was a local lad who made good six centuries ago and whose name keeps cropping up all over France and is far from forgotten in his home territory. Dinan was his home but it was at Rennes that he first won fame in the jousting lists and at Rennes that he was subsequently knighted for his successes in a series of military campaigns against France's enemies, particularly the English. He ended up High Constable of France. They say **Ti-Koz** was his home, as well it might have been, in all its crooked, dark beaminess. Americans love it, of course, but it doesn't rely entirely on its antiquity to bring in the customers. The 128f weekday menu with wine is the one I recommend – marinaded raw salmon and haddock surprisingly delicious, then a hot fish terrine, *magret* of duck with blackcurrants, cheese and *pâtisserie* but prices range from 98–225f. Wines are splendid but pricey and service leisurely, so pick the right occasion.

La Cotriade
(R)M   *40 r. St.-Georges   99.63.34.76   Cl. Sat. lunch; Sun. lunch; Mon.   EC*

The r. St.-Georges is one of the most picturesque in Rennes. It runs eastwards from the pl. du Palais, is cobbled, bordered with immensely old buildings, and newly blessed with a selection of small restaurants; something for everyone, from *crêperies* to Italian, and half a dozen bistros, the best of which is *La Cotriade*, one of Rennes' most popular restaurants. Not hard to see why – small, beamed, very pretty indeed, original cooking – leave room for their *feuillantine de poires caramélisées et son coulis de fruits rouges* – and a warm welcome from the moustachioed patron. Good house wine – Muscadet, Bordeaux or Burgundy – *en carafe*. Menus from 70f (lunch) to 175f.

La Chope
(R)S   *3 r. de la Chalotais   99.79.34.54   Cl. Sun.   AC, EC, DC*

The best-known brasserie in Rennes, near the pl. de la République, and popular with the students, since it doesn't throw them out until midnight. It was founded in 1936 by the grandfather of the present owners, Michel and Jean-Claude. Straightforward brasserie staples like *choucroute* or *cassoulet*, all well done but some more individual items too, like *rouelles de coquilles St.-Jacques*. Good value at 70f.

South of the river down the r. de Nemours to the pl. H. Commeurec are the central markets, open every day except Sundays and fêtes. After a stroll around, sniffing, admiring, envying, some light refreshment might be in order. Make for:

La Pâtisserie
(R)S   *34 blvd de la Liberté   Cl. Sun.*

Not only a pâtisserie, good for elevenses or tea, but a good choice for a light lunch. So good in fact that the queues start to form, so get there early or late to get a table, and enjoy a set lunch for 45f, which includes not only service but wine too.

Le Piano Blanc
(R)M   *rte de Saint-Foix   99.67.37.74   Cl. 1/1–7/1; Sun.*

A very unusual restaurant indeed, and especially useful if you do not wish to get embroiled in the centre of the city. Take the Route de la Prévalaye off the western ring road (next after the Vannes exit) to find an unprepossessing exterior disguising one of the most attractive, and certainly the most original, restaurants around. It gets its name from the white grand piano which dominates one of the dining-rooms – all *fin de siècle*, lacquered walls, potted palms. In summer it is particularly popular because of the courtyard area where it is most agreeable to sit by the fountain and sip and sup, but the value of the lunch menu – 125f (lunch only) or 168f for three interesting courses – draws businessmen from the city all year round, and it is wise to book.

In the evenings there is sometimes music, centering round that piano and then the *à la carte* will cost around 250f. The food is as attractive as the surroundings, leaning towards *nouvelle cuisine*, with dishes like *coussin de loup à la mousseline de persil*, and *terrine de fruits en crème d'amandes au sirop de framboise*.

Well worth discovering. Coming from the centre of the city, the rte. de la Prévalaye is the extension of the bd. Voltaire.

The above are the entries from FE5, updated and re-assessed. Since the time when they were compiled Rennes has blossomed gastronomically. The fact that this is a working town and not a tourist honeypot ensures a regular year-round trade from locals who will promptly move over to the opposition if standards drop and prices increase. There are now dozens of excellent restaurants, too many to describe in detail in this book; students and families prefer to eat in that bastion of provincial French life – the brasserie – and there are plenty of those too. So below is a list of the best of the considerable bunch, each one recommended by a local, with the basic facts attached. Any reader's recommendation will lead to further inspection and a more comprehensive account in the next edition.

list following

(New)

l'Escu de Funfao   (L)   *11r. Chapitre   99.79.13.10*   Lunch menu at 115f, next one up 195f

Le Florian   (M)   *r. Arsenal   99.67.25.35*   Midweek menu at 97f, otherwise 115f.

Le Gourmandin (M) *4 pl. Bretagne 19.30.42.01* Eat on the terrace. 75f lunch, 98–150f.

l'Ouvrée *18 pl Lices 99.30.16.38* On the main market square. Great atmosphere. 80f, 125f, 170f.

Le Piré *23 r. Mal-Joffre. 99.79.31.41m* Generally considered Rennes' no. 1. Bargain menus at 90f up to 200f.

l-Avant Scène (S) *8 Galeries Arcades 99.79.44.63* Carte from 70f.

Le Cortez (S) *11 pl. Champ Jacquet.* Good grills and salads on terrace of pleasant old square.

Le Galopin (S) Good brasserie.

Le Grain de Sable *2 rue Dames 19.30.78.18* Charcoal grills, carte from 70f.

Le Kerlouan (S) *99.36.83.02.* Near the parliament. Best crêperie.

Le Serment de Viun (S) *20 bd. La Tour d'Auvergne* 19.30.99.30 Brasserie with good wines. Menus from 70f.

Le Tire Bouchon *15 pl. Ste Anne 99.79.43.43* Take the plats du jour. Good wine carte from 60f.

Map 1F   LA RICHARDAIS 35780 (I. et V.) 3 km S of Dinard on the D 114

If approaching from St.-Malo don't follow the signs to la Richardais after the barrage, but turn right towards Dinard to find:

Le Petit Robinson
(HR)M *99.46.14.82 Cl. 15/11–15/12; Tues. p.m. o.o.s.; Wed.*

Previously recommended as a popular restaurant but now with seven good rooms. One I liked particularly overlooking the rear garden had a bath and cost 280f. Others range from 240–330f. Friendly M. Nicol does the welcoming. His 95f menu is the locals' favourite – it was packed when I was last there, but there for 120f you get five courses including sole of a size that would alone write off the menu price back home.

Au Puits des Gourmets
(R)S *37 r. de Dinard. 99.88.54.45 Open every day in summer, by reservation only winter evenings.*

One of those roadside cafe bars that you would pass by every time unless someone had suggested a longer look. Fortunately someone did and what I believe is going to be a treasure was revealed. For a start all the terrines for starters are home-made – always a good sign – and the plats du jours are barbecues on the terrace, or cous-cous, or just crepes if that's what you fancy. The vibes were highly propitious – more reports please.

Map 4C   **RIEC-SUR-BÉLON** 29340 (Finistère) 4.5 km SE of Pont Aven

4 km away on the right bank of the river Bélon, via the D 24, well
signed:

➤ **Chez Jacky**
(R)M *98.06.90.32   Cl. 1/10–Easter.*

Jacky, alas, has gone to the great oysterbed in the sky, but he could
have no fitter memorial than this adorable little restaurant (no longer
just a degustation/bar) built over the sweetest curve of the sweetest
river in Brittany. The view from the picture window is of verdant banks,
pines, fishing boats, yachts, and the bubbling tanks where the doomed
crustaceans spend their last pampered days.

It is such a treat to eat glorious simple food in glorious simple
surroundings. The effect at Chez Jacky is deliberately rustic, the china
and napkins are white, seating is on slatted benches and there are no
cloths on the tables. The menu of course is fittingly fishy. Belon oysters
are famous and there is no more appropriate place to enjoy them than
beside the Belon. You can freak out on nothing but. Cheapest are the
creuzes at 70f a dozen; *les plats* the prime specimens cost 100f.
Mussels and several varieties of clam come raw, *à la meuniere* or
stuffed. There are lobsters, crabs and spider crabs. Three 'fish of the
day' offered us sole, skate and haddock. And thats about it. Wonderful.

Its perfectly possible to get away with a bill of under £10 – say fish
soup and a huge bowl of mussels, both superb. Its perfectly possible to
spend 300f on a boggling *plâteau de fruits de mer*, including oysters,
lobsters – you name it. Forget the puds – boring.

Such excellence means that Jacky is always full. Midweek in a
dismal spring period when generally restaurateurs were wringing their
hands and wondering if the recession was going to be the end of them,
Jacky was packed. We were chuffed that we had booked a window
table in good time.

A very special place and arrowed accordingly.

Map 5F   **LA ROCHE-BERNARD** 56130 (Morbihan) 40 km SE of Vannes,
95 km SW of Rennes

A perfect anchorage, with old and new harbours, on the river Vilaine,
upriver of the *barrage.* The river is particularly attractive just here, wide
and tree-lined; two ancient cannons defend the entrance, many masts
swim in the early morning mists beneath the great new bridge.

The main street is dull, but the old quarter leading down from the
pl. du Bouffay to the creek is picturesquely cobbled and geraniumed.

Market day is Thursday, in the square flanked by:

Auberge des deux Magots

(HR)M   *pl. du Bouffay   99.90.60.75   Cl. 6/10–22/10; 15/12–15/1; Sun. p.m.; Mon. o.o.s.;*   P.

Large comfortable bedrooms, well furnished, with lots of character. One luxurious double with bath and loo costs 485f and the cheapest with bath is 290f. M. Joel Morice is patron-chef and prepares copious and good menus from 85f.

Hôtel de Bretagne

H(S)   *15 Crespel de Latouche   99.90.60.65   Cl. Sat.; Nov–Easter.*

At the other end of the town, near the new bridge. Without the character of the Deux Magots perhaps, but the rooms are spotlessly clean, good-sized, well-equipped with excellent bathrooms 280–330f.

L'Auberge Bretonne

HR(L)   *2 pl. Dugesclin.   99.90.60.28   Fax 99.90.85.00   Cl. 9/1–26/1 and 14/11–2/12; Thurs. and Fri. lunch*

At the top of the main street in a small square.

Established as a top Breton restaurant, with patron-chef Jacques Thorel now the proud owner of two Michelin stars and an 18 rating in Gault-Millau. His particular line is fresh, vegetables and herbs – the restaurant overlooks a 'jardin potager', which supplies his customers with a dewy-fresh choice. He also insists on buying most of his other ingredients locally or raises them himself on the farm, bought expressly to make sure that he gets exactly the breed and variety her prefers. His other passions are drag horses and the clarinet, so as you can see he is a man of many parts.

In order to earn a second rosette it is not enough just to cook perfectly perfect ingredients; you must add a touch of imagination, preferably well sauced with genius. And this Jacques achieves. To couple lobster with pineapple is dicing with perfect balance. And this Jacques achieves. To stuff a guinea fowl with macaroni and truffles is risking losing the savour of all three. Which Jacques does not do. To combine angelica, melon, fraises des bois and rhubarb in one crème glacée is asking to be accused of overdoing it. And this Jacques avoids. If you can catch his 120f lunch-time menu you're in tremendous luck, otherwise it will be 210, 350, 400 or 450f.

There are now nine rooms, with varying degrees of elegance and comfort, reflected in the wide price range of 450–850f.

Le Cardinal

(R)M   *99.70.79.41   Cl. Mon. lunch; Tues. 3/1–4/2*

In a prime position overlooking the river, this was once the custom house. Nowadays it houses a large bar, whose wares can be sampled on the terrace, a pizzeria land and on the first floor a vast light-flooded restaurant, with food surprisingly good considering that the proprietors might well consider they had got it made without bothering to cook well. Lots of good fish on menus from 85f and a sensible wine list.

Map 5F   **ROCHEFORT-EN-TERRE** 56220 (Morbihan) 25 km NW of Redon

---

Clinging to a spur overlooking the deep valleys of the Arz and Gueuzon rivers, this is one of the prettiest villages in Brittany. The main street is lined with 17th-century granite houses, whose owners vie with one another for the Best-Kept-Windowbox. Flowers tumble everywhere, their geranium-reds and hydrangea-blues enlivening the greyness of mediaeval fortress ruins, old gateway, horseshoe covered market, and Our Lady of Tronchaye's Church. A *tronchaye* is the bole of a tree, where a statue of the Virgin was found by a shepherd a thousand years ago; the church was built on that spot. There is a famous *pardon* here on the third Sunday in August.

It's a favourite excursion for tourists and to cater for their needs is:

Lion d'Or
(R)M   *97.43.32.80   Cl. 15/11–31/11; 25/2–15/3; Mon. p.m.; Tue.*

A 16th-century coaching inn, as flower-bedecked as the rest of the village. Menus from 90f (lunch) or 120f.

Cafe Breton
(R)S   *97.43.32.60   Open for meals from Easter to 15th September and out of season only for crepes.*

In the main street, one of those old houses, with typical beamy, rustic interiors that seem too good to be true. Can anything as picturesque as this also serve good food. It does, it does. You sit at old oak tables or barrels on benches or dark wood chairs in a wine cave and tuck into 'repas campagnard'. Terrines, salads, casseroles, or just very good galettes and crêpes. Obviously a popular tourist halt, so although its quite a sizeable operation, go early or late if you want to be certain of a table. There are menus from 85f.

Map 2B   **ROCHE MAURICE** 29800 (Finistère) 4 km NE of Landerneau

---

Rearing high on a rock outcrop above the river Élorn and dominated by the ruins of the mediaeval castle built to protect Landerneau. The church of St.-Yves has a Renaissance roof screen with finely carved grotesque figures and a beautiful 16th-century Passion Window; its *enclos paroissial* includes an ossuary with a macabre skeleton issuing a warning to those who gape: 'I'll get you all.' Make hastily for:

Le Vieux Château
(R)S   *4 Grand' pl.   98.20.40.52   Cl. 1/11–20/11; 6/3–27/3*

> For 110f you could have six oysters, *Langoustines armoricaines, gigôt* with *flageolets* and *tarte maison*, but this menu is for weekdays only. Otherwise it's 160f.

Milin an Élorn
(R)S   *Ancienne rte. de Landivisiau   98.20.41.46*

> A picturesque old watermill on the river Élorn, converted into a good *crêperie* and modest grill.

Map 1B   **ROSCOFF** 29211 (Finistère) 5 km N of St.-Pol-de-Léon

---

> Roscoff is foremost a port, or rather a series of ports – the old harbour, the ferry terminal and the new harbour with the gangway into the deep water for the **Ile de Batz** boats at low tide (see p. 38).
>
> This island is the biggest of many, some mere reefs, that lie off the coast, a panorama of unfailing interest. Little coves and beaches surround the headland – you pick the one to suit the weather conditions and your mood.
>
> Most of the animation centres around the quays, where the cafès and bars are always full and the families parade in the early evening sunshine. Or not, as was the case on my last visit, blighted with fog and drizzle. Still the stalwarts battled out to the end of the jetty, more in search of exercise than a view, but when the weather fails – and that is bad luck because the climate is unusually gentle – the town comes into its own and the shops selling souvenirs and fishermens' sweaters do good trade. Even the old 16th-century church gets visited and the plaque commemorating Mary Stuart's landing in 1584 noted.

Le Brittany
(H)M-L   *blvd Ste.-Barbe   98.69.70.78   Fax 98.61.13.29   Rest. cl. Sun. p.m. p.o.s.; Mon. lunch*

> An unexpectedly luxurious hotel overlooking the old harbour. Lovely galleried entrance hall, elegant lounges, stone-walled panelled breakfast room with seaviews framed in its arched windows. Lovely bedrooms from 380–590f with seasonal adjustment and a swimming pool make it worth every penny if you can run to it.
>
> The restaurant has been considerably upgraded since the last edition, and is now known as Le Yachtman. It has been cleverly contrived to make the most of the character of the heavy granite walls without sacrificing light and air. A series of arches allow the sea view to become part of the decor.
>
> Elegant table-settings and cooking by a student of the great Senderens makes this the classiest restaurant in town, but the young waiters see to it that it is never pompous.

A very fishy menu indeed – John Dory cooked with oriental spices, plaice with leeks and cod with bacon are original interpretations of old favourites.

Not too frightening a bill. Menus start at 95–145f.

Bellevue
(HR)M *blvd Jeanne-d'Arc 98.61.23.38 Fax 98.61.11.80 Cl. 15/11–15/3; rest. cl. Wed. o.o.s. CB*

A pleasant little hotel, recommended primarily for its superb view over the port and convenience for the ferry. The 20 rooms are simply but adequately furnished and cost from 260–390f. Demi-pension at 290–330f is obligatory in season. Otherwise menus are from 110f.

'This was a very useful little hotel close to the ferry. We had the 112f menu (there were cheaper and more expensive ones) and thought the food good and varied. Very pleasant atmosphere and service. Good for a one-night stop.' – Kay and Richard Johnson.

➤ **Temps de Vivre**
(R)M *pl. Lacaze-Duthiers 98.61.27.28 Cl. Sun. p.m. o.o.s.; Mon. CB*

It's time that so delightful a little town as Roscoff had its star restaurant and this is it. The view from the windows over to the Ile de Batz alone would make it worth a visit, but there's more, much more. The decor is most conducive to happy eating – all caramel, and vanilla, and Line Crenn's cooking is easily the best in the neighbourhood.

Of course he concentrates on seafood – who wouldn't with such an abundance there for the picking? – but with unusual imagination. His oysters are served warm, on a bed of crunchy just-cooked cabbage, and his lobster comes with artichoke chips. Desserts are something special. Menus from 98f weekdays, or 160f, or 250f.

Arrowed for good cooking in a charming setting.

Reader's Recommendation:

Map 3C   **ROSTRENEN** 17 kms W of Carhaix-Plouguer on the N 164

'Here we found a charming hotel and restaurant, Le Henri IV. The restaurant was immaculate and with a wide range of choice in interesting menus'. Sir Ian and Lady Hogg.

Map 1G   **ROTHÉNEUF** 35400 (I. et V.) 6 km N of St.-Malo

The Rothéneufs were pirates and smugglers who lived here in the 16th-century, a powerful and much respected family. On a rocky headland nearby a priest, Father Foure (who died in 1910) sculptured their legend. His gigantic granite fresco depicting 300 characters makes a unique memorial.

Follow the coast road further west towards Cancale and by turning down an unmarked lane to the left discover an almost landlocked sea, fringed with pines, sheltered, ideal for water sports at high tide and with a lovely beach at low water. Perfect for kids.

There are several hidden beaches, sheltered mini-harbours and tiny islands in this region – look at a map to see all the bays and headlands to give you an idea of which way to head. The drive all the way to Grouin is quite lovely and there are good walks among the sand dunes, along the beaches, through the pine woods.

Hotel Terminus
16 r. des Goëlands   19.56.97.72.   Fax 99.40.59.17   Cl.11/11–13/3

No restaurant here but a very pleasant breakfast room and good value in this generally pricey area. The rooms have all been recently refurbished and cost 260f for one with bath (229f with shower). The beach is a mere 200 metres away. A good family choice, about which I would value some more reports.

Map 1F   **SABLES-D'OR-LES-PINS** 22240 (C. d'A.) 44 km NW of Dinan

---

Well-named indeed. Golden sands and pine trees are what this little resort is all about. The beaches must be a strong candidate for being the finest in Brittany. On a blustery May day, when the sand yachts had the main north-facing beach all to themselves, I found, by climbing over the sand dunes, through the pine woods, another splendid beach, facing due south, so sheltered that sweaters and trousers soon gave way to bikinis. I could easily have spent all day there (and will another time) but a picnic in the pines' shade and wonderful walk following the twists and turns of the river through the sands, round the headland, right over to the little harbour, did very well indeed.

The 'town' is virtually one street, often dusted with fine flying sand when the wind is strong. Not very exciting – all new buildings, custom-built to make the most of the natural advantages of the town's name.

La Voile d'Or
(HR)M   *96.41.42.49   Fax 96.41.55.45   Cl.15/11–15/3; rest. cl. Tue. lunch; Mon. H. cl. mon. o.o.s.*

The rooms are vast and well-equipped, with a superb view of the coast. 50 metres away there is an annexe, La Lagune, with smaller rooms but equally comfortable. Good value at 195–400f.

The restaurant is unusually good and stands on its own merits, not just as an adjunct to the hotel. The sea actually laps the building, so plenty of waves to admire. Lots of fish on the menu, as you might expect. The cheapest menu is 92f, but the quality merits the prices.

Diane
(H)M   *96.41.42.07   Cl. 1/9–1/4   Fax 96.41.42.67*   Some sea views if you crane a little, no restaurant, with a wide choice of rooms to suit all tastes and pockets, from 150–360f.

Morgane
(H)M   *96.41.46.90   Cl. 1/9–1/4*   Smaller, pristine new, no restaurant, garden, terrace, parking. 20 rooms with bath cost from 300–400f.

Les Pins
(HR)S   *96.41.42.20   Cl. 2/10–26/3*   Nice terrace, lots of balconies, 22 rooms at 200–270f. Restaurant 75–170f.

Au Bon Accueil
(H)M   *96.41.42.19   Fax 96.41.57.59   Cl. Oct.–Easter*

Run by the same family for fifty years. All the 38 rooms have recently been modernised and now most have their own bathrooms, for 290–350f. No longer has a restaurant.

Le Manoir St.-Michel
(H)M   *96.41.48.87   Fax 96.41.41.55   Cl. Nov.–1/4*

At **Le Carquois**, 1.5 km NE on the Fréhel road. A converted 16th-century manorhouse – a bit over-converted perhaps, to give a brand new look. The rooms are a bit stereotyped and small for the 250–550f price tag, but they are spotlessly clean and well equipped and there's an expensive air about the terrace furniture. Comfortable, guaranteed quiet, with no obligation to eat in – for those who want a dead safe bet this could be the answer.

Map 5D   **STE.-ANNE-D'AURAY** 56400 (Morbihan) 16 km W of Vannes on the D 779

The largest *pardon* in Brittany is on July 25 and 26 when pilgrims come here from all over France and beyond to pray to the mother of the Virgin Mary. The legend is that Anne was born in Armorica, was married, widowed, travelled to Palestine and re-married producing a daughter, Mary; when she came back to Armorica, she was visited by Jesus.

There are other smaller *pardons* throughout the year and if you are lucky enough to witness one, the costumes and colour are unforgettable. Michelin says severely 'visitors to the pilgrimage closes must respect local traditions and be circumspectly dressed.'

The present elephantine basilica was built in the last century.

➤ **L'Auberge**
(HR)M *56 r. Vannes   97.57.61.55   Cl. Tue. 9/10–23/10 p.m. & Wed. o.o.s.*

Worth making a pilgrimage. Copper pans, Breton lace, a huge log fire gently smouldering provide a welcome on a chill autumn evening. All very bright and cheerful.

Allow plenty of time for decisions. Repas 80f. Every one of the four alternatives had particularly interesting components. As it was the last night of the holiday, I pushed the boat out on the most expensive, at 195f, and relished every mouthful of a terrine of three different mushrooms, chunks of tender *cêpes* contrasting with the puréed *champignons* and *chanterelles*, then superb baby *coquilles St.-Jacques* – lots of 'em swimming (*à la nage*) in a sea of *beurre blanc*, then *magret de canard* sharpened with raspberry vinegar. Unusually, lots of good vegs, including an excellent potato *gâteau*, a hot *crottin* (goats cheese, just melting) with expensive salad, and then a wicked assortment of desserts – six *dégustations* of hot *tarte normande, marquise au chocolate, sorbet d'orange, charlotte aux fraises* and fresh strawberries (o.o.s.).

A note from the chef on the menu, craving clients' patience over the fact that everything depended on the market and was freshly cooked to order, proved unnecessary – the first was quite obvious and the waits not excessive (and in my case welcome between so many courses).

Husband was more than happy on the cheapest menu at 80f, with perfect *oeufs pochés*, a shoulder of lamb braised with fennel and a good cheese board. With cheap house wine, or the alternative of a well-chosen wine list, this all adds up to an unusually good stop, especially since the value of the nine rooms upstairs is as good as the food. A spacious and comfortable double costs 300f and a more modest version is 220f. Aim for one at the rear.

Friendly and helpful owners, the best food I found for miles around at reasonable prices, and excellent bedrooms make this a certain arrow.

'Best meal ever.' Jill Day.

Map 3B   **STE.-ANNE-LA-PALUD** 29127 (Finistère) 16 km N of Douarnenez

---

Turn west of the D 63 towards the Bay of Douarnenez. In the midst of the rather desolate undulations stands Ste.-Anne's chapel, the destination for the great *pardon*, one of the most spectacular in Brittany, that takes place on the last weekend in August, when thousands of pilgrims, stallholders, sightseers flock to this lonely site.

Carry on to the coast for wonderful walks in all directions, along the spectacular sandy beach or above it amongst the dunes. Solitarily stands:

La Plage
(HR)L   *98.92.50.12   Fax 90.30.81.79   Cl. Mid Oct–mid April*

Supposing that absolute peace and tranquillity, allied with supreme comfort, along with superb food, in an outstandingly beautiful natural setting, and supposing again that around 450f for a double room were no object, make for **La Plage**. I have yet to hear of a visitor who did not love it and wish to return.

The building is ugly, modern, white, right on the beach. Inside all is spaciousness, light and luxury, taking full advantage of the marine aspect by having the dining-room overlooking the sea. This is the territory of a combination of talented young local chef, Jean Pierre Glouanec, the patron M. Le Coz, and his son and daughter-in-law. Between them they prepare and serve a remarkable menu at 180f which has clients queueing up to book. The emphasis, predictably, is on seafood – *Salade de rougets à l'huile de noix, bar grillé au beurre blanc, pânaché de poissons*, all faultless, with sauces enhancing not disguising their immaculate freshness. The dessert course is also star quality, particularly the *pâtisserie*. I find it exactly the right combination of traditional ingredients in their prime, with exciting inventiveness not just for inventiveness sake, all totally professional but not pompous. Menu 210f.

All the rooms, as you would expect from a Relais et Château hotel, are comfortable and well equipped, but this is a case for pushing the boat out and going for one on the front. The hotel faces due west and to catch that most spectacular sunset from your own balcony is worth a lot. The best rooms cost 980f and the cheapest 650f. Demi-pension, at 1300–1610f, is obligatory in high season.

There is a swimming pool, tennis court, sauna and games-room, but the biggest attraction of all is the silence.

The rooms have been fully booked, so I cannot confer a personal arrow, but I look forward to doing so soon.

'We enjoyed a quite wonderful stay at the Hotel de la Plage. We found the hotel exactly as you have described it. We took your advice and booked a room overlooking the bay – quite small, but extremely comfortable' Sir Ian and Lady Hogg.

Map 1C   **ST.-ANTOINE-PLOUEZOC'H** 29250 (Finistère) 6 km N of Morlaix on the D 46

The most attractive way to arrive is *via* the D 76 from Morlaix, following the valley of the Dourdouff ('Black Water' in Breton).

Hotel Menez
(H)M   *98.67.28.85   Closing times uncertain*

A substantial granite house standing at a cross roads in the middle of nowhere. Well tended hydrangea garden and immaculate inside too. Ten comfortable well-furnished rooms from 240–270f with bath. No restaurant makes life easier for those who like to eat out.

Map 1F   **ST.-BRIAC-SUR-MER** (I. et V.) 16 km W of St.-Malo

I could wax lyrical about St.-Briac. Dammit, I will wax lyrical about S.-B. After all it's not often you find two perfect horseshoe bays, facing west and south, fringed with pines, fine sand shelving down to water clearer, bluer than the Aegean (if perhaps not quite so warm), blessed with a vista of islands, other bays, many other beaches.

Follow the signs to Les Plages and choose between them, taking a stroll round the headland with the funny château to get bearings, confused by such a plethora of inlets and no glimpse of the way the Channel lies.

The village of St.-Briac, mercifully, slumbers away with only a passing nod at the tourists. Its signposts seem intent on evasion and a wrong turn will lead down narrow streets of little granite houses and cottage gardens. Only one modest hotel and that nowhere near the beach or I might take up residence in it. It's the **Hotel de la Houle** in the main street, but as it was shuttered on the day I wanted to check the bedrooms, I cannot vouch for them. They cost from 120–180f, and the menus start at 85f. Phone 99.88.32.17 and please report to me.

Map 2E   **ST.-BRIEUC** 22000 (C. d'A.) 58 km W of Dinan

A rapidly growing town – the largest in the area, with a busy Saturday market. I don't think I would choose to stay here in summer, but if the coastal weather were dreary I suppose it might make sense to look inland.

Ker Izel
(H)M   *20 r. Gouet   96.33.46.29   AE, DC, EC, V*

In a quiet pedestrianised street not far from the cathedral, with all the rooms recently and most attractively redecorated. A double with bath costs 230–330f. Good breakfasts.

'Yes, a delightful seaside resort, especially for children. The one hotel was very adequate; not full in September and only the French using it. There is a modern single-storey annexe at the back, basic chalet-type rooms with shower and wc. Serviceable if not charming.' Barry Russell.

Reader's Recommendation:

➤ **La Vieille Tour**
(R)M-L   *Port de St. Brieuc 75 r. de la Tour, Plérin   96.33.10.30   Cl. 2/5–10/5 1/10– 7/10; Sun. p.m.; Mon.*

Follow the river on the north bank along the D 24 for 3 unprepossessing kms to find the best restaurant in the area. The *vieille tour* in question is the Cesson tower, now in ruins.

The patron, Michel Hellio, has won a Michelin star for his inspired seafood cooking, duck with homemade pasta, and inventive desserts, all served in a first floor restaurant overlooking the bay of St.-Brieuc, menus at 110, mid-week 175–350f, justify an arrow for outstanding food.

Map 2H **ST BRICE EN COGLES** 35460 I. et V.

Lion d'Or (HR)S
r. Chateaubriand   99.98.61.44   Cl. Sun. p.m. o.o.s.

'We had an entrée of excellent langoustines, followed by salmon and raspberry mouse. With half a bottle of Bordeaux this came to 158f. We can certainly recommend this restaurant.' J. H. Brooks.
Menus from 65f. 22 rooms from 110–250f.

Map 1F **ST.-CAST-LE-GUILDO** 22380 (C. d'A.) 36 km NW of Dinan. –
Mkt: Tues., Fri.

St.-Cast and Le-Guildo together cover the narrow peninsula pointing to St.-Malo at the Pointe de St.-Cast. All round the promontory are scattered beaches of fine sands and rocks and some spectacular views, making it a popular resort.
The most promising hotel, unfortunately, is in the little town, only a step or two from the beach admittedly, but lacking those sea views:

Hotel des Dunes
(HR)M   *r. Primauguet   (96) 41.80.31   Fax 96.41.85.34   Cl. 5/11–20/3; Sun. p.m. & Mon. in Oct.*

Modern, bright, cheerful, efficient, nice patron, M. Feret, and above-average food, much appreciated by the regular *pensionnaires*, who tuck in appreciatively to grilled scallops, *gigôt de lotte à l'ail*, extra good desserts: their demi-pension costs from 335–375f. O.o.s rooms are 310–360f, some with balconies. Menus 100–370f.

Notre · Dame · le · Guildo

On the beach of Pen Guen to the east of the promontory is:

Le Biniou
(R)M   *96.41.94.53   Cl. 21/9–20/3; Tues. o.o.s.*

A trim little restaurant, well recommended locally, with a terrace above the beautiful beach, which judging by the size of the parking must be pretty busy. Rustic but quite smart – not the place for a damp bathing suit. Fishy menus from 98f.

Map 3H   **ST DIDIER** 35220 Châteaubourg. I. et V. 6 kms E of Châteaubourg by D857 and D105.

Pen'Roc
(HR)M   *99.00.33.02   Fax 99.62.30.89   Cl. Sun. p.m. o.o.s.; school holidays.*

An attractive stone built building, sympathetically modernised, set in peaceful countryside near the village of St. Didier. M. Froc is patron-chef, offering interesting dishes contrived from local ingredients, some from his own garden. Excellent menus from 105f.

The rooms are deliberately rustique but well modernised, with good bathrooms, comfortable and warm in winter, when prices for a double room start at 330f. In high season it goes up to 380f, with a top price of 500f for an apartment. These prices seem justified when the new heated swimming pool, gym and sauna are taken into consideration – sprats to catch the conference mackerel, I suppose. The usual impersonality that goes with catering for numbers not people is missing here though. I found the Frocs and the staff friendly and helpful.

Map 1F   **ST.-JACUT** 22750 (C. d'A.) 8 km SW of Dinard

Set on a long spit of land between two deep bays, with an unsurpassed panorama of wild rocks, sands and neighbouring headlands. Boasts eleven beaches, so there should always be one out of the wind.

Le Vieux Moulin
(HR)M   *96.27.71.62   Cl. 1/11–15/3*

Set in a colourful garden, a truly individual hotel, contrived from a 15C windmill, whose circular walls give eccentric charm to some of the rooms.

There are two annexes, one opposite the hotel and one facing the sea open only from June–mid Sept. The rooms vary greatly in comfort, views and amenities. Demi-pension costs from 285–330f per person per day. Menus start at 90f.

Readers' letters speak volumes: *'I was recently at the Moulin, which is run by Monsieur and Madame Papin. I am now 43 and have been going there on a regular basis about twice a year since I was 6. It is an unpretentious place with top quality food cooked entirely by M. Papin. Excellent value. So I tend to go there to unwind. Many other regular guests have been going there for years. From father to son.'* Beatrice Potter.

'We ventured en famille – grandparents, ourselves, two children of three and 1½ and my sister, for a special holiday to celebrate my parents' fortieth wedding anniversary. After the most exhaustive scrutiny of FE5 we agreed on the Vieux Moulin and were not disappointed. Our specific comments are:-

'Wonderfully peaceful location on a quiet peninsula with eleven clean sandy beaches. Ideal in this respect for children. Building of great character and interesting history. Rooms not very large but beaufifully furnished. Food is typically good French cuisine – not tremendously varied but of high standard and extremely plentiful. Beautiful soups and fish. Very much a traditional family-run hotel – M. & Mms Papin with their daughter and son in law. Great attention to detail – lovely flowers and garden. Magnificent special anniversary dinner for my parents – an evening to remember. We also particularly appreciated the excellent and most friendly staff.' Fiona Yeomans.

Well, M et Mme Papin – you couldn't have written a better testimonial yourselves. I think these two letters say it all.

Map 1C   **ST.-JEAN-DU-DOIGT** 29228 (Finistère) 17 km NE of Morlaix

This village, nestling in the shelter of a deep valley which later widens out to the sea, derives its curious name from the story that 500 years ago a young man from the neighbouring parish of Plougasnou chanced upon the finger of St. John the Baptist, no less, and bequeathed it to the village. By so doing he ensured that every year on St. John's Day those who bathe their eyes in 'the water of the finger' that flows from the gorgeous Italianate fountain in the parish close will have perfect eyesight. The villagers must have got tired of the sceptics, for a tetchy notice pinned upon the church says 'contrary to what is written in many guidebooks, the finger of St. John is not on public display.'

Le Ty Pont
(HR)S   *98.67.34.06   Cl. 15/10–Easter; 30/10–30/3; Sun. p.m. & Mon. o.o.s.*

A modest little pub in the village centre, popular with the locals, and offering some of the cheapest accommodation I found in the area. A double room – and they are all perfectly adequate – costs from 140–230f and the menus start at 65f.

Map 1F **ST.-MALO** 35400 (I. et V.) 65 km from Avranches – *Mkt: Thurs., Fri.*

For the British, probably the best-known of all Breton towns, and deservedly so. But far from typically Breton.

The Malouins have always been a breed apart, noted for their independence, with a motto 'Malouin first and foremost, Breton perhaps, French if there is anything left.' This distinctive character really does still exist, deriving from centuries of sea and land battles, and the fact that until the 18th-century the rock on which the town is built was linked to the mainland only by a sandbank, tide-covered for most of the day. Follow the signs to *Intra Muros* (Within the Walls) and you step into another world, which certainly accounts for some of the town's appeal.

The rebel Malouins fiercely resisted the idea of being linked to either Brittany or France, refusing to recognise Jean de Montfort as Duke of Brittany and defending the town under the leadership of privateers like Du Guesclin and Morfouace, still local heroes. Jean IV had to blockade the town, building the Solidor Tower in St.-Servan in the process, before the inhabitants finally submitted, but at the first opportunity they broke away to become French subjects. Their reluctant allegiance to either side swung to and fro as Charles VI gave the troublesome town back to Brittany in 1415, reverting again to France when Duchesse Anne of Brittany married Charles VIII. It was she who had engraved on the castle tower 'Quic en groigne, ainsi sera, c'est mon plaisir' – 'Grumble as you may, it will be thus because I wish it so', but the loyalty of the citizens was to remain to St.-Malo first and foremost.

The Quic-en-Groigne museum is now installed in this tower, with waxwork figures of local historic scenes. The Musée d'Histoire contains relics of some of the unusually large number of famous sons of the town, like Jacques Cartier, who almost by accident (he was looking for a northern passage to India) discovered Newfoundland in 1534. The subsequent opening up of the St. Lawrence seaway and of Canada brought great prosperity to St.-Malo, based on cod-fishing off Newfoundland and the fur trade. In the 17th century it was France's largest port.

The obstinate Malouin character produced a number of privateers (licensed pirates), like Surcouf, the last and greatest of them all, who, after legendary feats of dering-do, like capturing the treasure-laden *Kent* from the English in 1800, became the richest ship-owner in France and a Baron of the French Empire.

The air of St.-Malo seems to have produced a fine crop of men devoted to the pen as well as to the sword. Chateaubriand was born here and is buried on the island of Le Grand Bé, his grave facing out to sea as he wished. At low water you can walk out to le Grand Bé, one of a string of islets surrounding the town, some only visible when the tide goes down. Anyone who has sailed into the harbour will be aware of the hundreds of dragons' teeth hazards that severely test navigation skills.

Saint-Malo

An excellent viewpoint for this offshore panorama is from the ramparts, and two walks right round the town are a must, with completely different aspects at low and high water. The walls are one of the few relics of the original town. the greatest battle of all in St.-Malo's colourful history was fought, sadly, within living memory, in 1944, when three-quarters of the town was destroyed, but subsequently skilfully rebuilt in the solid 18th century style. Its cathedral, St. Vincent's, has now been fully restored from 12th century nave to 18th century façade.

It's altogether a most agreeable place to stroll around, to shop and then to sit in one of the cafés in the square, resting cobble-tired feet and watching all the invariable activity. Lively all the year round, so a good off-season choice.

The beaches, sandy and rocky, are wonderful here just below the walls, at nearby Paramé and *via* a delightful ferry ride, at Dinard, so it's ideal for children too.

Just outside the walls is the vast yacht harbour, with some mighty impressive boats tied up, and the lock into the Rance. Many's the frustrated hour we've spent there shaking fists at the lock-keeper, who, green light or no, is knocking off early for lunch, condemning us to another unscheduled day locked in, when the plan was to be out to sea or exploring the river.

A trip up the Rance to Dinan by whatever means is a must. With highly attractive towns at either end of the voyage and the most gorgeous scenery in between, it's worth doing some homework on the timetables at the tourist office. It's a longish trip, very dependent on the tides; a car at the other end would be ideal.

Through the massive gateway into the heart – the cobbled Place Richelieu. This is first choice for breakfast, drinks, tea and, at any time of day, people-watching. In April after a stuffy night on the ferry, we decanted into the Cafe de l'Ouest for our first outdoor breakfast of the year, the first crunch of baguette, the first bitter coffee, to the accompaniment of screeching gulls, with the flag of St. Mâlo – a white lion on red quarter and three blue quarters – fluttering above the Hôtel de Ville. The salty air revived our short-of-sleep spirits and we thankfully gulped lungfulls of Gallic air.

Generally I would recommend staying outside the walls and strolling into the town for dinner at one of the many restaurants. (Check up the menus along the ramparts and preferably choose the one with a babble of French voices.) For FE5 I investigated the choice along the beach stretching all the way round la Grande Plage, a truly fabulous beach, extending through Paramé to Rothéneuf, picking out those with sea views, but this time around I did find a few possibilities within the walls:

INTRA MUROS

Hotel de la Cité
(H)M   *Pl. Vauban.   99.40.55.40   Fax 99.40.10.04*

At last someone has converted an old building just below the ramparts, near the Aquarium and beaches, into a comfortable hotel. There are 39 rooms, small but pretty, partly sound-proofed (not a busy road), for 435–515f. The price reflects the shortage of accommodation in the old town. Good breakfasts for 40f.

Quic en Groigne
(H)M   *8 r. Estress   99.40.86.00   Fax 99.40.11.65   open year round*

In the heart of the old town, peaceful at night, 15 pleasant well-equipped rooms are supervised by a pleasant patronne. The 384–444f price tag includes two breakfasts, so this is a good buy. In low season try negotiating.

Ajoncsd'Or
(H)M   *10 r. des Forgeurs   99.40.85.03   Fax 99.40.80.70   Cl. 16/11–16/12*

There are only 22 rooms here but if feels bigger. Modern fairly boring decor but well-equipped rooms and a central position with good parking and a bar. Cheerful. M. & Mme Robin are proprietors.
  Cheapest prices for a double room in low season is 300f, 350 in mid season and 400–520 in late June to mid September.

Hotel du Palais
(H)M   *8 r. Toulier   99.40.07.30   Fax 99.40.29.53   Cl. 7/12–22/11; 8/11–25/12*

Central again, 18 rooms, functional but well equipped with baths, tv etc. Run by M. & Mme Guegueniat. 290–370f.

ON THE BEACH

Logis de Brocéliande
(H)M   *43 chaussée du Sillon   99.62.62.00   Fax 99.40.42.47   Cl. Dec.*

A stylish little 19C hotel with smart furnishing, a garden, and only nine bedrooms which means the personal touch from Mme Auffret. They are named after Arthurian characters – Guinevere, Lancelot etc. Absence of a restaurant gives you the chance to sample St.-Malo's many possibilities, even in high season. There are three apartments and two family rooms 300–500f.

Les Charmettes
(H)S   *64 blvd Hébert   99.56.07.31*

There have been considerable changes here since I first wrote about Les Charmettes. A new owner, Gilles Lécuyer, has certainly upgraded some of the rooms and twelve of them now have showers and loos, at 120f.
  The position, of course, is still prime and the prices still put Les Charmettes in a most unusual category in this area – a cheap hotel overlooking the sea. At 320f for a family room or 150f for a double – at the very least it must be a good budget base.
  'We had two rooms with basin loo and shower, very good value for the 200f we paid. I booked in advance and I must admit when we first arrived at the road entrance I was slightly concerned about the setting,

but the beautiful sea view, along with the friendliness of Gilles Lecuyer, more than compensated for adverse first impressions. I would thoroughly recommend Les Charmettes. The late night drinks session with Gilles in his bar nearly made us miss the ferry home!' Anne Bailey.

'Our room faced the sea and had a balcony. The en suite shower was very clean, the towels changed every day. M. Lecuyer served our continental breakfast. He was very pleasant and there was a good atmosphere. The garden area facing the sea had tables and chairs but no flowers, one thing I missed. It was a simple hotel, not plush, but all we needed. Very cheap for France. I would recommend it.' Sylvia Nicoll.

➤ **Le Villefromoy**
(H)M-L *34 blvd Chateaubriand 99.40.92.20 Fax 99.56.79.49 Cl. 15/11–3/3*

I think this must be one of the nicest hotels I know. It stands one road back from the sea, but from my balcony a gap allowed a fabulous view of the water and coastline. A drink in the evening sunshine there completed the purring satisfaction at having discovered such a gem.

La Villefromoy.

Jean-Guillaume Douët de la Villefromoy was an *antiquaire*, as was his father before him, and when he converted their 1860s house in 1984, he furnished it with beautiful pieces of polished furniture and objects d'art. But this is no museum. The rooms are light and bright, from the yellow of the staircase to the sky-blue of the salon; there is spaciousness along with the graciousness.

The bedrooms are all furnished with luxury but restraint (perhaps I appreciated the cool creams and whites all the more after a regime of the orange and black vinyl beloved by so many French hoteliers). The only hint of decadence was the mock marbling in the splendid bathrooms but even that was discreetly, beigely, inoffensive.

The hotel is really two houses joined by a clever glass passageway. The rooms in the older house, facing the sea, are obviously the best in this expensive area, and I didn't begrudge a franc of the 700f for mine, no. 3. Those facing the road (not a busy one) are equally comfortable and attractive but, without the view, they cost only 420f.

Breakfast came with a unique linen cover, drawstrung like a pudding cloth, over the hot croissant dish. Pity the jam and butter were plastic but really that was the only fault I could find with the whole experience.

M. Douët de la Villefromoy is a friendly and attentive host, but like other members of the *Châteaux Independants* who have turned their lovely homes into lovely hotels, he does not set out to offer the kind of service that goes with a big staff. If you insist on having your bed turned down and pyjamas spread out, with a chocolate on your pillow, you will be disappointed here. But you'd be missing a beaut.

In fact I found it hard to leave, after an early morning walk along that fabulous beach, tide obligingly well out, heading towards the pleasing prospect of the turrets and towers of St.-Malo, with only a jogger and a little boy turning cartwheels to share the bay. Here's one I shall certainly return to, given half an excuse. Meanwhile a certain arrow.

Alexandra

(HR)M   *138 Boul. Hébert*   99.56.11.12   Fax 99.56.30.03   Cl. 15/12–31/12

An imposing modernised hotel of 43 efficient bedrooms, near the Thalosso centre, with direct access to the beach and terrace for sunning and enjoying a light meal from the 'carte brasserie'. There is an adjoining restaurant l'**Etrave**, more expensive . . . All bright and cheerful, with pleasant lounge and breakfast room overlooking the sea. 500–950f depending on size and season.

Beaufort

(H)M   *25 chaussée Sillon*   199.40.99.99   Fax 99.40.99.52

Totally renovated in 1991, this 19C building now sports a charming pink and white facade and a light and airy peach and blue lounge, making the best of its superb position overlooking the beach, to which it has direct access. The terrace is a super location in which to have an evening drink or to catch up on the paperbacks. All the 21 rooms have good bathrooms and English T.V. channels, some have their own balconies. A very agreeable upmarket choice at 355–780f. Reports needed please.

The restaurant scene in St.-Malo is rapidly improving. The **Duchesse Anne** used to be the only quality choice and two years ago when I suggested to a local that there were plenty of smaller restaurants to choose from he looked over his specs and said firmly 'but not of quality, Madame'. He was right then perhaps but several new welcome possibilities have since appeared.

To the left of the Porte St.-Vincent stretches a row of eateries, tables on pavement, displays of shellfish, agreeable bustle; we have eaten at most of them over the years, when a pleasant situation in the heart of this most colourful town took precedence over a gastronomic experience. You can hardly go wrong there with a plateful of *moules* or a dozen oysters and you don't need any guide's advice when you can see for yourself what looks good on which plate. Indisputably the aristocrat of this bunch, crowned with a Michelin star, is:

➤ **La Duchesse Anne**
(R)M-L *5 pl. Guy La Chambre   99.40.87.53   Cl. Dec.; Jan.; Wed.; Sun. p.m. o.o.s.*

I hardly dared go back to the **Duchesse Anne**. It was our port in many a storm. From earliest sailing days, I remembered its familiar old-fashioned décor, comfortable *patronne*, delicious straightforward food, with great affection. But for many years now it has been *the* destination for English yachties, who telephone weeks ahead from London to book a table, and gain sublime courage in the face of all manner of marine adversity at the thought of the meal ahead. They sit there in their brass-buttoned blazers happily braying brave experiences and weather forecasts to their fellow mariners across the room, while crunching through their annual fix of lobster and oysters. Weekends are planned around the **Duchesse Anne**, Jersey millionaires hovercraft across for lunch, Rolls are parked outside. Surely by now this fame must have changed the place, they must have 'smartened' it up a bit, *noove cuis.* must have arrived, the prices must be sky-high?

But, miraculously, no. There were the remembered varnished walls, tiled floors, lace curtains, coat-rail in the middle of the two small rooms, buttercups and forget-me-nots on the tables. Best of all, it is still very, very French. Prudent locals book well ahead to defend themselves against the Brit take-over, as I realised to my cost when I tried to get a booking for the same day; I had to re-arrange an entire week's schedule to come back later for the first available space, but I'm very glad I did.

No set menu, everything cooked to order, but no long wait for the first course; the service, under Madame's all-seeing eye, is so efficient that if you don't deploy delaying tactics you could be out in an hour.

I had fresh asparagus – and I mean fresh – generous, with perfect hollandaise, then a superb sole stuffed with lobster. Desserts proved dull and it would be well worth accepting the invitation to order the speciality *Tarte Tatin* at the start of the meal. It arrived, before my envious eyes, on the next table, oozing caramel, surmounted with *crème fraîche*.

Allow around 200f to eat from the carte.

> *'Superb, and exactly as you state in every respect, from the
> buttercups and Madame's supervision, to the heavenly Tarte Tatin.'*
> Mrs P. Quayle.

Chez Gilles

(R)M   *2 r. Pie qui boit   99.40.97.25   Cl. 17/11–30/11; 2/2–8/2. Sun. p.m. o.o.s.;
Thur.*

Bright, modern, efficient, full of locals, it offers an excellent three-course menu for 115f.

We chose *langoustines* with perfect home made mayonnaise, all in lavish quantity, and a good *terrine de poissons*, then *vol au vent* overflowing with scallops, *lotte* and prawns, excellent steaks and the house speciality – a *crème caramel* with coconut.

Le Chalut

(R)M   *8 r. de la Corne de Cerf (99) 56.71.58   Cl. Mon.; Sun. p.m. o.o.s.*

Determinedly nautical in theme, with lifebelts and nets on walls, a small lively restaurant in the centre of town. Excellent seafood and more. But be warned. If you find something congenial on the limited-choice menu, the news is very good; if not it involves 170f (again only two choices) or the carte, say 250f. Fish lovers have nothing to fear because one option is always something piscine. For me it was raw smoked haddock 'petals' marinaded and served with cockles and *frisée* salad, then pearly fresh cod (do you remember when cod was despised as poor man's fish? An elevation of price has meant an elevation of esteem. and quite right). This came cooked *à point* on a bed of spring cabbage with a topping of tomato coulis surrounded by a yellow buttery sauce – pure technicolour. A healthy gratin of prunes or crème brulée was the dessert. Only 15 covers, very popular, so book.

Les Écluses

(R)M   *Gare Maritime   89.56.81.00*

Superb position behind the locks in the Bassin Vauban; the huge plate glass windows make the most of the stunning view across the water to Dinard, facing due west into the evening sun. Very modern and glossy and not particularly cheap, but quite different from St.-Malo's other serious restaurants and already popular with discerning locals, who praise its fish above all other. Menus 90–150f.

A pleasant place to drop in for *le five o'clock* tea with home-made cakes, light lunches, English breakfasts, is **Tea-Time**, 4 Grand'rue, open every day 11 a.m.–6.30 p.m. The best *pâtisserie* in town, though, is undoubtedly **Cheflet**, 10 rue Porcon (up Grand'rue, turn left), with delectable specialities like *Le Mâlo*, to bring home as presents, perhaps, or to eat in their teashop. Wonderful fruity ices and chocolates too, all made by the son of the family. Opposite is a good present shop, **Le Vaisseloire** for classy household desirables, but a real find is **Le Mazagran**, 9 Grand'rue, that has porcelain seconds at knockdown prices. Lots of expensive shops for model clothes and yachties gear but try **Dégriffés** in r. des Marine for bargains (*dégriffés* are model clothes with the labels removed.) And for cheeses it's the **Boutique des Fromages** in r. de l'Orme that has the best choice, in best condition.

Map 4B   STE.-MARINE (Finistère) 5.5 km W of Bénodet

Over the new bridge, seemingly a handshake away from Bénodet on the other side of the river Odet, is the nice little harbour of Ste.-Marine, with its complement of simple hotel, restaurant, bars, and an unusually good *crêperie*, **La Cremaillère**.

What I did investigate further was the stunning beach nearby, the Plage du Téven. Given a few palm trees and a grass skirt or two, this could well be a South Sea Islands poster. Miles of fine white sands round a gently curving, south-facing bay. A choice of outstanding walks here, along the beach towards the promontory of Île Tudy, or a totally contrasting scene round the headland towards the harbour. This gives a unique view of sea, estuary, bridge and river, with the picturesque Bénodet just across the water. Make a considerable detour if necessary for this one.

Map 1C   ST.-MICHEL-EN-GRÈVE (C. d'A.) 18 km SW of Lannion

A most impressive bay, three miles long and backed by high cliffs. When the tide goes out, it does it with a vengeance for 1½ miles, so it's a long hike for a swim. The sand is so firm that it is used as a race track for the Lannion races.

Prominently overlooking the bay is:

Hotel de la Plage
(HR)S   *96.36.74.43   Cl. 3/1–1/4*

A long established favourite family hotel, with simple rooms made special by their astounding view. Good value at 190–280f with bath. Full pension is not insisted on but is usually taken, because it offers such consistently good food.

Basic 'nosh' and lots of it is what the customers were evidently enjoying the night we ate there. Our three courses cost 100f, with house wine at 42f, but the most popular dish seemed to be their renowned *plateau de fruits de mer* for 140f.

One suggestion: we felt decidedly cheated, having driven some way to enjoy the waterside situation on a beautiful summer evening, to find all the blinds down to keep out the sun! The cleverdicks were sitting outside on the super terrace, where they serve 'snacks', but as these seem to include everything from a bowl of soup to the loaded *plateau*, my advice for a fine night is to book a table there rather than in the distinctly fuggy dining-room. The *patronne* and her staff are the essence of friendliness and will do all they can to accommodate the odd English taste for fresh air.

Hotel de la Plage

Map 4D   **ST.-NICHOLAS-DES-EAUX** 56930 (Morbihan) 16 km SW of
Pontivy on the D 1

A hamlet built on the hillside above the river Blavet, with old thatched
cottages either side of a 16th-century church. The whole area is green
and attractive and would make a peaceful inland stop.

Le Vieux Moulin
(HR)S   *97.51.81.09   Fax 97.51.83.12   Cl. Feb.; Sun. p.m.; Mon. o.o.s.*

A nice old converted farmhouse with guaranteed tranquillity, highly
recommended by an English friend who visits Pontivy regularly and
chooses always to stay here. Menus start at 70f and the 12 rooms cost
from 195–287f.

*'We ate lieu with tartare sauce which was served with a herby sorbet
that really worked. Then veal in cream sauce served with a terrine of
vegetables. Finished with a chocolate gâteau called Negus. The service
was 'okay' – they didn't appear to take their restaurant seriously
despite the food being excellent value for money and a high standard
for the price. The surroundings were a bit plasticky though.'*

Map 5B   **ST.-PHILIBERT** (Finistère) 5 km S of Trégunc

Le St.-Philibert
(R)S   *98.50.06.77*

New owners are working hard to make a success of this little village bistro. They write to tell me that they specialise in fresh fish and home-made desserts on menus from 90f. At lunchtime there is a 'formule rapide' at 60f including wine, and they offer a take-away service, which should be useful for self-caterers. Nice terrace.

More reports please.

'This was our third visit – much improved. The 86f menu include a Kir, much appreciated while waiting for our order – moules Provencal, gigôt *– all excellent. Côtes du Rhone 60f'.*

Map 1B   **ST.-POL-DE-LÉON** (Finistère) 5 km S of Roscoff

'Capital of the Artichoke' is the town's title and it's not hard to see why. That delicious edible thistle sways proudly in many a field for miles around. In summer farmers' carts stagger under twice their width of pruned foliage, frustrating those motorists with a ferry to catch, while swarms of farm workers are to be seen planting out the fledgling plants for next year's crops. How odd that never once in the region were we offered that simple, wholesome, cheap vegetable as an *hors d'oeuvre.*

St.-Pol is the market centre for other vegs too of course, sending early crops of cauliflowers and potatoes all over France and providing the onions and garlic strings from the Roscoff 'Onion Johnnies', those archetypal beret-ed Bretons-on-a-bicycle.

Don't miss the Tuesday market which fills the main square with colourful produce and overflows into the surrounding streets with household goods stalls and untrendy garments.

It's a lively likeable town – a refreshing change from tourist-orientation – whose unique spires dominate the flat countryside for kilometres around. We could certainly locate them from as far away as Trébeurden. They belong to two of the most impressive Breton Gothic buildings, the Kreisker chapel (Kreis-ker means lower town) and the former cathedral, their gracefulness attributable to Norman influences; that of the Kreisker chapel survived its originator, St.-Pierre in Caen, which was destroyed in the war (but now reconstructed). The pale stone of the 13–16th-century cathedral came for Caen and its layout is based on that of Coutances.

Pity about the hotels & restaurants.

Map 1G   **ST.-SERVAN** 35400 (I. et V.) 3 km S of St.-Mâlo – *Mkt: Thurs., Fri.*

Having always approached St.-Mâlo by sea before and being without land transport, I had no idea of the size of the town and was amazed and distressed at the amount of traffic to be negotiated on the approach roads. St.-Servan, which used to be called Aleth, is now virtually a suburb and a very noisy and fume-ridden main street it has. But take time to explore the little harbour and another altogether more agreeable impression emerges. It's a picturesque little horseshoe facing across the river, with lovely views of Dinan from the cliff path, the Corniche d'Aleth, flanked by the unique Solidor tower – three towers in one in fact, built in 1382 by Duc Jean IV de Bretagne, to keep an eye on the troublesome pirate city next door. Facing the port is:

Le Valmarin
(H)M-L   *7 r. Jean-XXIII   99.81.94.76   Cl. Feb.   P.   AE, V*

In a quiet side street, near a small park. It is a pleasant old grey house set in its own garden, with charming owners, M. and Mme Le Gal who have never run a hotel before and make you feel you are their guests not customers. Unlike some erstwhile private houses turned hotels, the **Valmarin** gleams with new paint, and the bathrooms work. The rooms are spacious, the ceilings high, the atmosphere delightfully calm. All this warrants, I feel, a price of 500–680f for a double room. Breakfast is the only meal, and a very good one too, served on a silver tray, with good china and linen, and real butter and jam.

An unusual hotel, full of character, but perhaps too pricey in this un-smart area to merit an arrow.

L'Ascott
(H)M   *35 r. du Chapitre   99.81.89.93   Fax 99.81.77.40*

The only asset the Ascott lacks is a seaview. Situated near the Solidor tower, it is a lovely 19C town house, freshly painted in sparkling white and grey with admirable cast iron balconies and entrance gates. The fact that its caring and helpful patronne, Mme Christine Haidouin, is the daughter of Mme Jaclin of Le Manoir de la Rance (see p. 90) means that she has imbibed the principle of making her guests feel welcome.

She has achieved wonders in restoring the elegant old building, using cheerful colours but never losing the period feel bestowed by the lovely cornices and room proportions. China for the excellent breakfast is top quality, as is everything about this establishment. The rooms are comfortable, with good bathrooms and justify their price of 500–600f, with a 20% reduction out of season.

St. Mâlo is only ten minutes away and the little harbour of St. Servan has lots of character in its own right.

An excellent new find that I am sure will be very popular.

Le Válmarin.

 St Placide

(R)M   *Pl. du Poncel, St. Servan   99.81.70.73   Cl. Wed. Thurs. p.m.; o.o.s., Sat. lunch in season; 23/6–30.6*

Staying at l'Ascott, St. Placide is the obvious choice of restaurant, seconded by my hostess who claimed that she had never known a guest displeased yet. But this is far too good to use only when in the St. Servan area – a detour is well merited to what I believe is the best restaurant in the St. Mâlo district. The outside is unpromising – on a busy street corner – but things look up immediately once inside, with a light beige decor, smart cutlery and glass, and fresh flowers on the tables. Odile Lemperieure welcomes warmly and one settles down in happy anticipation of what her husband Didier can produce.

For Husband on the 148f menu it was a croustade filled with smoked salmon, fricasse of guineafowl in sherry vinegar and a ginger and saffron ice cream served with a superb flaky pastry version of rhubarb tart. Whatever you do leave room for dessert, which is Didier's passion. I did equally well with one of the best rabbit terrines ever sampled.

Didier had incorporated sundried tomatoes and this daring innovation really worked. Then lovely fresh cod and scallops in a curry sauce. The cheese in both menus was outstanding – a blue cheese served in a feuillete with walnuts and the patisserie skills were evident again in the sable with strawberries. Faultless. Arrowed.

L'Âtre Port Solidor
(R)S *99.81.68.39 Cl. Tues. p.m. o.o.s.; Wed.*

A genuine little local restaurant, with good fishy menus from 78–188f and lots of atmosphere.

l'Amadeus
(R)S *7 Pl. Monseigneur Juhel. St. Servan 19.82.22.00*

Another discovery while getting to know the St. Servan area. This one has a youthful feel about it – clean and fresh and wholesome with lots of scrubbed wood and a bistro feel. Excellent imaginative menus from 70f. A winner I do believe.

Map 1G **ST.-SULIAC** 35340 (I. et V.) 9 km S of St.-Malo

The peninsula that sticks out into the river Rance west of Châteauneuf is rich in history and legend. It was a settlement in prehistoric times but was named after a Welsh monk, who built a monastery here in the 6th century. In the interesting church high above the river is a strange granite head, perhaps St. Suliac's. A very popular gutsy monk was he who rid the district of a terrorising dragon.

The traditional Gargantua, many years prior to Rabelais' character, lived in this area and you can see his tooth-menhir in the village of Chablé. So much earth was needed to bury him finally in his burial mound at Mont Garot that the Baie de la Baguais was created. Or so they say.

Nowadays St.-Suliac is a delightful old village of granite cottages sliding down a hill to the landing stage; not much here except a cluster of houses, a few boats and:

➤ **La Grève**
(R)M *99.58.33.83 Cl. Sun. p.m. o.o.s.; Mon. Jan.; 4/10–21/10*

We must be grateful to M. and Mme Louedec for rescuing this gem from the shambles it was only a year or so ago. The position has always been prime, with substantial terrace overlooking a superb view, but now a transformation has been wrought, restoring the shabby old building into a typical Malouin residence, and giving us the added bonus of the inspired cooking of M. Louedec.

The interior of the two little stone-walled rooms is distinctly boaty with models on the walls and rather dubious oil paintings of ships and sails. The view of the sea provides all the decor that is necessary.

There are only eight tables so booking is essential, even in summer when the superb terrace gets pressed into action and of course this is first choice on a balmy night.

On the 95f menu I happily devoured first oysters, then a lovely salad of warm scallops, then a skilful presentation of layers of white and dark chocolate terrine in a sauce anglaise. Next price up is 130f.

My favourite in the region for ambiance, position and food. The arrow is well justified.

Map 2B   **ST.-THÉGONNEC** 29410 (Finistère) 9 km SW of Morlaix

---

For an unforgettable, uniquely Breton experience no-one, however uninterested in churches, should omit a visit to an *enclos paroissial* or parish close. To encounter, in a humble grey granite village, as gateway to the parish church, a monumental Renaissance triumphal arch, to enter the tiny cemetery and find a colossal elaborately carved calvary, flanked by a dignified decorated *ossuaire* or funeral chapel, to penetrate the gloom of the church's porch and be taken aback with the impact of light and colour – gold and red and blue and green and white – is to gain a first-hand interpretation of a slice of history.

Intense rivalry existed in these villages in the 17th century; unprecedented prosperity based on international trade *via* Morlaix, flax, canvas-making and agriculture, encouraged the rich merchants and parish councils to vie with one another in elaborate and expensive memorials. The competition between two of the most noteworthy – Guimiliau and its neighbour St.-Thégonnec – went on for two centuries. Village triumphs were not confined to arches, each in turn superseded by yet another costlier embellishment. Imagine the local goings-on!

The interior of St.-Thégonnec is disappointing but it wins hands down on its calvary, the last word, the last calvary to be built in the Léon region, in 1610. Its grinning, frowning, blindfolded, bound, threatening, busy, posing, intensely individual carved mannekins feature on many a postcard and guidebook cover. The funeral chapel came some 70 years later, and even if you have no wish to go inside to see the painted life-size figures representing the Entombment, spare a glance for the decoration on the façade – you'll see no finer Renaissance architecture in Brittany.

All this makes a visit to the otherwise unremarkable village a good idea, but St.-Thégonnec has another jewel:

Auberge St.-Thegonnec
(HR)M   *pl. de la Mairie   98.79.61.18   Fax 98.62.71.10   Cl. Mon. p.m.; Tue. o.o.s.; 20/12–3/2*

Utterly changed and gone upmarket since it was my 'S' Hotel of the Year, but now again recommended by readers. 20 rooms, 300–500f. Menus 98–200f.

'A jewel still, perhaps a more precious one now, with a long wing at

*the back with 20 bedrooms, beautifully furnished. No longer 'simple'
but all the praise you heaped on it still well deserved. Fabulous food,
imaginative and delicately presented (now a rest. gastronomique).
Alain and Thérèse Le Coz as courteous and welcoming as ever. I
suspect it has now become very popular so booking ahead for table
and rooms in the season might be advisable. (They must need a rest –
now have three growing boys!)' Shirin Court.*

Map 2B   **SIZUN** 29450 (Finistère) 33 km SW of Morlaix

On the banks of the Élorn, with an outstanding 16th-century triumphal
arch to its parish close, impressively floodlit on summer evenings.
    There is a fairly basic restaurant, **Les Voyageurs**, near at hand but in
a much more attractive setting is an excellent *crêperie*:

Milin Kerroch
98.68.81.56   Cl. Tues. o.o.s.

In the Centre de Loisirs at the entrance to the village. It's all very
agreeable to sit in the old converted watermill overlooking a lake and
sample the variety of *crêpes* on offer. Lots of amusements for the
juvenile.

Map 2B   **TAULÉ** 29670 (Finistère) 7 km NW of Morlaix

Relais des Primeurs
(HR)S   *98.67.11.03   Cl. Sept.; Fri. p.m. & Sat. lunch o.o.s.*

Turn off the *route express* towards the station of Taulé to find this little
grey stone hotel, whose rooms at 145–245f and menus from 75f might
well make an economical and agreeable alternative to the coastal hassle.
Locals recommend the food as being reliably fresh and *copieuse*.

Map 2H   **LA TEMPLERIE** 35310 (Î et V.) 11 km from Fougères,
              174 km from Cherbourg

On the N 12 east of Fougères:

Chez Gallover 'La Petite Auberge'
(R)M   *99.95.27.03   Cl. 7/2–13/2; Sun. Mon. p.m.*

Menus from 99f now in this reader-recommended little restaurant.
More reports please.

Map 3A **TELGRUC-SUR-MER** 29560 (Finistère) 23 km W of Chateaulin

A small fishing village on the Crozon peninsula. The Auberge is on the D 887.

Auberge du Gerdann
(R)M *98.27.78.67 Cl. Mon. p.m. o.o.s.; Tues.; 1/10–22/10   EC, V*

This is an area strong on character but weak on cuisine, so I was pleased to know about l'Auberge. Menus include good meat dishes as well as fish – another rarity – and start at 78f.

Map 5D **TOUL-BROCHE** 56870 (Morbihan) 2 km E of Baden, 7 km SE of Vannes, 9 km SW of Auray, on the D 101

Le Gavrinis
(HR)M *97.57.00.82   Fax 95.57.09.47   Cl. Mon. lunch Mon. p.m. o.o.s.; 3/11–30/11*

Modern bright Logis, approved of by readers for its wholesomeness and good food. We found it efficient, if a little clinical; certainly it's the kind of hotel a guidewriter could recommend without fear of retribution.
Menus are 139–230f.
Rooms are irreproachably clean and functional, at 340–454f.
If I sound a little unenthusiastic, it is probably partly because of the **Gavrinis'** position, on the road, in a dull patch of countryside. With such a gorgeous coastline nearby, it seems a shame not to stay within sight of the sea, but that depends where priorities lie.

Map 1C **TRÉBEURDEN** 22566 (C. d'A.) 9 km NE of Lannion, 72 km NE of St.-Brieuc – *Mkt: Tues.*

If it weren't so stunningly beautiful, I would say it was scruffy; it's as though the owners of the lovely villas set in the shade of the pine trees, comfortable on their own terraces looking out at their private vistas of sea and rocks and sand and yachts and islands, have decided that their town should have no amenities to attract the hoi-polloi, that the straggly grass sprouting on the front, the broken wire fences, the hot dog stalls are no concern of theirs. But neither need they be to anyone else who has an eye for Trébeurden's extraordinary natural amenities.

Three gorgeous main beaches to choose from, according to wind direction, inclination to swim, to sunbathe, to clamber over rocks, for sun or shade. For children a veritable paradise, with little islands to reach at low water, causeways to explore, rock pools to delve in, hard sands to dig, fine sands to picnic upon.

It's a surprisingly big town, straggling in all directions, with no real heart, few shops, few restaurants. The new developments of modern flats have been tackled haphazardly, tucked in amongst the old villas at random, with considerable scrub in between. All sounding most unattractive and yet somehow managing unconcernedly to over-ride these lapses. Even in the 'bourg', seemingly several kilometres away from the beaches, a turn of the head to left or right will win a glimpse of water, so eccentrically indented is this coast. The viewing table upon the Pointe Bihit is a must for a unique panoramic view of all the ins and outs as far as Roscoff.

Trébeurden may not be perfect but I could never tire of the place, not least because of:

➤ **Ti al-Lannec**
(HR)L-M   *96.23.57.26   Fax 96.23.62.14   Cl. 15/11–20/03; rest. cl. Mon. lunch.*
AE, V

It stands high in the pine trees, a dignified granite house with a modern extension built on to the rear; encircling the plate-glassed dining room unfolds the sparkling watery panorama. A luxurious lounge next door shares the view and makes after-dinner fraternising easy. The whole hotel is furnished with perfect taste, antiques mingling with high quality modern, classy drapes and carpets. Not too large, so that a country-house atmosphere prevails, encouraged by deep armchairs, flowers, chat and the concern of M. et Mme Joanny and their efficient band of helpers.

I don't know how they pick them or train them, but I have never come across such friendly staff. The girls who bring breakfast and clean the rooms smile and chat and wish you the equivalent of Have a Nice Day; nothing is too much trouble.

The 'little touches' are manifest everywhere. I often amuse myself by considering how I would furnish the perfect hotel room, to make it as comfortable as home. Mme Joanny has put all my ideas into practice. (What do other hotels expect you to do with drip dry shirts and knickers? Drape 'em on the curtain pole?) **Ti al-Lannec** provides a drying rack in the bathroom, a full-length mirror, lots of deep towels, good soap, efficient lighting – basic enough you would think, but how rarely does one find them all?

And the breakfasts! How often have I railed against plastic butter and jam, not enough coffee served with cold sterilized milk? How often have the jammy croissant crumbs prickled in bed because there was no plate? At **Ti al-Lannec** breakfast comes served on pink and white porcelain; the jam is a different home-made flavour every day, the honey runs from a practical little glass and silver jug (buy them in the market for good take-home presents), the butter and the coffee are copious, the croissant buttery-flaky, the hot brioche home-made.

The bedrooms and two suites are all different; all are charming but mine had french windows opening on to a little, almost-private, corner lawn, so we could lie in bed and admire our own personal view, or sit outside underneath a white umbrella in a white deck chair for a magical aperitif hour, facing west across the bay into the evening sun that made us reluctant to stir enough to change for dinner.

ti al lannec.

Dinner in that dining room is worth stirring for. We ate on the menu that changes every three weeks. *Pensionnaires* can stay that long and never have the same dinner twice. Their menu is a three-course no-choice but everyone I spoke to said that, where necessary, alternatives had been willingly and helpfully substituted. Lots of fish appears of course and the cooking I would call traditional with interesting variations.

All this is good – very good indeed – but the best thing of all about **Ti al-Lannec** is its owners. The Joannys, she with a hotel-keeping background, brought 'the House on the Moor' with fingers crossed and since then have been constantly improving, never missing a pointer to perfection. They are ideal hosts – attentive, efficient, friendly.

All the above I wrote when I made Ti al-Lannec my Hotel of the Year in 1985–6. The astonishing thing is that I need not alter a word in 1995. Here is one much-praised hotel that has never once let me down. Every reader that has been there and reported back has been equally enthusiastic. If I were to choose a new Hotel of the Year for this book, it would not be new at all – the Ti al-Lannec is still top of the pops.

The only material changes have been the addition of a health centre, with gym, solarium, sauna, jacuzzi, and that prices have inevitably risen. A double room now costs from 370–950f, demi-pension is from 405–730f per person and menus start at 190f.

'We loved it. They are so nice, helpful and friendly and as we had our sometimes rather anti-social baby with us, their kindness to her was especially appreciated. We thought the place offered very good value and particularly liked the 3-course set menu, where in fact you can easily swap dishes for those on the carte. The only things we could fault them on were their cheeses – which were poor – and the cost of a simple picnic – £18 for four hard boiled eggs, tomatoes, some bread, a melon and slices of ham and a bottle of mineral water, all presented unattractively in a 'panier picnique' – a plastic bag.
Otherwise, wonderful, and the decor of our first-floor room – no. 7 – was delightful – striped blue wallpaper with pale turquoise flowered curtains and upholstery.' Tessa Stuart

There are two new hotels overlooking the water: the **Aigue Marine**, 5 r. M. Berthelot. 96.23.39.39. (HR)M and the **Roches Douvres**, 17 r. M. Berthelot. 96.92.27.27, (H)M.

Creperie du Cloitre
(R)S   *1 Placedu Martray   96.92.33.18   Cl. Mon.*

A very popular crêperie and tea bar run by the Quivoron family in the main square. You sit at long tables and choose from a list of 39 savoury and 43 sweet crêpes, plus the day's specials. Some are special – butter and tomatoe costs 14f – some are elaborate – 'Crêpe Maison' involving coquille St. Jacques, moules, lotte and mushrooms rate 46f. Pottery bowls were the preferred receptacle for excellent demi-sec cider made in nearby Roche-Derrien.

Husband hates crêpes so I always have to find a crêperie that offers omelettes as well. His came crispy round the edge, soft in the middle, stuffed to overflowing with ham and served with a salad for 30f. No grumbles there and I was equally pleased with my onion-filled sarrasin crêpe. Highly recommended particularly o.o.s. when the (very pleasant) service can cope best.

Ker-An-Nod
(HR) M   *r. de Pors Termen*   96.23.50.21   *Cl. 1/1–10/3*

 H

Mme Brigitte Penven has changed the policy of her nice old hotel, with the best situation in the town facing right on to the beach. She no longer takes *pensionnaires* but has transformed her old dining-room into Le Jardin, a charming fresh trellissed room, green and airy, looking out to sea, where light snacks can be taken at any hour from '*midi à minuit*'. Interesting salads and omelettes or just one dish like *langoustines mayonnaise* are easy on the pocket, but there is a good three-course daily menu too at 85f. No compulsion for residents to eat in, but they could do far worse.

The rooms are lovely, with smashing sea views from the more expensive ones – 305f for one of good size with modern bathroom, 260f for those at the back, with showers. A pleasant lounge makes possible bad weather more bearable.

Exceptional value in this generally expensive area for those who like to eat out sometimes, and another potential Trébeurden arrow.

ÎLE GRANDE

A few kms north of Trébeurden, juts out the one-time island where Joseph Conrad spent his honeymoon, now a strange promontory edged with rocky coves, surrounded by islets. Easy to get disorientated with so much sea in so many directions. The little fishing port still provides many of the local restaurants with their catch and the island still benefits from the character of the many grey stone fishermens' cottages dotted about. Fishermen still live in some no doubt, but now there are more bathing drawers than nets draped from their windows; the farmers let out their land to campers and it is from holiday makers that most of the ready money comes.

This is DIY territory; with hotels yielding to food and souvenir shops, but it's still worth a visit for the never boring endless variations on the same watery theme. I could spend months walking, swimming, exploring and even then there would be yet another beach, yet another little harbour.

Map 3F **TREFFENDEL** 35380 (I. et V.) Plélan-le-Grand. 8 km NE of Plélan by the N 24 and D 63

A village near the forest of Broceliande, and a pleasant place to stop on the way to Rennes, 39 km to the north-east.

l'Auberge du Presbytere
(R)M *99.61.00.76 Fax 99.61.00.48 Cl. Sun. p.m.; Mon. CB*

This one-time presbytery is picturesquely covered by an ancient vine. There are two dining-rooms, one the 'Salle du curé' and the other the 'Salle du catéchisme'. Both are charming. The menu is admirably limited to specialities, of which particularly famous is the chicken raised by M. Le Guehénnec, chef/patron, and the beef, served in sizeable ribs of excellent quality. Pigeon is grilled with wild mushrooms; asparagus and tarragon come from the garden. This would make a pleasant change from the almost totally fishy diet imposed throughout most of Brittany.

The menus, including splendid desserts, are commendable. There is a lunchtime version at 100f; from 168f otherwise.

Map 1C **TRÉGASTEL** 22730 (C. d'A.) 8 km W of Perros Guirec

The coast along here is dominated by the power of its smooth pink granite rocks, crumpled into hints of all manner of strange beasties – the Witch, the Puffin, the Pile of Pancakes, the Corkscrew and King Gradlon's Crown, near the Grève Blanche. To add to the fairytale cornucopia, on a small island beyond the Baie de Ste.-Anne there is an extraordinary pastiche of the mediaeval castle, Costaëres. The only hope of working out the convulations is to climb up to the *table d'orientation* for a view all along the coast.

Inland, a little away from the beaches, in verdant calm:

Hôtel Bellevue
(HR)M *20 r. des Calculots 96.23.88.18 Fax 96.23.89.51 Cl. 15/10–10/4*

An upmarket family hotel, particularly popular for its unusually good food. Nice garden, well-furnished comfortable rooms from 300–460f. Demi-pension from 340–500f per person is obligatory in season. Menus from 100f.

Map 1D **TRÉGUIER** 22220 (C. d'A.) 30 km N of Guingamp

A smashing little town, high above the confluence of two rivers which together form the river Tréguier – Breton for 'three corners'.

St.-Yves, a local lad, is the patron saint of barristers, many of whom, stately in gowns and wigs, attend his annual fête here on May 19.

The picturesque little town, all nice old houses and cobbled streets, centres on St. Tugdual's cathedral, with its exquisite nave, surely the most beautiful Gothic building in Brittany. The difficult unpliable local granite has somehow been worked here to achieve the lightness and delicacy which I sadly miss from the Norman Caen stone architecture. Look at the marvellous tracery of the 15th-century cloisters to see what I mean.

Not much down by the water, except a marina from whence cometh all those blazers and Docksiders reading the *Daily Telegraph* in the cafés in the square. They, poor things, having only marine transport, can't drive out to the best restaurant two km away:

➤ Kastell Dinech

(HR)M *rte. de Lannion   96.92.49.39   Fax 96.92.34.03   Cl. 11/10–27/10; Jan–15/3; Tues. p.m.; Wed. o.o.s.*

Signposted right off the Lannion road. A real old Breton farmhouse that has miraculously retained its character while becoming a deservedly popular hotel and restaurant. The honeysuckle still rambles untamed over the grey stone walls, there are dried flowers in pottery jugs, straw hats pinned on the wall; the dining-room is long and low and raftered, brightened with coral tablecloths and country flowers, and the bedrooms have been decorated with unsophisticated Laura Ashley prints, a shining example of how 'inexpensive' does not have to mean orange vinyl and brown lino. Those bedrooms in the main house are largest and prettiest with particularly good bathrooms. I liked the

Hotel Kastell Dinec'h.

converted barn wing, simple but bright with yellow paint, good bathroom, for 390f. Demi pension 390–460f.

The three arms of the farmhouse enclose a garden and a terrace with lots of reclining chairs and tables which lead to regular meeting-ups over drinks and the comparing of the day's discoveries; the clientèle has a strong English complement.

Dinner costs 120f and is imaginative and varied. A swimming pool is a welcome new institution.

'Better if you are staying there. The ambience is exquisite but we found the food disappointing; the wine waiter was excellent.'

POINTE DU CHÂTEAU

Don't fail to take a memorable drive out along the river from Tréguier for 10 km to this most extraordinary sight on this extraordinary coast. The atmosphere of the bay is distinctly eerie, with dozens of strange menhir-type rocks rearing sheer out of the water, like the backgrounds of early Florentine paintings, two-dimensional. The atmosphere silences even the children, who stop in their tracks and gaze wide-eyed at the spectacle; perhaps the spirits of the shipwrecked still haunt. Twice I've seen it, both times at low water, both in calm weather. In a storm it must be terrifying.

The first time we picnicked on the turf high above, with a much-travelled friend who said he'd never in all the world seen anything like it; this summer we drove out after dinner to see if the rosily setting sun might soften the menace that perhaps we had imagined. Not at all. The fierce colours made the scene even more awe-inspiring. See if you don't agree.

Map 4B   **TRÉGUNC** 29910 (Finistère) 9 km W of Pont Aven

A fairly uninteresting village, but well situated for coastal excursions.

Le Menhir
(HR)M   *17 r. de Concarneau   98.97.62.35   Cl. 1/10–1/4; Mon. o.o.s.*

A little hotel on the main road but with a pleasant dining-room looking over the rear garden, as do most of the rooms.
Rooms 160–310f. Menus from 85f.

L'Auberge les Grandes Roches
(HR)M   *98.97.62.97   Fax 98.50.29.19   Cl. 15/11–10/3; Mon. & lunchtime o.o.s. Hotel cl. Christmas & Feb. hols. Rest. cl. Mon. & lunchtime except weekends 15/11–30/3*

Signposted from the church down the V 3. Aptly named indeed; the menir shaped rocks in the front garden are gigantic.

It's a sophisticated/rustic kind of building, well-tended, efficient, quiet, with modern rooms at 260–390f. A safe bet if you can get in – it's a popular conference hotel, which perhaps makes it a bit impersonal. Menus from 90f.

Map 2H   **TREMBLAY** 35460 (I. et V.) 42 km N of Rennes on the N 776

Turn right (west) in the village and follow the clearly marked signs to:

Roc Land
(HR)M   *99.98.20.46   Fax 99.98.29.00   Cl. Sun. p.m.; Mon. 15/10–30/10, 15/2–28/2*

Spic, modern, *soignée*, calm, pine-encircled; Swings in the *parc*, elegant dining-room. Altogether a safe and useful overnight stop on the main road south. Rooms 290–350f, menus start at 98f.

Map 2E   **TRÉMUSON** 22440 (C. d'A.) 8 km W of St.-Brieuc on the N 12

Le Buchon
(R)M   *96.94.85.84   Cl. Sat. lunch from 15/11–15/3, Sun. p.m.; Tue. p.m. 5/11–20/11*

If you don't want to get involved in the St.-Brieuc traffic hassle, this could be a useful stop, situated as it is on the *Nationale* just outside the town, with easy parking. It's a smart little restaurant, specialising in fish, with good menus from 78f.

Map 1D   **TRÉVOU-TRÉGUIGNEC** 22660 (C. d'A.) 12 km E of Perros Guirec

---

Yet another wide sandy bay, high above which stands:

Ker Bugalic
(HR)M   *96.23.71.15   Fax 96.23.74.71   Cl. 30/9–Easter*

Creeper-covered old Breton house whose verandah makes the best of the view; nice gardens unusually good menus at 100f, no compulsion to eat in. Friendly trouble-taking management. Eighteen rooms, all full when I tried to look, at 255–385f. Good vibes.
There are now an additional four rooms in the annexe at 310f.

Map 6D   **LA TRINITÉ-SUR-MER** 56470 (Morbihan) 4.5 km NW of Carnac

A famous yachting centre in a gorgeous position at the mouth of the
Crach river. Pontoons are lined with hundreds of boats, from the family
sailer to the ocean racer, and its very pleasant to stroll alongside being
nosy. When a big race is on you will see lots of famous names here
and the town hums but it's a very short season (the French aren't
natural frostbite sailors like our inured Solent hardies) and even on a
fine June Sunday there was little activity, with the bars along the front
depressingly empty. There are some beautiful sheltered bays for a
day's excursion but I found the town too artificial for a longer stay and
failed to find a hotel that might make it worth while.

Surprisingly no little fishy restaurants along by the harbour either, so
what *do* the yachties do? With any sense, head for:

➤ **L'Azimut**
(R)M   *1 ru. Men-Du   97.55.71.88   Fax 97.55.80.15*

Having just relished the comfort and welcome of one of the best
chambres d'hôtes in my new b. and b. book (you'll have to buy it to
find out which but its not a million kms from La Trinité) it seemed that
fortune was smiling that day when we ate at l'Azimut. Everyone said it
was the best, and everyone was right. It stands a little above the town,
so that there is a fine view from the terrace of masts and sparkling
water and white sails in the sunset. Inside is more rustique, with
panelled walls, lace table cloths, hanging converted oil lamps. In April
we appreciated both the ambiance and the warmth from the crackling
wood fire on which Hervé Le Calvez cooks his much-appreciated grills
of meat and fish. The three menus are admirably concise. The Menu
Terroir, at 98f, has two choices in each of three courses, plus the
amuse bouche that comes with every menu, the Menu Marin of 168f
has no choice but enticing four courses, like mixed shellfish with
asparagus, stuffed crab, *panaché* of sole and plaice with a *compôte* of
shallots in ginger and a chocolate marquise with mint coulis. It is not
till you reach the 195f level that you get the gamut of Hervé's repertoire
spread throughout four courses. Whichever you choose, leave room
for the dessert – he is a dab hand at the pâtisserie, some of which
appears gratuit with the excellent coffee. Arrowed for great ambiance
and cooking. In case you wondered – an azimut is a sextant.

Map 1E   **VAL ANDRÉ** 22370 (C. d'A.) 16 km N of Lamballe

A sizeable town, with a sheltered beach of fine sand. It's all very
pleasant to sit by the west-facing harbour and watch the fishing boats
busy about. Just here is:

La Cotriade
(R)M-L *96.72.20.26 Cl. 11/1–11/2; 31/5–18/6; Mon. p.m.; Tues.*

A seemingly unassuming little restaurant with plastic tables outside for itinerant drinkers, giving little hint that it boasts a Michelin star for its predominately fishy cooking. If the 190f menu happens to suit your tastebuds, you've got a bargain. For me it was *salade tiède de St.-Jacques* (could have been oysters hot or cold or *plateau de fruits de mer*), followed by a no-choice *feuilleté de barbue, crème d'oseille.* This was very good news indeed; the bad is that the menu does not change for several days at a time with no notice given what and when, and the next one up is 260f; *à la carte* is even more pricey, with starters and main courses costing 95-ish apiece, and lobster a heady 230f.

So best to study the menu before commitment and then rub hands and congratulate yourself.

Mer
(HR)S *r. Admiral Charner 96.72.20.44 Cl. Tues. o.o.s.; 15/11–15/12; 10/1–4/2 All credit cards*

A restaurant with rooms really, very popular with the locals for the good local produce cooked there. Menus start at 69f (lunch), including plenty of seafood, and the newly decorated rooms from 175–225f.

The annexe, Nuit et Jour has 8 modern studios for 240f with kitchenettes.

➤ Au Biniou
(R)M *121 r. Clémenceau 96.72.24.35 Cl.- Dec–March, Thurs o.o.s.*

Its a rule worth mentioning – in a seaside town if you want to eat good value cooking with the locals not the tourists, forgo the marine view and head into the town centre. It certainly applies with Pléneuf-Val André, twin towns mostly André. Le Biniou is a funny little building in the main street, with a thatched canopy over the door, all very cottagey and folksy – the kind of place I'd give a wide berth to were it not for a local nudge and wink.

The interior does nothing to dispel doubts; there are lots of awful oil paintings and rustic photos, lace tablecloths, red ceiling, heavy patterned wallpaper, and leather banquettes. But after a while you settle down to enjoy the fussiness, the bustling atmosphere full of good will, and when the food starts to arrive you will be completely won over. "Cosy," you would say rather than "naff", I do think it is a winter place though, all warm and fuggy.

The 80f menu yielded a superb *tourte aux crabe aux légumes*, with escellent home-made flaky pastry. Then a *papillote de truite* came enclosed in foil with a butter sauce – yummy, and that did us nicely. I did notice a fantastic *plâteau de fruits de mer* (175f) being served to lustier trencher persons. I really loved this one and will certainly return to sample their other menus at 145, 175 and 240f. Arrowed for charming kitsch and good cooking.

Map 5E   **VANNES** 56000 (Morbihan) 107 km SW of Rennes – *Mkt: Wed.,*
Sat.

You have only to look at a map to guess at Vannes' perfect setting. At
the head of the Gulf of Morbihan this is a good place to check up on
the various alternatives offered by the *vedettes vertes* to see the gulf. I
am told the gastronomic tour is well worth the money. See Morbihan
(p. 103).

The canalised waterway drives into the heart of the town. The
approach along the quays lined with masts and rigging and old grey
houses is already full of charm, leading directly to the main square full
of café tables facing into the sun and ideally placed for getting
bearings and deciding on routes.

The obvious one is to pass through the 16th-century St. Vincent's
Gate into the shade and calm of the mediaeval town. Or comparative
calm, because although there are fewer cars here, there are many
more tourists – some say too many. Personally I like the liveliness of
the place, particularly after a spell beach-combing, and have wandered
round some of the ancient cobbled streets, shaded by gabled houses
nearly meeting overhead, almost alone, except in high summer.

Everyone takes his camera up to the House of Vannes to photograph
the carved rubicund peasants, 'Vannes and his Wife', projecting like
figureheads from the eaves. Then on to the photogenic pl. Henri IV,
lined with 18th-century gabled houses, and then to gape, not knowing
what to say, at the cathedral St.-Pierre, an incongruous hotchpotch of
ideas from the 15th to the 19th centuries.

Then down to the Postern Gate and ramparts, particularly impressive
in summer, when floodlighting throws the ancient towers into dramatic
relief. The moat has been filled with flower gardens. Look down upon it
from the narrow bridge and don't miss the old wash-houses built 300
years ago and looking like a film set for that period.

Hotels are sparse in Vannes. You could try the Marebaudière, 4 ru. A.
Briand 97.47.26.46, in the town centre (but quiet), whose 40 rooms cost
a reasonable 260–400f, but here is a personal recommendation for:-

Hotel de France
(H)M   *Av. V. Hugo   97.47.27.57   Fax 97.42.59.17   Cl. Sun. o.o.s.*

25 rooms for 195–300f.
    *'Immaculate, the bedrooms well furnished, with bath, toilet etc en
suite. Horrendous colour scheme. No restaurant but a cheerful
breakfast room and patio bar. The patronne and her staff were most
welcoming. Prices very reasonable. Disadvantages: on a busy one-way
street with a bus lane so that rooms at the rear should be chosen. Car
parking could be a problem at peak seasons. About 7 minutes walk
from the town centre' A. W. Deakin.*

Arnaud Lorgéoux
(R)M *Le Pave des Halles, 17 r. Halles 97.47.15.96 Cl. Sun. p.m. o.o.s.; Mon. 2/1–17/1*

> Confidently named after the chef-patron, who cooks divinely. The best advice I can give anyone is to make a beeline for the 109f menu which features oysters, a definitive *'hochepot'* flavoured with salt from the Guérande, good cheeses and pears cooked in honey and spices. There is also an attractive 69f menu, which should certainly not be despised. Go for a table downstairs if you can.

Le Lys
(R)M *51 r. Maréchal Leclerc 97.47.29.30 Cl. Sun. p.m.; Mon. o.o.s. AE, DC, V*

> New owners in this delightful little restaurant in the centre of Vannes are trying hard to please, and all reports have been favourable.
> Three courses for 120f (mid-week), or four on the 180f, and Menu Savour 280f, the latter including specialities like Barbary duck stuffed with bay leaves and local herbs, and an individual casserole of scallops and clams in a creamy sauce based on seaweed.
> The outstanding cellar inherited from the previous owners still pleases readers.

Le Pressoir
(R)M *7 r. de l'Hopital 56890 St. Avé (5km N by D 757 and D 135) 97.60.87.63 Cl. Sun. p.m.; Mon.; 4/3–14/3; 1/10–18/10 St. Avé 5 kms N ly D767 & D135*

> Now one of the best restaurants in the Vannes conglomeration and blessed with a Michelin Star. Bernard Rambaud's cooking is highly inventive, using seafood in new ways – a galette of red mullet with potatoes and rosemary, warm oysters with quail eggs and caviar. He does not ignore meat dishes, however, and in cold weather his beef stews and tripe would make a welcome change from an exclusively fishy diet. The 120f weekday lunch menu is a bargain, as is the next one up at 175f, but you can pay as much as 400f if you want lobster.

Marée Bleue
(R)S *8 pl. Bir-Hakeim 97.47.21.23 Cl. 17/12–7/1; Sun. p.m. o.o.s.*

> This no-nonsense, strictly functional, eating place in a noisy ugly street just outside the old walls offers the best value for kilometres around. At lunchtime it is packed with office workers, eating their way through a remarkable four courser for 75f, which includes expensive items like *langoustines*, oysters, *gigot*. Service is brisk, wine is cheap, it's a Vannes institution.

Map 3H   **VITRÉ** 35500 (I. et V.) 37 km E of Rennes, 30 km S of Fougères

---

> No doubt about the mediaeval origins of this hilltop town, fortressed against its Norman neighbours – it is probably the best preserved and

intact in Brittany, from towering 15th-century castle, to ramparts, to old streets a-tangle with dignified top-heavy houses.

Impressive from any approach, have cameras ready arriving from Fougères, on the hill looking down, or from the west from the top of the Tertres Noirs, for a fine panorama of castle, town and Vilaine valley.

Petit Billot
HR(S) *5 pl. Mar-Leclerc   99.75.02.10   Fax 99.74.72.96   Cl. 15/12–15/1; Sun. o.o.s.*

Central, with bedrooms that vary considerably in price according to size and position. Those in the new wing, with bathroom, are a good-value 250f; in the older part they start as low as 175f.

There is now a highly recommandable restaurant at Le Petit Billot, with some of the best value menus in the district. For example the 70f menu offers a lovely vegetable terrine with a fresh tomato sauce, followed by brains (I love them but I know it's a minority choice) or escalope for the more conservative. Like all good thrifty Frenchmen the chef makes good use of the more obscure parts of the animal, so tripe and ox-cheek also feature. This is conclusive proof to my mind that the freezer is not involved, but long slow traditional cooking is. Spend 120f to get at the more expensive ingredients like a terrine of salmon with red peppers and a *panaché* of fish with shellfish *coulis*, then salad with three cheeses and home made pâtisserie. Even here the offal affiliation is evident (try saying that after your petit verre). *Aumonière de cervelle de veau aux grisets, salade de gesiers confits, foie de veau aux petits oignons*, and *ouileletée*. If I describe the menu at length it is because it is such an unusual one and to be commended.

Friendly management and such unusually good food make this a potential arrow, lacking only a few reports.

Map 1C   **LE YAUDET** 22300 (C. d'A.) 5 km W of Lannion on the D 88

At the head of a little bay of altogether different character from the beaches all around. Picnic on the grassy headland by the little chapel and take in the view; chances are that even in high season nothing more brash than the chug of a fishing boat or the lyricism of a lark will disturb the calm. Down far below is a perfect horseshoe bay, rocks, sand at low water, surmounted with conifers, rare in these parts. Wonderful walks. The coast road to Locquémeau is a must. Back in the village:

Les Genêts d'Or
(HR)S   *96.35.24.17   Cl. 15/11–15/12; 15/1–15/2; Sun. p.m.; Mon. o.o.s.   V, MC, CB*

A pretty little hotel, used by locals as well as summer visitors, which I would choose in preference to any of the Lannion alternatives. Readers agree. Fourteen rooms cost from 180f. Menus from 68f.

Wines and spirits by John Doxat

AN INTRODUCTION TO FRENCH WINES

Bonne cuisine et bons vins, c'est le paradis sur terre. (Good cooking and good wines, that is earthly paradise.)

King Henri IV

French food positively invites accompaniment by wine, albeit only a couple of glasses because one is driving on after lunch. At dinner one can usually be self-indulgent. Then wine becomes more than a sensory pleasure: with some rich regional meals it is almost imperative digestively. Civilised drinking of wine inhibits the speedy eating that is the cause of much Anglo-Saxon dyspepsia.

The most basic French wine generically is *vin ordinaire*, and very ordinary indeed it can be. The term is seldom used nowadays: *vin de table* is a fancier description – simple blended wine of no particular provenance. *Vins de table* often come under brand-names, such as those of the of the ubiquitous Nicolas stores (Vieux Ceps, etc.) – and highly reliable they are. Only personal experience can lead you to your preference: in a take-away situation I would never buy the absolute cheapest just to save a franc or so.

Nearly every restaurant has its house wines. Many an owner, even of a chain of establishments, takes pride in those he has chosen to signify as *vins de la maison*, *vin du patron* or similar listing. In a wine-rich area, house wines (in carafe or bottle) are likely to be *vins de pays*, one step up from *vins de table*, since this label indicated that they come from a distinct certificated area and only that area, though they may be a blend (thus sometimes an improvement) of several wines.

Ever since they invented the useful, if frequently confusing, *Appellation d'Origine Contrôlée* (AC) the French have created qualitative sub-divisions. An AC wine, whose label will give you a good deal of information, will usually be costlier – but not necessarily better – than one that is a VDQS. To avoid excessive use of French, I translate that as 'designated (regional) wine of superior quality'. A newer, marginally lesser category is VQPRD: 'quality wine from a specified district'.

Hundreds of wines bear AC descriptions: you require knowledge and/or a wine guide to find your way around. The intention of the AC laws was to protect consumers and ensure wine was not falsely labelled – and also to prevent over-production, without noticeable reduction of the 'EEC wine lake'. Only wines of reasonable standards should achieve AC status: new ones are being regularly admitted to the list, and the hand of politics as much as the expertise of the taster can be suspected in some instances. Thus AC covers some unimportant wines as well as the rarest, vastly expensive vintages.

Advice? In wine regions, drink local wines. Do not hesitate to ask the opinion of patron or wine-waiter: they are not all venal, and most folk are flattered by being consulted. By all means refer to a vintage chart, when considering top class wines, but it cannot be an infallible guide: it has no bearing on blended wines.

OUTLINE OF FRENCH WINE REGIONS

Bordeaux

Divided into a score of districts, and sub-divided into very many *communes* (parishes' The big district names are Médoc, St. Emilion, Pomerol, Graves and Sauternes. Prices for the great reds (châteaux Pérus, Mouton-Rothschild, etc.) or the finest sweet whites (especially the miraculous Yquem) have become stratospheric. Yet château in itself means little and the classification of various rankings of châteaux is not easily understood. Some tiny vineyards are entitled to be called château, which has led to disputes about what have been dubbed 'phantom châteaux'. Visitors are advised, unless wine-wise, to stick to the simpler designations.

Bourgogne (Burgundy)

Topographically a large region, stretching from Chablis (on the east end of the Loire), noted for its steely dry whites, to Lyons. It is particularly associated with fairly powerful red wines and very dry whites, which tend to acidity except for the costlier styles. Almost to Bordeaux excesses, the prices for really top Burgundies have gone through the roof. For value, stick to simpler local wines.

Technically Burgundies, but often separately listed, are the Beaujolais wines. The young red Beaujolais (not necessarily the over-publicised *nouveau*) are delicious, mildly chilled. There are several rather neglected Beaujolais wines (Moulin-à-Vent, Morgon, St. Amour, for instance) that improve for several years: they represent good value as a rule. The Maçonnais and Chalonnais also produce sound Burgundies (red and white) that are usually priced within reason.

Rhône

Continuation south of Burgundy. The Rhône is particularly associated with very robust reds, notably Châteauneuf-du-Pape; also Tavel, to my mind the finest of all still *rosé* wines. Lirac *rosé* is nearly as good. Hermitage and Gigondas are names to respect for reds, whites and *rosés*. Rhône has well earned its modern reputation – no longer Burgundy's poorer brother. From the extreme south comes the newly 'smart' dessert *vin doux naturel*, ultra-sweet Muscat des Beaumes-de-Venise, once despised by British wine-drinkers. There are fashions in wine just like anything else.

Alsace

Producer of attractive, light white wines, mostly medium-dry, widely used as carafe wines in middle-range French restaurants. Alsace wines are not greatly appreciated overseas and thus remain comparatively inexpensive for their quality; they are well placed to compete with popular German varieties. Alsace wines are designated by grape – principally Sylvaner for lightest styles, the widespread and reliable Riesling for a large part of the total, and Gerwürtztraminer for slightly fruitier wines.

Loire

Prolific producer of very reliable, if rarely great, white wines, notably Muscadet, Sancerre, Anjou (its *rosé* is famous), Vouvray (sparkling and semi-sparkling), and Saumur (particularly its 'champagne styles'). Touraine makes excellent whites and also reds of some distinction – Bourgueil and Chinon. It used to be widely believed – a rumour put out by rivals? – that Loire wines 'did not travel'; nonsense. They are a successful export.

Champagne

So important is Champagne that, alone of French wines, it carries no AC: its name is sufficient guarantee. (It shares this distinction with the brandies Cognac and Armagnac.) Vintage Champagnes from the *grandes marques* – a limited number of 'great brands' – tend to be as expensive in France as in Britain. You can find unknown brands of high quality (often off-shoots of *grandes marques*) at attractive prices, especially in the Champagne country itself. However, you need information to discover these, and there are true Champagnes for the home market that are *doux* (sweet) or *demi-sec* (medium sweet) that are pleasing to few non-French tastes. Champagne is very closely controlled as to region, quantities, grape types, and is made only by secondary fermentation in the bottle. From 1993, it is prohibited (under EEC law) to state that other wines are made by the 'champagne method' – even if they are.

Minor regions, very briefly

Jura – Virtually known outside France. Try local speciality wines such as *vin jaune* if in the region.

Jurançon – Remote area; sound, unimportant white wines, sweet styles being the better.

Cahors – Noted for its powerful *vin de pays* 'black wine', darkest red made.

Gaillac – Little known; once celebrated for dessert wines.

Savoy – Good enough table wines for local consumption. Best product of the region is delicious Chambéry vermouth: as an aperitif, do try the well distributed Chambéryzette, a unique vermouth with a hint of wild strawberries.

Bergerac – Attractive basic reds; also sweet Monbazillac, relished in France but not easily obtained outside: aged examples can be superb.

Provence – Large wine region of immense antiquity. Many and varied *vins de pays* of little distinction, usually on the sweet side, inexpensive and totally drinkable.

Midi – Stretches from Marseilles to the Spanish border. Outstandingly prolific contributor to the 'EEC wine lake' and producer of some 80 per cent of French *vins de table*, white and red. Sweet whites dominate, and there is major production of *vins doux naturels* (fortified sugary wines).

Corsica – Roughish wines of more antiquity than breeding, but by all means drink local reds – and try the wine-based aperitif Cap Corse – if visiting this remarkable island.

Paris – Yes, there is a vineyard – in Montmartre! Don't ask for a bottle: the tiny production is sold by auction, for charity, to rich collectors of curiosities.

HINTS ON SPIRITS

The great French spirit is brandy. Cognac, commercially the leader, must come from the closely controlled region of that name. Of various quality designations, the commonest is VSOP (very special old pale): it will be a cognac worth drinking neat. Remember, *champagne* in a cognac connotation has absolutely no connection with the wine. It is a topographical term, *grande champagne* being the most prestigious cognac area: *fine champagne* is a blend of brandy from the two top cognac sub-divisions.

Armagnac has become better known lately outside France, and rightly so. As a brandy it has a much longer history than cognac: some connoisseurs rate old armagnac (the quality designations are roughly similar) above cognac.

Be cautious of French brandy without a cognac or armagnac title, regardless of how many meaningless 'stars' the label carries or even the magic word 'Napoléon' (which has no legal significance).

Little appreciated in Britain is the splendid 'apple brandy', Calvados, mainly associated with Normandy but also made in Brittany and the Marne. The best is *Calvados du Pays d'Auge*. Do take well-aged Calvados, but avoid any suspiciously cheap.

Contrary to popular belief, true Calvados is not distilled from cider – but an inferior imitation is: French cider (*cidre*) is excellent.

Though most French proprietary aperitifs, like Dubonnet, are fairly low in alcohol, the extremely popular Pernod/Ricard *pastis*-style brands are highly spirituous. *Eau-de-vie* is the generic term for all spirits, but colloquially tends to refer to local, often rough, distillates. Exceptions are the better *alcohols blancs* (white spirits), which are not inexpensive, made from fresh fruits and not sweetened as *crèmes* are.

Liqueurs

Numerous travellers deem it worth allocating their allowance to bring back some of the famous French liqueurs (Bénédictine, Chartreuse, Cointreau, and so on) which are so costly in Britain. Compare 'duty free' prices with those in stores, which can vary markedly. There is a plethora of regional liqueurs, and numerous sickly *crèmes*, interesting to taste locally. The only *crème* generally meriting serious consideration as a liqueur is *crème de menthe* (preferably Cusenier), though the newish *crème de Grand Marnier* has been successful. *Crème de cassis* has a special function: see *Kir* in alphabetical list.

Condensed glossary
of French wine and ancillary terminology

Abricotine – Generic apricot liqueur. Look for known brand-names.

Alcool blanc – Spirit distilled from fruit (not wine); not to be confused with fruit-flavoured cordials.

Aligoté – Burgundy wine (from grape of same name); light and dry.

Anis – Aniseed; much used in aperitifs of Pernod type.

Apéritif – Any drink taken as an appetiser (literally 'opener'). France has a huge range of proprietary aperitifs.

Appellation (d'Origine) Contrôlée – AC; see An Introduction to French Wines.

Armagnac – Superb brandy of the Gascon country, now achieving something of a rediscovery. See Hints on Spirits.

Barsac – Sweet Bordeaux wine (officially part of Sauternes); wide range from excellent to sickly boring.

Basserau – Sparkling red Burgundy; unusual if nothing else.

Beaune – Prestigious Burgundy name (red), the best very costly.

Blanc de Blancs – White wine from white grapes only. White wine is often made from black grapes, skins being removed before fermentation – as this is.

Blanc de Noirs – See immediately above: these are essentially type descriptions; some prestige accrues to *Blanc de Blancs*.

Bordeaux – See An Introduction to French Wines.

Bourgogne – Burgundy, see An Introduction to French Wines.

Brut – Very dry; particularly with good Champagne.

Cabernet – Noble grape, especially Cabernet-Sauvignon. Just its name on a label denotes a sound red wine.

Cacao – Cocoa; usually as *crème de cacao*.

Calvados – Apple brandy; see Hints on Spirits.

Cassis – Blackcurrant; *crème de cassis* widely favoured, notably in Kir (q.v.).

Cave – Cellar.

Cépage – Indication of grape variety; e.g. *cépage Sauvignon*.

Chai – Ground-level wine store, exclusively used in Cognac, frequently also in Bordeaux.

Champagne – See An Introduction to French Wines.

Clairet – Unimportant little-known Bordeaux wine, but probably origin of English word Claret (red Bordeaux).

Clos – Principally Burgundian word for vineyard enclosed, or formerly protected, by a wall.

Cognac – see Hints on Spirits.

Côte – Vineyard on a slope; no particular quality significance.

Coteaux(x) – Hillside(s); much the same as *côte*.

Crème – Sweet, mildly alcoholic cordials of many flavours. Not rated as true liqueurs, but one exception is *crème de menthe* (mint). See also *cassis*.

Crémant – Sparkling wine, without lasting champagne-style effervescence.

Cru – Literally 'growth'. Somewhat complicated term. *Grand cru* only meaningful if allied to good name. *Grand cru classé* (officially classified great wine) covers greatest wines, but not all *cru classé* is *grand*.

Cuve close – Sealed vat; describes production of sparkling wine by bulk secondary fermentation as opposed to bottle fermentation of 'champagne method'.

Cuvée – Wine from one vat, unblended. Another confusing word; *cuvée spéciale* can have more than its literal meaning.

Demi-sec – Translates as 'medium dry'; in practice means sweet.

Domaine – Mainly Burgundian word; broadly equivalent to château.

Doux – Very sweet.

Eau-de-vie – Generic term for all distilled spirits.

Frappé – Drink served on finely crushed ice.

Glacé – Iced by immersion of bottle, or other refrigeration.

Goût – Taste. In some regions also describes rough local spirit.

Haut – 'High'; denotes upper part of wine district. Not necessarily a mark of quality, though Haut-Medoc produces notably better wines than its lower areas

Izarra – Ancient, Armagnac-based Basque liqueur.

Kir – Excellent, now very popular aperitif: very dry chilled white wine (properly *Bourgogne Aligoté*) with a teaspoon of *crème de cassis* (q.v.) added, Kir Royale employs champagne.

Liqueur – originally *liqueur de dessert*, denoting post-prandial digestive use. Always sweet, so to speak of a 'liqueur Cognac' is absurd.

Litre – 1.7 pints; 5 litres equals 1.1 gallons.

Méthode Champenoise – Wine made by the champagne method.

Marc – Usually roughish brandy distilled from wine residue, though a few *Marcs* (pronounced 'mar') – notably *Marc de Bourgogne* – have some status.

Marque – Brand or company name.

Mise – As in *mise en bouteilles au château* (bottled at the château) or . . . *dans nos caves* (in our own cellars), etc.

Moelleux – On the sweet side.

Mousseux – Semi-technical term for sparkling; applies to the greatest champagne and to artificially carbonated rubbish.

Nouveau – New wine, particularly Beaujolais; made for drinking within a few months of harvest.

Pastis – General description, once more specific, for strong anis/ liquorice-flavoured aperitifs originating in Marseilles; Ricard is a prime example.

Pétillant – Gently effervescent; sometimes translated as 'prickly' or 'crackling'.

Pineau – Unfermented grape juice fortified with grape spirit. Made in many regions: *Pineau des Charantes* (Cognac area) is best known. Well chilled, an attractive aperitif.

Porto – Portwine. The French are very big consumers, often using it (chilled) as an aperitif.

Primeur – Basically the same as *nouveau*. However, much fine Bordeaux and Bugundy is sold *'en primeur'* for long maturing by buyer.

Rosé – 'Pink wine'. Made by leaving skins of black grapes briefly in contact with juice; also by addition of red wine to white.

Sauvignon – Splendid white grape.

Sec – 'Dry', but wines thus marked will be sweetish. *Extra sec* may actually mean what it says.

Sirop – Syrup; akin to non-alcoholic *crème*.

Vermout – Vermouth.

Vin de Xérès – 'Vin de 'ereth'; sherry.

Glossary of cooking terms and dishes

(It would take another book to list comprehensively French cooking terms and dishes, but here are the ones most likely to be encountered)

Aigre-doux	bittersweet
Aiguillette	thin slice (aiguille – needle)
Aile	wing
Aïoli	garlic mayonnaise
Allemande (à l')	German style, i.e.: with sausages and sauerkraut
Amuses-gueule	appetisers
Anglaise (à l')	plain boiled. Crème Anglaise – egg and cream sauce
Andouille	large boiling sausage
Andouillettes	ditto but made from smaller intestines, usually served hot after grilling
Anis	aniseed
Argenteuil	with asparagus
Assiette Anglaise	plate of cold meats
Baba au Rhum	yeast-based sponge macerated in rum
Baguette	long thin loaf
Ballotine	boned, stuffed and rolled meat or poultry, usually cold
Béarnaise	sauce made from egg yolks, butter, tarragon, wine, shallots
Beurre Blanc	sauce from Nantes, with butter, reduction of shallot-flavoured vinegar or wine
Béchamel	white sauce flavoured with infusion of herbs
Beignets	fritters
Bercy	sauce with white wine and shallots
Beurre noir	browned butter
Bigarade	with oranges
Billy By	mussel soup
Bisque	creamy shellfish soup
Blanquette	stew with thick white creamy sauce, usually veal
Boeuf à la mode	braised beef
Bombe	ice cream mould
Bonne femme	with root vegetables
Bordelais	Bordeaux-style, with red or white wine, marrow bone fat
Bouchée	mouthful, i.e. vol au vent
Boudin	sausage or black pudding
Bourride	thick fish soup

Braisé	braised
Brandade (de morue)	dried salt cod pounded into a mousse
Broche	spit
Brochette	skewer
Brouillade	stew, using oil
Brouillé	scrambled
Brulé	burnt, i.e. crème brulée
Campagne	country style
Cannelle	cinnamon
Carbonade	braised in beer
Cardinal	red-coloured sauce, i.e. with lobster or in pâtisserie with redcurrant
Cassolette or cassoulette	small pan
Cassoulet	rich stew with goose, pork and haricot beans
Cervelas	pork garlic sausage
Cervelles	brains
Chantilly	whipped sweetened cream
Charcuterie	cold pork-butcher's meats
Charlotte	mould, as dessert lined with spongefingers, as savoury lined with vegetable
Chasseur	with mushrooms, shallots, wine
Chausson	pastry turnover
Chemise	covering, i.e. pastry
Chiffonade	thinly-cut, i.e. lettuce
Choron	tomato Béarnaise
Choucroute	Alsatian stew with sauerkraut and sausages
Civet	stew
Clafoutis	batter desert, usually with cherries
Clamart	with peas
Cocotte	covered casserole
Compôte	cooked fruit
Concassé	i.e. tomatoes concassées – skinned, chopped, juice extracted
Confit	preserved
Confiture	jam
Consommé	clear soup
Coque (à la)	i.e. oeufs – boiled eggs
Cou	neck
Coulis	juice, puree (of vegetables or fruit)

Court-bouillon	aromatic liquor for cooking meat, fish, vegetables	Friture	assorted small fish, fried in batter
Couscous	N. African dish with millet, chicken, vegetable variations	Froid	cold
		Fumé	smoked
Crapaudine	involving fowl, particularly pigeon, trussed	Galatine	loaf-shaped chopped meat, fish or vegetable, set in natural jelly
Crécy	with carrots		
Crême Pâtissière	thick custard filling	Galette	Breton pancake, flat cake
		Garbure	thick country soup
Crêpe	pancake	Garni	garnished, usually with vegetables
Crépinette	little flat sausage, encased in caul		
		Gaufre	waffle
Croque Monsieur	toasted cheese and ham sandwich	Gelée	aspic
		Gésier	gizzard
Croustade	pastry or baked bread shell	Gibier	game
Croûte	pastry crust	Gigôt	leg
Croûton	cube of fried or toasted bread	Glacé	iced
		Gougère	choux pastry, large base
Cru	raw	Goujons	fried strips, usually of fish
Crudités	raw vegetables	Graine	seed
		Gratin	baked dish of vegetables cooked in cream and eggs
Demi-glâce	basic brown sauce		
Doria	with cucumber	Gratinée	browned under grill
		Grêcque (à la)	cold vegetables served in oil
Emin</br>cé	thinly sliced		
Entremets	sweets	Grenouilles	frogs; cuisses de grenouille – frogs' legs
Etuvé	stewed, i.e. vegetables in butter		
		Grillé	grilled
		Gros sel	coarse salt
Farci	stuffed		
Fines herbes	parsley, thyme, bayleaf	Hachis	minced or chopped
Feuillété	leaves of flaky pastry	Haricot	slow cooked stew
Flamande	Flemish style, with beer	Hochepot	hotpot
Flambé	flamed in spirit	Hollandaise	sauce with egg, butter, lemon
Flamiche	flan		
Florentine	with spinach	Hongroise	Hungarian, i.e. spiced with paprika
Flute	thinnest bread loaf		
Foie gras	goose liver	Hors d'oeuvre	assorted starters
Fondu	melted	Huile	oil
Fond (d'artichaut)	heart (of artichoke)	Île flottante	floating island – soft meringue on egg custard sauce
Forestière	with mushrooms, bacon and potatoes		
		Indienne	Indian, i.e. with hot spices
Four (au)	baked in the oven		
Fourré	stuffed, usually sweets	Jambon	ham
Fricandeau	veal, usually topside	Jardinière	from the garden, i.e. with vegetables
Frais, fraiche	fresh and cool		
Frangipane	almond creme patisserie	Jarret	shin, i.e. jarret de veau
Fricadelle	Swedish meat ball	Julienne	matchstick vegetables
Fricassée	(usually of veal) in creamy sauce	Jus	natural juice
Frit	fried	Lait	milk
Frites	chips	Langue	tongue

Lard	bacon	*Pâte*	pastry
Longe	loin	*Pâte brisée*	rich short crust pastry
		Pâtisserie	pastries
		Paupiettes	paper-thin slice
Macedoine	diced fruits or vegetables	*Pavé*	thick slice
Madeleine	small sponge cake	*Paysan*	country style
Magret	breast (of duck)	*Perigueux*	with truffles
Maïs	sweetcorn	*Persillade*	chopped parsley and garlic
Maître d'hôtel	sauce with butter, lemon,		topping
	parsley	*Petits fours*	tiny cakes, sweetmeats
Marchand de vin	sauce with red wine, shallot	*Petit pain*	bread roll
Marengo	sauce with tomatoes, olive	*Piperade*	peppers, onions, tomatoes
	oil, white wine		in scrambled egg
Marinière	seamen's style, i.e. moules	*Poché*	poached
	marinières (mussels in	*Poêlé*	fried
	white wine)	*Poitrine*	breast
Marmite	deep casserole	*Poivre*	pepper
Matelote	fish stew, i.e. of eel	*Pommade*	paste
Médaillon	round slice	*Potage*	thick soup
Mélange	mixture	*Pot-au-four*	broth with meat and
Meunière	sauce with butter, lemon		vegetables
Miel	honey	*Potée*	country soup with cabbage
Mille feuille	flaky pastry, lit. 1,000 leaves	*Pralines*	caramelised almonds
Mirepoix	cubed carrot, onion etc.	*Primeurs*	young veg
	used for sauces	*Printanièr(e)*	garnished with early
Moëlle	beef marrow		vegetables
Mornay	cheese sauce	*Profiteroles*	choux pastry balls
Mouclade	mussel stew	*Provençale*	with garlic, tomatoes, olive
Mousseline	Hollandaise sauce,		oil, peppers
	lightened with egg white	*Purée*	mashed and sieved
Moutarde	mustard		
		Quenelle	pounded fish or meat,
			bound with egg, poached
Nage (à la)	poached in flavoured liquor	*Queue*	tail
	(fish)	*Quiche*	pastry flan, i.e. quiche
Nature	plain		Lorraine – egg, bacon,
Navarin	stew of lamb with spring		cream
(*d'agneau*)	vegetables		
Noisette	nut-brown, burned butter		
Noix de veau	nut of veal (leg)	*Râble*	saddle, i.e. rable de lièvre
Normande	Normandy style, with	*Ragout*	stew
	cream, apple, cider,	*Ramequin*	little pot
	Calvados	*Rapé*	grated
Nouilles	noodles	*Ratatouille*	provencale stew of onions,
			garlic, peppers, tomatoes
		Ravigote	highly seasoned white
Os	bone		sauce
		Rémoulade	mayonnaise with gherkins,
			capers, herbs and shallot
Paillettes	straws (of pastry)	*Rillettes*	potted shredded meat,
Panaché	mixed		usually fat pork or goose
Panade	flour crust	*Riz*	rice
Papillote (en)	cooked in paper case	*Robert*	sauce with mustard,
Parmentier	with potatoes		vinegar, onion
Pâté	paste, of meat or fish	*Roquefort*	ewe's milk blue cheese

Rossini	garnished with foie gras and truffle	*Suprême*	fillet of poultry breast or fish
Rôti	roast		
Rouelle	nugget	*Tartare*	raw minced beef, flavoured
Rouille	hot garlicky sauce for soupe de poisson		with onion etc. and bound with raw egg
Roulade	roll	*Tartare (sauce)*	mayonnaise with capers, herbs, onions
Roux	sauce base – flour and butter	*Tarte Tatin*	upside-down apple pie
		Terrine	pottery dish/baked minced, chopped meat, veg., chicken, fish or fruit
Sabayon	sweet fluffy sauce, with eggs and wine	*Thé*	tea
Safran	saffron	*Tiède*	luke warm
Sagou	sago	*Timbale*	steamed mould
St.-Germain	with peas	*Tisane*	infusion
Salade niçoise	with tunny, anchovies, tomatoes, beans, black olives	*Tourte*	pie
		Tranche	thick slice
Salé	salted	*Truffes*	truffles
Salmis	dish of game or fowl, with red wine	*Tuile*	tile, i.e. thin biscuit
Sang	blood	*Vacherin*	meringue confection
Santé	lit. healthy, i.e. with spinach and potato	*Vallée d'Auge*	with cream, apple, Calvados
Salpicon	meat, fowl, vegetables, chopped fine, bound with sauce and used as fillings	*Vapeur (au)*	steamed
		Velouté	white sauce, bouillon-flavoured
Saucisse	fresh sausage	*Véronique*	with grapes
Saucisson	dried sausage	*Vert(e)*	green, i.e. sauce verte with herbs
Sauté	cooked in fat in open pan		
Sauvage	wild	*Vessie*	pig's bladder
Savarin	ring of yeast sponge, soaked in syrup and liquor	*Vichyssoise*	chilled creamy leek and potato soup
Sel	salt	*Vierge*	prime olive oil
Selle	saddle	*Vinaigre*	vinegar (lit. bitter wine)
Selon	according to, i.e. selon grosseur (according to size)	*Vinaigrette*	wine vinegar and oil dressing
		Volaille	poultry
Smitane	with sour cream, white wine, onion	*Vol-au-vent*	puff pastry case
Soissons	with dried white beans	*Xérès*	sherry
Sorbet	water ice		
Soubise	with creamed onions	*Yaourt*	yoghurt
Soufflé	puffed, i.e. mixed with egg white and baked		
Sucre	sugar (Sucré – sugared)		

FISH – Les Poissons, SHELLFISH – Les Coquillages

Aiglefin	haddock – also Églefin	*Langouste*	crawfish
Alose	shad	*Langoustine*	Dublin Bay prawn
Anchois	anchovy	*Lieu*	ling
Anguille	eel	*Limand*	lemon sole
Araignée de mer	spider crab	*Lotte de mer*	monkfish
Bar	sea bass	*Loup de mer*	sea bass
Barbue	brill	*Maquereau*	mackerel
Baudroie	monkfish, anglerfish	*Merlan*	whiting
Belon	oyster – flat shelled	*Mérou*	grouper
Bigorneau	winkle	*Morue*	salt cod
Blanchaille	whitebait	*Moule*	mussel
Brochet	pike	*Muge, mulet*	grey mullet
Cabillaud	cod	*Murène*	moray eel
Calmar	squid	*Nonat*	tiny fish similar to
Carrelet	plaice		whitebait
Chapon de mer	scorpion fish	*Ombre*	grayling
Claire	oyster	*Orade*	gilt-headed bream
Clovisse	large clam	*Oursin*	sea urchin
Colin	hake	*Pageot*	sea bream
Congre	conger eel	*Palourde*	clam
Coques	cockles	*Perche*	perch
Coquille	scallop	*Petoncle*	small scallop
St. Jacques		*Plie*	plaice
Crabe	crab	*Portugaise*	oyster
Crevette grise	shrimp	*Poulpe*	octopus
Crevette rose	prawn	*Praire*	small clam
Daurade	sea bream	*Raie*	skate
Donzelle or Girelle	a brightly coloured eel-	*Rascasse*	scorpion-fish
	like Mediterranean fish	*Rouget*	red mullet
Écrevisse	crayfish	*St. Pierre*	John Dory
Encornet	cuttlefish, squid	*Sauclet*	sand smelt
Éperlan	smelt	*Saumon*	salmon
Espadon	swordfish	*Saumonette*	rock salmon
Etrille	baby crab	*Scipion*	cuttlefish
Favouille	spider crab	*Seiche*	squid
Fiecas	conger eel	*Sole*	sole
Flétan	halibut	*Soupion*	inkfish
Fruits de mer	seafood	*Sourdon*	cockle
Gamba	large prawn	*Thon*	tunny
Grondin	red gurnet	*Tortue*	turtle
Hareng	herring	*Tourteau*	large crab
Homard	lobster	*Truite*	trout
Huitre	oyster	*Turbot*	turbot
Julienne	ling	*Turbotin*	chicken turbot
Laitance	soft herring roe	*Vernis*	clam
Lamproie	lamprey	*Violet*	soft-shelled shellfish